INTELLIGENT
CHARISMATIC®

Changing the way you think about your faith.

For more resources, please visit pastormike.nyc.

If you are looking for a book that you can have to learn about healing and even use as a guide, Michael's book is as complete as it gets. He has done an excellent job of covering the healing message that Jesus wants us to know and have. You will not only read about the Word of healing, but also the testimony of healing that will inspire you to receive your own healing and begin to bring healing to others. Be blessed as you read and learn from this great book.

Cal Pierce
Director, Healing Rooms Ministries

As far back as when he first began following Jesus, Pastor Michael White has had an uncommon passion for people to experience Christ's healing power in their physical bodies. This book was birthed out of a deep place of communion with the Lord, intense scriptural study, and over a decade of first-hand experience witnessing the miraculous power of Jesus' finished work on the cross. Read this book and both your faith and understanding in how to move in healing will go to another level.

Bojan Jancic
Lead Pastor, CityLight Church

Pastor Michael White is to be congratulated for this exciting and theologically rigorous presentation of God's power to heal in the present age. Having witnessed a number of spectacular healings that defied scientific explanation (including the complete recovery of two patients believed to be brain dead), I am inspired by Pastor White's book to pray for and expect more miracles in my medical work.

Meredith Hawkins, MD, MS
Professor of Medicine and Director, Global Diabetes Institute

I want to encourage you to add this encouraging and enlightening book to your library. I am so excited to see a new generation of apologists for healing arising. Younger men and women who not only are praying for the sick, but writing books defending healing's biblical basis, and its continuation in our 21st century world. Thank you, Michael White for a well-written, encouraging, and challenging book.

Randy Clark, D.D., D.Min. Th.D., Author, Overseer of the Apostolic Network of Global Awakening, and President of Global Awakening Theological Seminary

THE DIVINE MANDATE

Why Every Christian Should
Pray for Healing

MICHAEL D. WHITE

FOREWORD BY DR. RANDY CLARK

Jenny,
I speak the FIRE of GOD
over your life & your ministry
like never before!

Intelligent Charismatic

New York

For information about special discounts for bulk purchases, as well as inviting Michael White to speak at a special event, please visit pastormike.nyc.

Cover design by Chris Rosenberry @ Fifth Story Interactive
ISBN 978-0-578-79366-5

This book is dedicated to our Healing Rooms volunteers. Since the day we opened, you have run for the prize with us. You have refused to let sickness and disease take hold of anyone who walks in our doors. Countless lives have been touched, and innumerable bodies have been healed, because of your faithful devotion to God's mandate to "lay hands on the sick" (Mk. 16:18) that they might recover. Thank you! I know God will richly bless you in response to your passion for His mission.

Rachael, thank you for your endless love and support: not only for two books, but now for three. You truly are the woman of my dreams, and I love you with all my heart, today more than ever before.

Thank you to Allison Armerding for giving new life to my ideas, and expressing my thoughts better than I can express myself.

Thank you to the members of CityLight Church. This book is the result of our continuing journey together. You inspire me in the way you always pursue more of God! I truly love and cherish our church family.

TABLE OF CONTENTS

A NOTE

from the author

In 2017, I published <u>Intelligent Charismatic: The Believer's Guide to a Spirit-Filled Life</u>. My intent with my first work was to provide something I wish I had when I started to explore Spirit-filled Christianity—a guide. Though I found a lot of good books for new believers, the subject matter was often the same: *Do better. Try harder. Read the Bible. Make good Christian friends.* None of them had what I was seeking: Biblical proofs for everything we see in "Charismatic" church. If I was going to speak in tongues, I wanted to know everything I could about the subject. If I was going to tithe, I wanted to know every verse in Scripture that talked about money. If I was going to raise my hands in worship and sing *loud* to God, I wanted to find my example in God's Word. I wrote <u>Intelligent Charismatic</u> to answer the most common questions I had about Spirit-filled Christianity as a new believer.

What I quickly discovered in my first work is there is a lot of ground to be covered. A complete discussion of divine healing is not just a chapter in a book; it is a book in and of itself. I resolved to write a book for each chapter in my original work, explaining in detail the concepts presented in <u>Intelligent Charismatic</u>.

As such, this is the third installment in the Intelligent Charismatic Series. I will have forthcoming books on leadership, speaking in tongues, financial stewardship, and all the other concepts presented in my original book. I pray they bless you, and I hope you enjoy them.

FOREWORD

by Dr. Randy Clark

Michael White is a pastor and overseer of the Healing Rooms in New York City. Prior to his life as a pastor, he worked in finance. He is a well-educated millennial who is one of the first of his generation to write a full-length book on the subject of healing. Along with Michael's faith, integrity, passion, and love for God, I applaud his desire to show people the truth about healing being for today and the God of Christians being a healing God.

When I first received the manuscript and read the table of contents, I realized this was going to be a comprehensive book on healing. Michael covers all the major issues related to healing and also addresses why so many Christians and non-believers do not believe in healing or why they don't pray for healing today. He uses many Scriptures and personal stories, which makes the book both more authoritative and interesting.

Michael is definitely not only a teacher but an exhorter and encourager to those who have and have not prayed for the sick. The book strongly exhorts the reader to believe the Bible rather than their experience regarding healing. In 1996, God communicated to me very strongly, "Don't lower your theology to the level of your experience! Don't lower my Word to the level of your experience. Teach my Word and let your experience rise to my Word, but don't lower my Word to the level of your experience. Don't be an experienced-based preacher. Preach my Word, not your experience." Michael writes similarly, "When healing doesn't happen, please do not adjust your theology to match your life experience." I want to echo a strong "Amen" to Michael's words. I believe Michael has a Holy Spirit "Amen" as well as mine.

Throughout this book there are strong statements. With some, I initially felt a temptation to mitigate them with nuancing and make them less absolute, but then realized this would reduce the assurance of the promises of the Father and the Son, Jesus. This book is written to build faith, to confront churches influenced by a culture and theology that teaches the gift of healing has ended. Michael has thrown down the gauntlet, challenging the teaching that healing is possible since God is sovereign and can answer prayer, but is not to be normative. I agree with Michael—for the churches, healing should be normative, not the exception. I faced my temptation to nuance Michael, realizing I like to talk with people who believe more than I do about the power of God to heal, not with those who are full of doubt.

To the question of whether or not the Bible reveals God as desiring to heal people, Michael answers with a resounding Yes! He demonstrates that the source of sickness and disease is the devil, not God. He also writes a very interesting chapter on the diversity of how God heals and how healings are unique to each individual, explaining that God is not committed to models, but to relationships, and as a result we need to hear from God how to pray in different situations for different conditions and different people.

Michael presents the biblical proof that God has given His followers authority to heal through both the logos, the Bible, and through rhema words, prophetic words regarding healing. God has likewise anointed His followers with His very Spirit and presence to heal. This anointing is rooted in the cross of His Son, Jesus, and the resultant power of Pentecost.

Michael emphasizes the importance of perseverance for healing. He challenges us to believe not only in healing but also to believe for unusual miracles. He exhorts us to take healing beyond the walls of our churches into the secular places where we work and socialize.

He reminds us of the Scriptures indicating that general atonement applies to both forgiveness and healing. He roots both forgiveness and healing in the love of God and the work of Jesus on the cross. He reminds us that the name and blood of Jesus are powerful weapons against the enemies of disease and the demonic.

One subject that stood out to me was the relationship between healing and prophecy and words of knowledge, which are manifestations of God revealing information to the person praying or the person needing prayer. Michael illustrates how this information regarding the specific will of God for an individual is related to strong faith.

I was glad to see his chapter on the relationship between healing and Communion. There is great need for Christians to become aware of how Communion is related to healing.

A book on healing would not be complete without facing the issue of those who aren't healed and the issue of doubt. Michael does a great job of encouraging, exhorting, and giving examples from his own ministry on how to deal with doubt.

This book concludes by encouraging readers that they too can be used in the ministry of healing. The teaching in the book should inspire readers to engage the kingdom to enable them to see God heal the sick and diseased.

I encourage you to add this enlightening book to your library. I am so excited to see a new generation of apologists for healing arising— younger men and women who not only are praying for the sick, but writing books defending healing's biblical basis, and its continuation in our 21st-century world. Thank you, Michael White, for a well-written, encouraging, and challenging book.

— Randy Clark, D.D., D.Min., Th.D., Overseer of the Apostolic Network of Global Awakening, President of Global Awakening Theological

MICHAEL D. WHITE

Seminary of Family of Faith Christian University, author of *Destined for the Cross: 16 Reasons Jesus Had to Die*, *The Healing Breakthrough*, *Power to Heal*, *Authority to Heal*, *The Essential Guide to Healing* (coauthored with Bill Johnson), *There Is More*, and over 35 more books.

THE DIVINE MANDATE

Why Every Christian Should
Pray for Healing

INTRODUCTION

I still remember walking into the hospital room in Newark, New Jersey, and seeing Carl's shriveled body. Carl had always been athletic, with a strong, powerful frame. He had walked into our church about two years prior, smiling ear to ear, and immediately became one of our church's most active and devoted members. Everyone in our church loved him. He was passionate about Jesus and had a zest for life. The energy and enthusiasm he carried was contagious.

But at twenty-six, Carl was diagnosed with an aggressive form of cancer. In a matter of days, his condition grew worse and worse. News of his illness sent shockwaves through our church community. How was it even possible that someone as healthy and active as Carl could come down with such an aggressive illness? How was it fair that God would allow someone so insanely devoted to Jesus to be exposed to such a crippling disease? But the enemy doesn't play favorites. Disease shows no mercy. Satan "does not come except to steal, and to kill, and to destroy" (Jn. 10:10).

We prayed night after night for Carl in our church, and several months after his initial diagnosis, the miracle came. Carl was given a clean bill of health. We rejoiced as a church family! But the good news only lasted several weeks. A follow-up scan revealed that the cancer had returned, and was spreading more aggressively than ever.

As we walked into the hospital room, Carl managed to raise the corners of his mouth in a reluctant smile. He was happy to see us, and we were happy to see him. For half an hour, we asked him every question we could think to ask, caught up on life, and marveled at God's faithfulness, even in the midst of sickness and disease. Carl knew that God would use even this for His glory.

I believed with every fiber of my being that Carl would be healed. I had seen people in our church healed of stage IV cancer. I had seen blind eyes opened! I had seen unavoidable death sentences erased in favor of a new lease on life, and I believed God would do the same for Carl.

But several weeks later, Carl passed away.

How Will You Respond?

Have you ever had a heartbreaking experience like this? Have you seen someone you love and cherish succumb to the crippling effects of sickness and disease? Have you ever wondered why it just doesn't feel *fair* that people die before their time? Have you every stopped to consider that there is something innate within you— deep down and firmly rooted —that tells you that sickness and disease are *not* what we are meant to experience in life?

When I heard Carl had passed away, I was distraught. I was frustrated. I was confused! I had honestly believed with every ounce of my faith that Carl would be completely healed. He was a young man with a bright future, and he deserved to enjoy the rest of his life. But more than anything, I was angry. I was angry that the devil had stolen the life of such a precious man. I was angry because I knew that the outcome Carl had experienced was *not* God's best.

From that moment forward, I dedicated my life to seeing people healed through prayer. I decided I would stop at nothing until I prayed the same prayers Jesus prayed and got exactly the same results. Have you ever noticed that Jesus healed *everyone* He prayed for?

> *When the sun was setting, all those who had any that were sick with various diseases brought them to Him; and He laid His hands on every one of them and healed them. And demons also came out of many, crying out and saying, "You are the Christ, the Son of God!"*
> —*Luke 4:40-41*

Now listen to me: I am not there yet. Some people I pray for don't recover. That's why I opened this book with Carl's heartbreaking story, instead of one of the hundreds of miraculous healings I've seen with my own eyes. I have work to do, just like you!

But *I am going to spend my life trying to get there.* I am going to spend my time in prayer asking God why I'm not there yet! I am going to spend my days sitting at the feet of Jesus so I can move in the same power He displayed. I know I'm not Jesus! But I *want to be like Him.* And the question is, will I seek and study the ways and Word of God every day so I can become more like Him? Will I allow Him to change in me whatever needs to change so His power can come pouring out of me when I pray? Or will I settle for a watered-down version of Christianity where I talk myself out of miracles before they can even happen?

The State of the Church

Jesus *expected* His disciples to heal.

> *Then He called His twelve disciples together and gave them power and authority over all demons, and to cure diseases. He sent them to preach the kingdom of God and to heal the sick.*   —*Luke 9:1-2*

It was fair for Jesus to expect His disciples to heal, because He had given them everything they needed to heal in His name! He gave them power and authority "over all demons, and to cure diseases" (Lk. 9:1).[1]

So when the disciples ran into their first instance of *failed healing,* Jesus had some choice words for them:

---

[1] We will dive into this passage much more deeply later in this book.

Then Jesus answered and said, "O faithless and perverse generation, how long shall I be with you and bear with you? Bring your son here." And as he was still coming, the demon threw him down and convulsed him. Then Jesus rebuked the unclean spirit, healed the child, and gave him back to his father. —Luke 9:41-42

If we as disciples of Jesus cannot cast out demons and heal the sick, *there is a problem.* I am not saying that Jesus would consider you "faithless" or "perverse" just because you have prayers that don't get answered. But I am saying that there is a level of *power* Jesus wants the church to experience that we have yet to fully embrace. There are a select few men and women in the kingdom of God who have touched on the level of power Jesus experienced in His ministry![2] But I believe it is time for the body of Christ—the whole church!—to rise up with *authority and power* and do the things Jesus told us to do in His name.

If you pray for a sick person and nothing happens, don't condemn yourself. But *don't let yourself get comfortable* with the current state of affairs. Please do not allow yourself to believe that just because you prayed once and nothing happened, healing is not God's will for your life and your ministry!

Words of Encouragement

Carl's family invited me to speak at Carl's memorial service. I reflected that Carl was the strongest man I know. As his health deteriorated, he faced obstacles I would never dream of facing, and he did it all with a courageous smile and an attitude that was impossible to deflate. When he was diagnosed with cancer, he didn't complain; he believed. He believed with all of his heart that God would heal him! I remarked to Carl's family

---

[2] Katherine Kuhlman, John G. Lake, Smith Wigglesworth, and modern-day heroes like Dr. Randy Clark come to mind.

that by believing for his healing, they had given him the greatest gift he could have ever received: they had faith that he would be healed, right up until the very end.

From that day forward, I was on a mission to pray for every sick person I could find. I was on a mission to refuse to let the enemy ever steal the life from someone right under my nose. I was on a mission to constantly remind myself that God is not the Author of sickness and disease. He gives life! It is the enemy—not God—who takes life away.[3] There is a world full of people who need us to heal, because without a tangible display of the glory of God, they will not believe that Jesus is real! Are you ready to join me on this mission?

Here is the simple truth: people are dying because the church has forgotten that healing is God's will for His people. Instead of living to "a good old age" (Gen. 25:8), people are dying of sickness and disease all the time. In 2017, almost one third of people who died globally passed away from heart disease. Over *seventeen percent* of reported deaths were caused by cancer.[4] We're not staying healthy like we're supposed to! What ever happened to God's promise that He would satisfy us with "long life" (Ps. 91:16)? Why have we abandoned the promise that we, just like Abraham, are supposed to die "old . . . and full of years" (Gen. 25:8)?

God has not changed,[5] but perhaps we have. I believe it's time for the church to make it our mission to start praying for healing again. We cannot sit back and accept death and disease as inevitable outcomes when God asks us to press forward and pursue miracles in His name.

---

[3] "The thief does not come except to steal, and to kill, and to destroy. I have come that they may have life, and that they may have it more abundantly." —Jn. 10:10

[4] Global Burden of Disease Collaborative Network. *Global Burden of Disease Study 2017* (GBD 2017) Results. Seattle, United States: Institute for Health Metrics and Evaluation (IHME), 2018. https://ourworldindata.org/what-does-the-world-die-from.

[5] "Jesus Christ is the same yesterday, today, and forever." – Heb. 13:8

Believing that healing is possible is not enough. Experiencing healing is a *must* for every Christian who walks by faith. A recent Barna survey found that while two thirds (66%) of Americans believe that God *can* supernaturally heal, fewer than three in ten (27%) had ever experienced a "physical healing that could only be explained as miraculous."[6] It is my hope that by the time you finish this book, you will be in that small but growing group of believers who have seen the hand of God in your own body, or in the body of someone you know.

The fact that you picked up this book means that you are unique. You refuse to accept the status quo. You refuse to settle for anything less than the full hope that the gospel of Jesus Christ offers us. You refuse to believe that God is anything less than a Healer! And that means you are uniquely positioned to show the power of God to a generation of people who may have *no idea* that God can heal.

I believe *you* have been chosen by God to be an integral part of His healing mission. The apostle Paul reminded the church at Corinth, "Pursue love, and desire spiritual gifts" (1 Cor. 14:1). Our hearts should *ache* to see God's healing power on display! And we can launch into the journey of healing with full confidence that when we ask to see God move, He will respond.

I didn't see Carl healed. But I refuse to allow my experience to dictate my theology. Instead, I will humbly and boldly request that God will raise my level of experience to match what I see in His Word. Will you join me?

---

[6] Barna Group. "Most Americans Believe in Supernatural Healing." (Sep. 29, 2016). https://www.barna.com/research/americans-believe-supernatural-healing/

CHAPTER ONE

GOD WANTS TO HEAL YOU

For many years, I had no idea Jesus is the Healer. I grew up in church, but I had never met someone who had been healed as a result of prayer. I used to read stories about Jesus healing people in Scripture as if they were folklore. My response to the gospel accounts was, "Man, I wish I had been around when Jesus walked the earth!"

But once I started attending a Spirit-filled church, everything changed. The Holy Spirit started to show me that God is the Healer.[7] I learned that the same Spirit who raised Jesus from the grave gives life to my body (Rom. 8:11). If the Holy Spirit raised Jesus from the dead, how easy should it be for Him to heal my body?

I remember when I first realized divine healing was possible. I was experiencing a persistent sickness in my body—something that just wouldn't go away, no matter how hard I prayed. I had asked others to pray for me, but still no luck. Looking back, I now realize that part of my problem was I didn't *actually expect* God to heal me. I thought it would be nice so I could save money on doctor visits! But I didn't really believe in healing because I had never *seen it*.

But one Sunday when my fiancée (now my wife) and I were visiting a church outside of Syracuse, New York, I stopped in the bookstore. I stumbled[8] across a book of collected sermons by John G. Lake.[9] As I

---

[7] "For I am the Lord who heals you." —Ex. 15:26

[8] Now I clearly recognize this as God's sovereignty, even over seemingly random events.

[9] Roberts Liardon, *John G. Lake on Healing* (New Kensington, PA: Whitaker House, 2009).

flipped through the pages, I felt the presence of God. I knew this would be a significant moment. I bought the book, and for weeks I couldn't put it down.

John G. Lake founded the Healing Rooms in Spokane, Washington in 1915. People traveled there from all over the country to receive prayer because of how God was using Lake, along with the men and women who volunteered in his ministry. Gordon Lindsay reports that Lake's ministry in Spokane resulted in no fewer than 100,000 healing miracles within the span of just over five years.[10] Spokane was quickly dubbed the "healthiest city in America" because of what was happening in the Healing Rooms.

There was *power* in Lake's sermons. He boldly preached that sin, sickness, and death were never God's intention for His people. According to Lake, these three ailments that define our human condition made up the "devil's triumvirate,"[11] and to sit back and accept them was a mistake. Even worse, to invite them as lessons from God was an affront to the very nature and goodness of God.

I was immediately hooked. I told God, "I want to see testimonies like that in my own life." And as a result of this cry to God, I have seen some *amazing* testimonies. I have seen small children cured of life-threatening diseases. I have seen young men and women healed of terminal illnesses. I have seen old men and women cured of scoliosis, bone spurs, and other impediments to the "long life" (Ps. 91:16) with which God promises to satisfy us!

A Plea and A Challenge

Here is my plea to you: Don't accept sickness. Don't treat it as an inevitable part of life. For people who encounter Jesus, it doesn't have to be.

---

[10] Gordon Lindsay, *John G. Lake: Apostle to Africa* (London, UK: The Revival Library, 2014).

[11] Liardon, *John G. Lake on Healing*, 60.

And here is my challenge: You should live in perfect, divine health. What's more, the people you pray for should be healed. As you speak life over them, their bodies should come back into alignment with the perfect will of God.

I will spend the next several hundred pages doing my best to convince you of everything I have just said, and telling you about all the amazing things I have seen God do!

Here is why the subject of divine healing is so important. Sooner or later, you will be sick. Someone you know—a friend, family member, or co-worker—will be sick. The time to find out what God's Word says about healing is now, *before* sickness rears its ugly head. Because if you wait until you're sick to find out what God's posture is towards sickness, you will have already missed an opportunity to mount an effective initial response. You will have wasted valuable time grappling with how God feels about sickness and disease, instead of actively pursuing and declaring divine health for your body.

Our journey to healing starts with this simple truth: God wants to heal you.

Do you believe it? As much as you want to receive healing, God wants you to receive it all the more. Scripture shows that God isn't waiting to *give you* healing. In fact, He released healing to His people two thousand years ago through Christ's death on the cross.

God Is the Healer

If you want to understand divine healing, you have to understand that God is the Healer. He has gone to great lengths to establish this reality for His people over the course of human history.

For four hundred years, God's people lived in bondage as slaves under the Pharaoh of Egypt. But finally, freedom came. God raised up Moses and Aaron as His servants to deliver His people. The Lord "struck all the firstborn in the land of Egypt" (Ex. 12:12) and Israel was forced to leave.

Yet even as Israel was fleeing the Egyptians, they started to complain:

> *So Moses brought Israel from the Red Sea; then they went out into the Wilderness of Shur. and they went three days in the wilderness and found no water. Now when they came to Marah, they could not drink the waters of Marah, for they were bitter. Therefore the name of it was called Marah. And the people complained against Moses, saying, "What shall we drink?" So he cried out to the Lord, and the Lord showed him a tree. When he cast it into the waters, the waters were made sweet.* —Exodus 15:22-25a

Do you see the *first thing* God's people did with their freedom? They *complained*. "God, why have You done this to us?" they cried. But God would make provision.

God used Israel's predicament as an opportunity to provide. The waters were "bitter"—cursed—but as the people complained, God showed Moses a tree. Thousands of years later, we know what God was really pointing to—the cross of Jesus Christ.[12] God told Moses to cast the tree into the waters, and as He did, "the waters were made sweet" (v 26). The curse that God's people *assumed would haunt them forever* was completely done away with as they responded to God's command.

But God's encouragement to His people wasn't over:

---

[12] "Christ has redeemed us from the curse of the law, having become a curse for us (for it is written, 'Cursed is everyone who hangs on a tree'), that the blessing of Abraham might come upon the Gentiles in Christ Jesus, that we might receive the promise of the Spirit through faith." —Gal. 3:13-14

There He made a statute and an ordinance for them, and there He tested them, and said, "If you diligently heed the voice of the Lord your God and do what is right in His sight, give ear to His commandments and keep all His statutes, I will put none of the diseases on you which I have brought on the Egyptians. For I am the Lord who heals you."   *—Exodus 15:25b-26*

God's message to His people was profound: Freedom doesn't have to feel like slavery. "If you heed [My] voice," He said, "I will put none of the diseases on you which I have brought on the Egyptians" (v 26). God brought sickness on His enemies, not His friends. His goal was never to afflict His people with sickness, disease, and death. As long as they *stayed inside covenant* with Him, they would be healthy and whole. So, are you an enemy of God? Or are you His friend?[13] And if you are His friend, *why on earth* would you ever accept something that is meant for His enemies?

Notice also that divine health is *conditional.* God's word to Israel was, "If you diligently heed . . ." (v. 25). While healing is impossible to *earn* or *buy,* it is something for which you have to properly position yourself. Yes, Jesus already purchased your healing two thousand years ago on the cross! But yes, if you want to receive the healing He died for you to have, you have to accept God's invitation to live in covenant with Him. You do this by making a decision to believe in Jesus Christ.[14]

---

[13] "And the Scripture was fulfilled which says, 'Abraham believed God, and it was accounted to him for righteousness.' And he was called the friend of God." —Jas. 2:23

[14] ". . . that if you confess with your mouth the Lord Jesus and believe in your heart that God has raised Him from the dead, you will be saved." —Rom. 10:9

Healing Is Who God Is

In my eyes, the conclusion of verse 26 is the most powerful portion of the Scripture passage above. "For I am the Lord who heals you." In the original Hebrew language, God was giving His people a name by which to call Him: *Jehovah Rapha,*[15] the God who Heals.

What's in a name? For God, *everything.* Throughout the course of Old Testament Scripture, God gives Himself more than a dozen names. The purpose of this name-giving was to establish an important truth for His people: "This is not just something I do—it is *who I am.*"

Healing is not just something God does—it is *who He is.* Healing is not something that God *chooses* to do based on how His day is going, or what kind of mood He is in! Healing is who He is—an inseparable part of God's character.

My name is Mike. On Monday, when I wake up grumpy and irritable after a long Sunday of church services, I am Mike. On Thursday, when I wake up refreshed and flying on cloud nine on my day off (#churchlife), I am still Mike. I am usually in *much different moods* on those two days. Mondays I feel like I got hit by a semi tractor-trailer, and Thursday I feel light as a feather after a full night's sleep. But *who I am* does not change based on the mood I am in. My wife still comes to me as a husband. My kids still come to me as father. They know that the circumstances of life do not change my identity.

---

[15] From Blue Letter Bible: "Jehovah is translated as 'The Existing One' or 'Lord.' The chief meaning of Jehovah is derived from the Hebrew word *havah,* meaning 'to be' or 'to exist.' It also suggests 'to become' or specifically 'to become known' - this denotes a God who reveals Himself unceasingly. *Rapha* (râpâ') means 'to restore,' 'to heal' or 'to make healthful' in Hebrew. When the two words are combined - Jehovah Rapha - it can be translated as 'Jehovah Who Heals.' (cf. Jer. 30:17; Jer. 3:22; Isa. 30:26; Isa. 61:1; Psa. 103:3). Jehovah is the Great Physician who heals the physical and emotional needs of His people." Source: "The Names of God in the Old Testament," https://www.blueletterbible.org/study/misc/name_god.cfm.

In the same way, God is the Healer. He is *Jehovah Rapha,* the Lord Who Heals! It doesn't matter what day of the week it is! It doesn't matter what's happening in your life, or somewhere else across the world. His nature does not change based on circumstance.[16] No matter what is going on in your life, you get to *go to Him* and receive the healing He has already promised, and for which He has already made provision.

What Makes God's People Sick?

So if God is the Healer, and He has never changed, what made His people sick in the first place? Back to verse 26:

> *"If you diligently heed the voice of the Lord your God and do what is right in His sight, give ear to His commandments and keep all His statutes, I will put none of the diseases on you which I have brought on the Egyptians. For I am the Lord who heals you."*

Under the old covenant, what was the key to healing for God's people? Obedience! As long as they 1) listened to God and 2) did what He said, they would stay healthy! But as soon as they strayed from the safety of His covenant through sin and disobedience, they no longer had legal claim[17] to the protection He offered.

Now, to assume that God relates to us the same way under the new covenant as He did under the old covenant is a costly mistake. We'll

---

[16] "Jesus Christ is the same yesterday, today, and forever." —Heb. 13:8

[17] A covenant is more than a contract. But using legal language to describe our right to go to God and expect Him to deliver on His promises is helpful in our understanding of divine healing. Similarly, knowing our right to reject the work of Satan, which we often improperly attribute to God, is essential if we are to experience divine healing in our lives, and pray for it in the lives of others.

tackle that in a minute. But first, I need to properly frame our discussion by showing you where sickness and disease come from.

Back to the Beginning

Did you know that sin, sickness, and death were never God's intention for humans? Look at the original state of affairs designed by God in the Garden of Eden:

> *Then the Lord God took the man and put him in the garden of Eden to tend and keep it. And the Lord God commanded the man, saying, "Of every tree of the garden you may freely eat; but of the tree of the knowledge of good and evil you shall not eat, for in the day that you eat of it you shall surely die."* —Genesis 2:15-16

What I want you to see here is this: *Death* was never part of God's plan. *Sickness* was never part of God's plan! *Disease* was never part of God's plan! As far as God was concerned, Adam was welcome to live with Him in the Garden of Eden for all time, *completely healthy* and walking in perfect intimacy with God. The Garden of Eden didn't have a cancer ward just in case Adam's cellular development took a hard right turn. There was no hospice for when Adam was old and confined to bed rest! Do you see my point? Divine health has *always been* God's original intention for His beloved.

Do you see how *simple* life was supposed to be for Adam? Adam would have all his needs met. He would live in paradise! God gave him a beautiful garden with everything he needed. All Adam had to do was 1) tend and keep the garden and 2) stay away from one tree. The only requirements were to 1) listen to God and 2) do what He said! But oh, how complicated God's simple instructions become when we decide to play by our own rules!

Soon enough, Satan entered the picture. You know the story, so I'll get to the point. Adam and Eve decided *they* knew what was best for themselves more than *God* knew what was best for them. And when God's people chose disobedience, the consequences were tremendous:

> *To the woman He said: "I will greatly multiply your sorrow and your conception; in pain you shall bring forth children; Your desire shall be for your husband, and he shall rule over you." Then to Adam He said, "Because you have heeded the voice of your wife, and have eaten from the tree of which I commanded you, saying, 'You shall not eat of it': "Cursed is the ground for your sake; In toil you shall eat of it all the days of your life. Both thorns and thistles it shall bring forth for you, and you shall eat the herb of the field. In the sweat of your face you shall eat bread till you return to the ground, For out of it you were taken; For dust you are, And to dust you shall return."*
> —*Genesis 3:16-19, emphasis added*

This is the first time Scripture introduces the word "pain."[18] Do you see it? The problem wasn't that God wanted His people to be sick! The problem was that He set us up for perfect health, but we opted out of His plan by not *listening* to God and not *doing* what He said.

Life would now get harder for Eve. She would have pain in childbirth. The marriage union, which was originally designed to be a complementary and mutually respectful relationship between husband and wife, would be forever perverted.

Life would get harder for Adam, too. The ground he was to tend would now be cursed because the covenant had been broken. Adam

---

[18] Hebrew *etseb*: "pain, hurt, toil, sorrow, labor, hardship." "H6089 - 'etseb - Strong's Hebrew Lexicon (KJV)." Blue Letter Bible. Accessed 11 Aug, 2020. https://www.blueletterbible.org//lang/lexicon/lexicon.cfm?Strongs=H6089&t=KJV

would have to *work hard* to make his living. He would have to *labor* for his food! And at the end of his life, he would face an obstacle he had never previously been forced to consider: death.

Adam and Eve were expelled from the Garden of Eden—not because God no longer wanted them there, but because He didn't want them to cause further damage. God *had to* expel Adam and Eve from the Garden so that they didn't eat of the "tree of life" in their fallen state, and carry their sinful nature into eternity:

> *Then the Lord God said, "Behold, the man has become like one of Us, to know good and evil. And now, lest he put out his hand and take also of the tree of life, and eat, and live forever."*   —*Genesis 3:22*

Do you see it? None of the things we struggle with—sin, sickness, and death—were God's idea! They are the rotten fruit of our choice to live outside of covenant with Him.

Why, God?

At this point in our discussion, a logical question should cement itself in the forefront of your mind. Why? Why would God allow this to happen? If God *knows everything*, surely He must have known that Adam would eat that stinking fruit! So *why* would He let Adam and Eve be exposed to temptation? Why would God allow them to make such a disastrous decision?

The answer is free will. True love means giving the people you love the ability to choose. God's desire was for His people to choose Him—to love Him with all their hearts, just as He loved them! But loving them fully also meant giving them the right to *choose something else*.

Love without choice is not love at all; it is abuse. If God *forced us* to choose Him, we wouldn't ever really love Him! In fact, we wouldn't be *human.* We would be automatons incapable of ever loving God fully and completely, the way He deserves to be loved.

You might also ask, why would God allow Satan to trick Adam and Eve—or even to enter the Garden in the first place? The answer to that question is the same. Free will. God created Satan to worship Him.[19] But because God fully loved Satan, even Satan had the choice to love God back. And instead of choosing to love Him, he chose to reject Him. Just as Adam and Eve did. Just as you and I have!

But aren't you so glad that God has made provision even for our disobedience? You see, the Second Adam, Jesus Christ, came to "redeem us from the curse of the Law" (Gal. 3:13). He came to rescue us from the consequences of our own bad decisions. In Him, "Behold, all things have become new" (2 Cor. 5:17)! Once we were destined to a life of toil, pain, and ultimately death, but now in Christ we lay hold of rest, divine health, and eternal life.

New Covenant Love

Do you remember why God's people ever got sick in the first place? They strayed from His covenant. They *removed themselves* from His umbrella of divine grace, love, and protection.

Does that mean that every time we mess up, God metaphorically casts us out of the Garden? Does that mean that when we make a bad decision, He puts sickness and disease on us until we learn our lesson?

No! Because the cross changes everything. To assume that God still relates to His people with an old covenant mindset on this side of the cross is a grave mistake. Under the old covenant, what kept God's people

---

[19] "You were in Eden, the garden of God; every precious stone was your covering . . . the sardius, topaz, and diamond, beryl, onyx, and jasper, sapphire, turquoise, and emerald with gold. The workmanship of your timbrels and pipes was prepared for you on the day you were created." — Ezek. 28:13

righteous was the same character trait that kept them healthy: obedience. But under the new covenant, it is no longer your own personal obedience that makes you righteous—it is *faith* in the perfect obedience of Jesus Christ:

> *But now the righteousness of God apart from the law is revealed, being witnessed by the Law and the Prophets, even the righteousness of God, through faith in Jesus Christ, to all and on all who believe. For there is no difference; for all have sinned and fall short of the glory of God, being justified freely by His grace through the redemption that is in Christ Jesus, whom God set forth as a propitiation by His blood, through faith, to demonstrate His righteousness, because in His forbearance God had passed over the sins that were previously committed, to demonstrate at the present time His righteousness, that He might be just and the justifier of the one who has faith in Jesus.* —Romans 3:21-26

Your faith—not your obedience!—makes you righteous. Likewise, it is no longer your *obedience* that keeps you healthy; it is your faith.

Jesus Died for Your Sickness

How do you tap into the healing God promised His people thousands of years ago on the shores of the waters of Marah?[20] The same way you tapped into the promise of salvation—by believing in Jesus Christ:

> *And if you are Christ's, then you are Abraham's seed, and heirs according to the promise.* —Galatians 3:29

---

[20] See Exodus 15 above.

You broke the covenant. *You* should have to bear the weight of the curse! But Jesus already took on the curse so you don't have to. He beat you to the punch! What a beautiful Savior! He died *as* the curse, and that means when you believe in Him, there is *no curse* left for you!

> *Christ has redeemed us from the curse of the law, having become a curse for us (for it is written, "Cursed is everyone who hangs on a tree"), that the blessing of Abraham might come upon the Gentiles in Christ Jesus, that we might receive the promise of the Spirit through faith.* —Galatians 3:13-14

Here is what happened two thousand years ago on the cross:

- Jesus died as your sin.[21]
- He died as your sickness.

We are quick to embrace the first, but slow to accept the second. But the scriptural truth is this: Healing and salvation happened on the same day. God sent Jesus to die not just *for,* but *as* your sickness and disease. The *cause* for sin and sickness were the same, so the *remedy* for sin and sickness is also the same! Jesus defeated both on the cross. And that means you are free to walk in newness of life.

Let me show you scriptural proof that Jesus died for your sickness:

> *Surely He has borne our griefs and carried our sorrows;*
> *Yet we esteemed Him stricken,*
> *Smitten by God, and afflicted.*
> *But He was wounded for our transgressions,*

---

[21] "For He made Him who knew no sin to be sin for us, that we might become the righteousness of God in Him." —2 Cor. 5:21

He was bruised for our iniquities;
The chastisement for our peace was upon Him,
And by His stripes we are healed.
All we like sheep have gone astray;
We have turned, every one, to his own way;
And the Lord has laid on Him the iniquity of us all.

—*Isaiah 53:4-6*

Verses 5 and 6 are easy enough to understand. Jesus was "wounded for our transgressions . . . bruised for our iniquities . . and by His stripes we are healed." Healed is the Hebrew *rapha*.[22] By now you should recognize that word! Do you remember what God told His people to call Him in Exodus 15? *Johova Rapha,* the God Who Heals! *Rapha* means "to heal" or to "make healthful." Jesus took on "stripes" (i.e., physical punishment) for something He never did. He took on *literal pain* as a consequence of being rejected on the cross!

But let's also look at verse 4: "Surely He has borne our griefs and carried our sorrows." We have a tendency in the modern church to *dilute* God's Word based on what is most comfortable for us to hear in our contemporary context. Over centuries of church history, we have unintentionally changed the meaning of Isaiah's original text.[23] In the New King James Version, when I read that Jesus has borne my "griefs" and "sorrows," I assume that Isaiah is referring to emotional ailments. I quickly interpret that to mean that whenever I am grieving because I have lost something or someone, I can go to Jesus and He will heal me. Whenever I am sad, I can go to Jesus and He will make me feel better.

---

[22] "H7495 - rapha' - Strong's Hebrew Lexicon (KJV)." Blue Letter Bible. Accessed 11 Aug, 2020. https://www.blueletterbible.org//lang/lexicon/lexicon.cfm?Strongs=H7495&t=KJV

[23] I will explain why we have done this in Chapter 10, "The Missing Ingredient."

That is all *true*, but that is not the *full extent* of everything the Holy Spirit was saying through the Old Testament prophet Isaiah!

In the original text, the Hebrew word for "griefs" is *choliy*.[24] Do you know what *choliy* means? Sickness! The Holy Spirit's mission through the prophet Isaiah was to tell us that Jesus *has already* borne our sickness on the cross! Isaiah wasn't referring to emotional ailments or the pain of loss; he was referring specifically to sickness and disease. Amazing, isn't it? But it doesn't stop there.

In the original text, the Hebrew word for "sorrows" is *makob*.[25] Do you know what *makob* means? Pain! This is the same "pain" described in Job 33:19 as Job was "chastened with pain on his bed, and with strong pain in many of his bones." Again, Isaiah was not referring to an emotional condition or subjective sadness. He was referring to the *physical pain* a person would feel as a consequence of being afflicted with sickness and disease!

Jesus not only took care of your sin on the cross—He also took care of your sickness and disease! What Isaiah 53 means is this: Healing and salvation happened on the same day! Jesus never sinned, yet He *became sin* on the cross and took the punishment for your sins. In the same way, Jesus was never sick! Yet He *became sickness and disease* on the cross and *died,* so that you and I would know we have a legal, scriptural right to expect physical healing and divine health as part of the atonement. And if Jesus took on sickness and disease on the cross, that means as far as God is concerned, there is *none left for you!*

---

[24] "H2483 - choliy - Strong's Hebrew Lexicon (KJV)." Blue Letter Bible. Accessed 11 Aug, 2020. https://www.blueletterbible.org//lang/lexicon/lexicon.cfm?Strongs=H2483&t=KJV

[25] "H4341 - mak'ob - Strong's Hebrew Lexicon (KJV)." Blue Letter Bible. Accessed 11 Aug, 2020. https://www.blueletterbible.org//lang/lexicon/lexicon.cfm?Strongs=H4341&t=KJV

When I preached this message in our church, I used a visual illustration to get the point across. Before service, I inflated a bright blue kiddie pool about four feet wide. After preaching on Isaiah 53, I brought out the kiddie pool from behind the stage, put a chair in the middle of it, and asked for a volunteer. An immaculately-dressed gentleman who is an exemplary member at our church came forward to help me out.

At first, he was smiling. But when I brought out a bright red bucket full of several gallons of water, his countenance immediately changed from joy to terror. I could only imagine what was going through this man's mind as he sat there in his expensive shoes and well-pressed shirt, watching me approach him with that giant bucket of water.

I asked the congregation to imagine that our volunteer had had a "bad week." He hadn't attended Life Groups. He had missed his Bible study. He had been too lazy to wake up in the morning for prayer. So as a consequence, he was going to get soaked! The bucket was bright red, I explained to the people, because it represented the fiery wrath of God.

As I went to pour the contents of the bucket over his head, I shouted, "Somebody better stop me if this is not the gospel!" The whole room erupted with desperate shouts of "No!" and "Don't do it!" Our volunteer looked up at me out of the corner of one eye, as if pleading for mercy. I asked someone to explain to me why this was *not* the gospel, and people tossed several Scripture references and short exhortations across the room.

I put down the bucket and asked our volunteer to take my hand. I helped him out of the pool, and invited him to sit in the front row. As he breathed a sigh of relief, I placed a giant wooden cross on the chair where he had been sitting.

"This is the gospel," I explained to a room full of relieved Christians. I poured out the entire contents of the bucket out on the wooden cross.

"This is the wrath of God, meant for you, but poured out on Jesus Christ instead," I explained. This was the consequence for our sin, poured out on the cross. And according to Isaiah 53, this was also sin, sickness, disease, and death, poured out on God's only Son, Jesus Christ.

I held the bucket upside down until *every last drop* trickled out of the bucket. Jesus took *every ounce* of God's wrath—all pain, all sickness, all disease, and even death— for us on the cross. Then I held the bucket over our volunteer's head. Relief flooded his face. He stayed dry, because *nothing* was left to be poured out.

This is the beauty of the cross. Because Jesus took it all, that means there is *nothing left for you.*

> *Christ has redeemed us from the curse of the law, having become a curse for us (for it is written, "Cursed is everyone who hangs on a tree"), that the blessing of Abraham might come upon the Gentiles in Christ Jesus, that we might receive the promise of the Spirit through faith.* —Galatians 3:13-14

Testimonies Follow the Word

When I originally preached this message in our church, I could feel spiritual eyes opening across the room. People who had never heard that Jesus heals suddenly grasped the revelation that Jesus is our Healer. After preaching, I called people up for prayer. Whenever I preach on healing, I test the message. What better way to prove to God you really believe His Word than to pray for the things you've just declared?

One young man approached me because he had lost hearing in both ears. His vision had also deteriorated since he had started experiencing symptoms of depression several months prior. We prayed, and his hearing and vision immediately improved.

An older woman came up for prayer because she had experienced complete loss of hearing in her right ear. Doctors had told her she had "a hole in her eardrum" after years of using ear drops following frequent ear infections. As we prayed and I released God's healing virtue over her, she said she "felt a release of pressure" in her right ear and could hear again!

Yet another woman came up for prayer because she had been experiencing constant gastrointestinal pain for several weeks. I asked her to put her hand on her own stomach, and I gently laid my hand on top of her hand. I released the power of God over her,[26] and the pain immediately left. She testified of the miracle in front of the whole church.

Do you need a touch from God in your body? Respond to God's Word. Test it! Declare by faith that Jesus is the Healer, and expect your body to respond. Try to move something that wouldn't move before, or do something you couldn't do before!

As you step out in faith in response to God's Word, He will respond.

---

[26] More on this in Chapter 8, "Power to Heal!"

CHAPTER TWO

WHO IS THE AUTHOR OF SICKNESS?

In the last chapter, I went to great lengths to establish that God is *not* the author of sickness and disease. He doesn't want you sick—He wants you healed! So at this point you should be wondering, *Well if God doesn't make me sick, who does?*

Here's why the answer to that question is so important. If God is the One who gives us sickness and disease, we should accept them as a gift. We shouldn't want to get better if sickness is His will. We shouldn't visit the doctor or pursue recovery! We shouldn't take medication to take the edge off the pain. Our response to everything from the common cold to terminal illness should be, *More Lord!* After all, if God is the One who wants you sick, why would you try and ruin His will by being healed?

But if God is *not* the author of sickness and disease, we should wholeheartedly reject it. We should demonstrate an outright refusal to stand for *anything less* than perfect health, and posture ourselves in prayer accordingly.

I know too many Christians who think God wants them sick. Earlier this year, I was in Boston for a wedding. One of my best childhood friends was getting married, and it was the first time many in our group of friends had been together in years.

Another of our friends, Ted, was notably absent.[27] He had grown callous and withdrawn over the past few years. Every time I went home

---

[27] Throughout the manuscript I have changed names wherever necessary to protect privacy.

to visit my parents, I reached out to Ted and asked him to meet up, but Ted always had something else to do.

On my way to the wedding ceremony, walking down a cobblestone street in historic downtown Boston, I heard Ted's voice ring out. "Whitey!"[28] I turned around, surprised but delighted to see Ted. We hugged and exchanged small talk for a few minutes. Then we went inside the church and sat next to each other during the wedding. During the cocktail hour after the ceremony, we finally had the chance to catch up.

Ted shared with me that his wife was struggling with long-term illness. Some months, she was in the hospital for ten days out of thirty. She and he were both suffering through this, and trying to keep their relationship intact. However, they were tired. Ted confessed that even though he had promised to love his wife in sickness and in health, things had gotten so bad that both he and his wife wondered if they should stay together. They were separated and headed towards divorce.

"What I can't wrap my head around," Ted eventually admitted, "is *why* would God do this to us?"

I took a deep breath and chose my next words very carefully. I wanted to support Ted and say something that would heal instead of hurt, so I offered this: "But what if it isn't God?"

Ted looked at me quizzically. After several seconds, he asked me what I meant. For the next fifteen minutes, we talked about the reality that Satan exists. I explained that he is the author of sickness and disease. He is the one who tries to ruin our lives, not God. Satan is the one who brings pain and suffering, and then tries to convince us that we have to live with it!

At the end of our conversation, Ted smiled and said, "I never thought of that."

---

[28] My last name is White, and this was my nickname for several years in high school.

26

Can you see it? Can you see how the enemy sneaks into our lives and we don't even know it? Can you see how Satan loves to trick us into pinning his work on God?

I cannot tell you how many people—*especially Christians*—have that same false notion about God. We think God wants us to suffer needlessly. We think He's out to get us! I wholeheartedly believe that *biblical* suffering[29] has a purpose, and God works through it, but to say that God is the *author* of suffering is, quite frankly, biblically inaccurate.

If you think your sickness is from God, you will accept it. You will rationalize that God is teaching you something through your pain, and refuse to do the hard work of praying for healing. But if sickness is *not* from God, you must reject it with every fiber of your being!

I will be the first to admit that there is *tension* that arises when we discover God wants us to be well, because we live in a world where people—*even Christians!*—are often very sick, and we all eventually die. But I believe it is our job to live in that tension. We should never read the Word of God through the lens of our imperfect life experience. Rather, we should view our life experience through the lens of God's perfect Word! Just because you are not healed *does not mean* that God's will is for you to be anything but healthy. And just because you are sick *certainly does not mean* that God is the author of your disease.

The Book of Job

The story of Job is perhaps the example in Scripture that people most often point to as "proof" that God puts sickness on His people. Job went through a lot, and he learned a lot. But to say that God "caused" Job's suffering is simply not true:

---

[29] "For I will show him how many things he must suffer for My name's sake." —Acts 9:16

There was a man in the land of Uz, whose name was Job; and that man was blameless and upright, and one who feared God and shunned evil. And seven sons and three daughters were born to him. Also, his possessions were seven thousand sheep, three thousand camels, five hundred yoke of oxen, five hundred female donkeys, and a very large household, so that this man was the greatest of all the people of the East. —Job 1:1-3

Job was "blameless and upright." The word we would use in contemporary theology to describe Job is "righteous." Job was about to suffer through incredible calamity, but we *have to understand* that it was not his fault. Everything that happened to Job was not the result of Job messing up, followed by God inevitably punishing him for his mistakes. If Job was "blameless and upright," that means he hadn't made any mistakes worthy of punishment.

This nips "retribution theology" in the bud. Retribution theology claims that we receive the reward we deserve for our actions from God. If we do good, we will get good things from God! But if we do bad, we will get bad things from God. Job's friends thought this was the case in Job's life.[30] They assumed Job's suffering was his fault. But if Scripture says Job was "blameless," that means his suffering was *not* the consequence of any mistake(s) he had made.

So if Job's suffering wasn't his own fault, then whose fault was it?

Now there was a day when the sons of God came to present themselves before the Lord, and Satan also came among them. And the Lord said to Satan, "From where do you come?" So Satan answered the Lord

---

[30] Job 4:7 provides one example, as Job's friend, Eliphaz, asks Job: "Remember now, who ever perished being innocent? Or where were the upright ever cut off?"

and said, "From going to and fro on the earth, and from walking back and forth on it."

Then the Lord said to Satan, "Have you considered My servant Job, that there is none like him on the earth, a blameless and upright man, one who fears God and shuns evil?"

So Satan answered the Lord and said, "Does Job fear God for nothing? Have You not made a hedge around him, around his household, and around all that he has on every side? You have blessed the work of his hands, and his possessions have increased in the land. But now, stretch out Your hand and touch all that he has, and he will surely curse You to Your face!" —Job 1:6-11

Here we see the true culprit, and the author of Job's suffering and sickness: *Satan.* Scripture identifies Satan as the "accuser of our brethren."[31] His primary objective is to accuse you before God. Here we see him doing *exactly that* with Job. God *loves Job!* He is proud of Job! In verse 8, we even see God *bragging* to the heavenly host about what an amazing man and servant Job is!

But Satan *hates it* when God loves you, because Satan can never fully receive the love of God. So Satan's retaliation is to try and bring pain and suffering into your life. He cannot take the love of God from you! But he can do his best to put you through so much pain and suffering that you are persuaded to *give up* your love for God.

---

[31] "Then I heard a loud voice saying in heaven, 'Now salvation, and strength, and the kingdom of our God, and the power of His Christ have come, for the accuser of our brethren, who accused them before our God day and night, has been cast down.'" —Rev. 12:10

And the Lord said to Satan, "Behold, all that he has is in your power; only do not lay a hand on his person." So Satan went out from the presence of the Lord. —Job 1:12

It was Satan's "power"—not God's—that caused sickness and suffering in Job's life. Satan comes to "steal, and to kill, and to destroy," but Jesus has come that you may have abundant life![32]

We know the rest of the story. In Job 1, Job loses all his property and children (see vv 13-22), but he refuses to "charge God with wrong" (v 22). Isn't it interesting that Job—the man experiencing the suffering—refused to attribute his calamity to God, yet so often, we assume God was the one who caused Job's mess?

In Job 2, Satan goes at it again. He "struck Job with painful boils from the sole of his foot to the crown of his head" (Job 2:7). Things got so bad that even Job's wife told him, "Curse God and die!" (Job 2:9). Yet even then, Job "did not sin with his lips" (v 10) by attributing Satan's work to God.

Now you may be wondering, why would God allow this to happen in Job's life? If God really loved Job so much, why would He let the enemy waltz in like that and steal everything that belonged to Job?[33] I don't have all the answers, and I won't trivialize your pain by attempting to offer an explanation of the "why" in this book. I will, however, give guidelines as to "where" we go from here.

For our purposes as it relates to healing, there are two primary takeaways from the Book of Job:

---

[32] "The thief does not come except to steal, and to kill, and to destroy. I have come that they may have life, and that they may have it more abundantly." —Jn. 10:10

[33] For a thorough treatment on the theology of suffering, I highly recommend the book *Why Suffering?* by Ravi Zacharias and Vince Vitale.

1) God restored double.

It is true that Satan stole *everything* from Job. It is also true that what Satan stole, God restored:

> *Now the Lord blessed the latter days of Job more than his beginning;*
> *for he had fourteen thousand sheep, six thousand camels, one*
> *thousand yoke of oxen, and one thousand female donkeys. He also had*
> *seven sons and three daughters. And he called the name of the first*
> *Jemimah, the name of the second Keziah, and the name of the third*
> *Keren-Happuch. In all the land were found no women so beautiful*
> *as the daughters of Job; and their father gave them an inheritance*
> *among their brothers.* —Job 42:12-15

Satan steals, but God restores. And God not only restores *fully*—He restores *double*. Because Job never lost his faith, God gave Job "twice as much" as he had before (Job 42:10). Double restoration is a constant refrain throughout Scripture.[34] Our role is not to *understand* everything God allows. Our job is to understand that whatever the enemy steals— whether health, relationships, or wealth—God will doubly restore.

Please do not accept your sickness as a gift from God. It is a curse from Satan, but God will remove it and install blessing in its place!

2) Job had no mediator . . . but you do!

Satan had it out for Job, and for whatever reason, God allowed Satan to take his best shot. But now that Jesus is here, *everything has changed.*

Job had no mediator. He had no one to step in and deny Satan access to his life. Yet because of the cross, you and I do:

---

[34] See Zech. 9:12; Isa. 61:7

For there is one God and one Mediator between God and men, the Man Christ Jesus, who gave Himself a ransom for all, to be testified in due time . . . —1 *Timothy 2:5-6*

When Satan asked for Job, Job had no one to advocate on his behalf. Yet because of the blood of Jesus, you and I do!

My little children, these things I write to you, so that you may not sin. And if anyone sins, we have an Advocate with the Father, Jesus Christ the righteous. And He Himself is the propitiation for our sins, and not for ours only but also for the whole world. —1 *John 2:1-2*

Don't you see that everything changes on this side of the cross? Job poses an old covenant question, but Jesus gives a new covenant answer! Jesus! Because Jesus came and died on the cross as your sickness and pain, you don't have to *worry* about Satan coming after you like he came after Job!

In fact, Scripture gives us a New Testament parallel of Job 1 to show us *exactly* what would happen if Satan came after one of Jesus' disciples:

And the Lord said, "Simon, Simon! Indeed, Satan has asked for you, that he may sift you as wheat. But I have prayed for you, that your faith should not fail; and when you have returned to Me, strengthen your brethren." —*Luke 22:31-32*

Now that Jesus is here, nothing is the same. "Simon" is the disciple we know as Peter. This is the same Peter who walked on the water before taking his eyes off Jesus and sinking.[35] This is the same Peter who told

---

[35] "And Peter answered Him and said, 'Lord, if it is You, command me to come to You on the water.' So He said, 'Come.' And when Peter had come down out of the boat, he walked on the water to go to Jesus. But when he saw that the wind was boisterous, he was afraid; and beginning to sink he cried out, saying, 'Lord, save me!'" —Matt. 14:28-30

Jesus he would follow Him even unto death![36] Satan knew the powerful destiny Peter had ahead of him, so he tried to sabotage it. Satan asked for Peter, just as he asked for Job!

But look at how the divine response changes on this side of the cross: *"I have prayed for you"* (v 32). Jesus is our Mediator! He is our Advocate! Jesus put His hand up, and said *no* to Satan. Where the old covenant said yes (Job 1:11), the new covenant says no! It wasn't that God changed His mind—it was simply that a new covenant was in place through Jesus Christ that facilitated a different measure of grace in response to Satan's request. *Not on My watch! Peter's with me!* And that is *exactly* what Jesus' response would be if Satan asked for you.

Aren't you so happy that you don't have to worry about Satan attacking you like he attacked Job? Aren't you so glad you have a Mediator and an Advocate who will resist Satan on your behalf? Aren't you amazed that Jesus, at this very moment, is "making intercession"[37] for you, and protecting you from the sickness and disease Satan wants you to have?

Under the new covenant, everything changes. Job had lots of questions, but in Jesus, you have the answer.

Why Did God Allow It?

If God is really good, why did He allow Job to go through so much? This is similar to a question I am asked quite a bit: If God is really so good, why does He allow people to get sick?

---

[36] "Peter said to Him, 'Even if all are made to stumble, yet I will not be.' Jesus said to him, 'Assuredly, I say to you that today, even this night, before the rooster crows twice, you will deny Me three times.' But he spoke more vehemently, 'If I have to die with You, I will not deny You!' And they all said likewise." —Mk. 14:29-31

[37] "Who is he who condemns? It is Christ who died, and furthermore is also risen, who is even at the right hand of God, who also makes intercession for us." —Rom. 8:34

The gospel of John gives us the same answer in two different places. In John 9, Jesus encountered "a man who was blind from birth." The disciples asked him, "Rabbi, who sinned, this man or his parents, that he was born blind?" (v 2). The disciples assumed that retribution theology was the way Jesus worked. If this man was blind, surely someone must have done something to deserve it!

But Jesus balked at their question. He provided His own answer that would forever change the disciples' mindset—and one that should forever change yours and mine:

> Jesus answered, "Neither this man nor his parents sinned, but that the works of God should be revealed in him."　　　　　—John 9:3

The purpose of this man's blindness was not to pay him or his parents back for sin! The express purpose of his blindness was so that the glory of God might be revealed.

We see the same truth illustrated in John 11, before Jesus raises Lazarus from the dead. Jesus heard that Lazarus was sick! And here was His comment on the matter:

> When Jesus heard that, He said, "This sickness is not unto death, but for the glory of God, that the Son of God may be glorified through it."
> 　　　　　　　　　　　　　　　　　　　　　　—John 11:4

The purpose of Lazarus' sickness was not to kill him or to teach him a lesson! It was to provide an opportunity for God to be glorified as Lazarus was healed.

So why does God allow sickness to exist? So that His glory will be revealed as He heals! That is where Jesus comes in.

Undoing Satan's Work

Throughout the Gospels, we see that Jesus spent His entire earthly ministry *undoing* the work of the devil:

> [H]ow God anointed Jesus of Nazareth with the Holy Spirit and with power, who went about doing good and healing all who were oppressed by the devil, for God was with Him.   —Acts 10:38

Healing is the release of God's "power." And it is also the *removal* of oppression caused "by the devil." The devil puts sickness on, and Jesus takes it off!

Jesus' mission was to eradicate sickness and disease. Everywhere He went, people were healed. Everywhere He went, the oppressed were set free. Everywhere He went, eyes were opened, ears were unstopped, and the dead were raised! Now if Jesus spent His time on earth eliminating the devil's work, what sense would it make for us to accept it into our lives with open arms here and now?

God and Jesus are One. So now that Jesus is seated at the right hand of the Father in heavenly places,[38] God is not going to turn around and put the same sickness Jesus removed back on His people! A house divided cannot stand![39] Jesus was not some rebellious teenager who spent His time on earth doing something His Father didn't want Him to do and trying to hide it from His Dad! He is the perfect Son of God, exercising His Father's perfect will. And do you know what His Father's will is? *Healing!*

---

[38] "[W]hich He worked in Christ when He raised Him from the dead and seated Him at His right hand in the heavenly places . . ." —Eph. 1:20

[39] "But Jesus knew their thoughts, and said to them: 'Every kingdom divided against itself is brought to desolation, and every city or house divided against itself will not stand.'" —Matt. 12:25

Paul's Thorn in the Flesh

Along with Job, Paul's "thorn in the flesh" is another example in Scripture to which people love to point and say, "See! God made someone sick!"

The apostle Paul describes his suffering in his second letter to the church at Corinth:

> *And lest I should be exalted above measure by the abundance of the revelations, a thorn in the flesh was given to me, a messenger of Satan to buffet me, lest I be exalted above measure.* —2 *Corinthians 12:7*

Paul had a *good problem.* He was getting such heavy doses of revelation straight from heaven all the time that Satan got frustrated. So, Paul was given "a thorn in the flesh . . . a messenger of Satan to buffet me." Notice again the author of Paul's suffering. This was a messenger of *Satan.* Messenger is the Greek *angelos,*[40] which is where we get our English word "angel." Paul's thorn in the flesh was not a sickness or disease from God meant to keep Paul humble! It was *demonic resistance*—a messenger sent by Satan to buffet Paul.

In another portion of the same letter to the Corinthians, Paul describes the suffering he experienced for the sake of the gospel:

> *From the Jews five times I received forty stripes minus one. Three times I was beaten with rods; once I was stoned; three times I was shipwrecked; a night and a day I have been in the deep . . .*
> —2 *Corinthians 11:24-25*

---

[40] "G32 - angelos - Strong's Greek Lexicon (KJV)." Blue Letter Bible. Accessed 11 Aug, 2020. https://www.blueletterbible.org//lang/lexicon/lexicon. cfm?Strongs=G32&t=KJV.

Paul was scourged with thirty-nine lashes on five separate occasions! That means he was whipped until the flesh hung off his back with a cat-o'-nine-tails, which typically had sharp pieces of bone and/or metal on the ends of the cords designed to rip the flesh from a man's body. Three times he was beaten with rods. He was stoned and left for dead![41] He was shipwrecked on three separate occasions, and on one of those occasions, he was stranded alone in the ocean for a day and a half!

Paul was not struggling with sickness—he was dealing with demonic resistance to his preaching of the gospel. So how did he respond?

> *Concerning this thing I pleaded with the Lord three times that it might depart from me.*   —2 Corinthians 12:8

If Paul's suffering was some sort of holy sickness from God, would he have begged God to take it away? If this "thorn in the flesh" was some disease that God wanted Paul to have, Paul wouldn't have said, "Lord, take it away!" His response would have been, "More, Lord!"

As Paul pleaded, here was the divine response:

> *And He said to me, "My grace is sufficient for you, for My strength is made perfect in weakness." Therefore most gladly I will rather boast in my infirmities, that the power of Christ may rest upon me. Therefore I take pleasure in infirmities, in reproaches, in needs, in persecutions, in distresses, for Christ's sake. For when I am weak, then I am strong.*   —2 Corinthians 12:9-10

---

[41] "Then Jews from Antioch and Iconium came there; and having persuaded the multitudes, they stoned Paul and dragged him out of the city, supposing him to be dead. However, when the disciples gathered around him, he rose up and went into the city. And the next day he departed with Barnabas to Derbe." —Acts 14:19-20

For whatever reason, God *permitted* Paul's suffering, but let's be clear that He did not cause it. And Paul's suffering had *nothing* to do with illness, and everything to do with demonic resistance to the work God had given him to do.

You see the word "infirmities" twice in verses 9 and 10 above. There again, Christians who advocate for their right to be sick love to point a finger and say, "Aha! See, Paul was sick!"[42] But "weakness" and "infirmity" are both the Greek word *astheneia*,[43] which refers to the human body's relative frailty in comparison to God's strength, as opposed to sickness compared to relative health.

God's exhortation to Paul was not, "Accept this sickness from Me!" It was, *"Don't lose faith"* — the same prayer Jesus prayed for Simon Peter in Luke 22! Paul was not supposed to hide what he was experiencing. He was to tell other people, so 1) they could be encouraged, and 2) he could become a magnet for the grace and power of Jesus Christ. The more you boast about your frailty, the more you will become a magnet for the Holy Spirit's strength!

Ananias and Sapphira

The *one and only* example of a "Christian" being struck by God with sickness, disease, or death of which I am aware in the New Testament is the story of Ananias and Sapphira. Acts 4:32 says that the members of the early church "had all things in common." When someone was in lack, those in the church who had abundance made up for it by giving a generous offering.

---

[42] These same proponents of misery also point to Galatians 6:11, "See with what large letters I have written to you with my own hand," as supposed evidence that Paul had an eye disease. But alas, Paul's comment refers to the length of his letters, and not the size of his handwriting.

[43] "G769 - astheneia - Strong's Greek Lexicon (KJV)." Blue Letter Bible. Accessed 11 Aug, 2020. https://www.blueletterbible.org//lang/lexicon/lexicon.cfm?Strongs=G769&t=KJV

In this atmosphere of supernatural generosity, Ananias and Sapphira claimed to be someone they were not. They sold a possession, and though they told church leadership they were donating all the proceeds to their faith community, they "held back part of the proceeds" (Acts 5:2). In response, God was upset. The Holy Spirit struck and killed Ananias (v 5). Then, just several hours later, God also struck down his wife, Sapphira (v 10).

But again, look who was really behind the whole attack:

> But Peter said, "Ananias, why has Satan filled your heart to lie to the Holy Spirit and keep back part of the price of the land for yourself?"
> — Acts 5:3

Ananias and Sapphira lied to the Holy Spirit, but it was Satan who had filled their hearts to do so. And if Satan had filled their hearts, were they really Christian at all? By my estimation, Ananias and Sapphira were no more "Christian" than was Judas when Satan filled his heart to betray Jesus.[44]

This was not, then, the case of God striking down His people. This was an instance of two people stepping outside the protective covering of God's covenant, thereby becoming subject to the curse Jesus would have gladly accepted in their place had they simply believed in Him.

Let It Ring

My wife and I live in Brooklyn along with our children. Our building has what's called a "Virtual Doorman." That's really just a fancy name for an intercom panel on the wall outside our building. When someone comes

---

[44] "Then Satan entered Judas, surnamed Iscariot, who was numbered among the twelve. So he went his way and conferred with the chief priests and captains, how he might betray Him to them." —Lk. 22:3-4

to visit, they type in our apartment number, and a bell in our apartment rings so we can unlock the door downstairs and let them in.

Several years ago, we had a problem in our building. People would come to the door dressed as employees from UPS, FedEx, or the US Postal Service. They really didn't work for those companies, but they wore the uniform to perpetuate a scam. They would ring the buzzers for apartments in our building, and wait for someone to let them in. Their goal was to steal packages full of things people had ordered from online retailers.

Unfortunately, time and time again, residents in our building would *let these people in*! This frustrated me to no end. After all, there was a *video feed* on the intercom system! All you had to do was look closely when your buzzer rang and see who was actually trying to get inside and refuse to let them in! But people weren't willing to *do the hard work* of *looking closely and saying no.* So, they would just let the thieves right in.

Sometimes we treat the door to our body the same way. The enemy shows up, pretending to be God, with sickness and disease! But because we haven't done the hard work of seeing what Scripture really says about sickness and disease, instead of turning Satan away, we let him right in! He walks right in and drops off sickness, disease, doubt, and unbelief. And because we're too scared to tell him to get out, he walks off with the gifts (peace, love, and divine health) God wants us to have.

The moral of the story is this: don't let Satan in! When he comes and tries to drop off something that doesn't belong to you, say no. Find the truth in God's Word, and tell the enemy to take a hike!

Testimony Time

When you understand that Satan—not God—is the one who wants you sick, everything changes. You will no longer be plagued with doubt and wonder, *Why did God do this to me?* Instead, you will understand that while the enemy wants to cripple you, God wants you healed and set free!

A woman struggling with pain all over her body came to the Healing Rooms at CityLight Church for prayer on Saturday, September 14th, 2019. She had so many different issues causing pain in her body that she didn't know where to start! So, we asked the Holy Spirit where He wanted us to begin, and one by one, He revealed points of pain and discomfort in this woman's body so we could see them healed in Jesus' name.

But before we could start to pray, we had to have a quick conversation about Scripture. You see, this woman thought that her sickness from God. She thought that He *wanted her* to have pain in her body so she could learn to be humble! We shared with her some of the same verses that I've just shared with you. As we did, things started to change. Her body started to loosen up, and one by one, every ache and pain she asked us to pray for was healed.

Here is the testimony she left us:

> "I came to the healing rooms and asked for prayer over my stomach, right heel, and my lower back pain. The [prayer team members] were persistent and cast out doubt, unbelief, and fear, and I received the love of Christ and the Holy Spirit healed me from all three things.
>
> I had a bone spur in my heel that always caused me pain and right now I feel nothing: no pain! I came with high expectancy and I got healed. I am so grateful and happy about what God did for me." —DN, 9/14/19

We should be a church that not only preaches healing, but also experiences it time and time again! Take a risk. Take God at His word. Believe Jesus heals! And watch what He does.

41

CHAPTER THREE

YOUR HEALING IS UNIQUE

So far we've laid the foundation of the biblical response to sickness and disease. God wants to heal you—so much so that He sent Jesus to die *as* your sin.[45] Satan wants to make you sick, but there is a limit to his power to touch you now that you have a Mediator.[46] This is the divine struggle, and you have been thrust in the middle with a mandate to not only cling to the Word of God for your own healing, but also to demonstrate God's power to people who don't know Jesus (yet!) as you pray and God heals them.

Now we're going to move from a theoretical discussion of healing into the practical. When God heals, how does He do it? What does healing look like? As we see people healed in Scripture, are there any commonalities across their experiences from which we can learn and grow? Does seeing how God has healed other people before us tell us anything we can use to pursue our own healing as effectively as possible?

How God Heals

Step one in the healing process is cultivating a desire to be healed. Do you want to be healed? That might seem like a silly question. Most of us would cry out in response with a resounding "Yes!" But a desire to

---

[45] "For He made Him who knew no sin *to be* sin for us, that we might become the righteousness of God in Him." —2 Cor. 5:21, emphasis added

[46] "For there is one God and one Mediator between God and men, the Man Christ Jesus, who gave Himself a ransom for all, to be testified in due time..." —1 Tim. 2:5-6

be healed must be present. Jesus healed all who "came to Him"[47] and all who were "brought . . . to Him""[48] (This will be the theme of our discussion in the next chapter.)

Step two in the healing process, which we will address first, is asking God, "What is my healing going to look like?" I'm intentionally addressing step two first, because I often meet people who are disappointed because they haven't already been healed. Their disappointment often leads to apathy or resentment, and they lose their desire to be healed altogether and/or rationalize that God must be trying to "teach them something" through their sickness. So before we can even address what is logically step one, we need to address the hurt and pain that sometimes surface as a result of a failure to understand step two.

The general thesis of this chapter is this: You should have a relationship with God in which you *expect* to hear from Him. What you expect will, in large part, dictate what you experience. This is paramount for your healing process. Even Jesus cultivated an expectation that His Father would *show Him* everything He wanted Him to do before He would go out and do it:

> *"Most assuredly, I say to you, the Son can do nothing of Himself, but what He sees the Father do; for whatever He does, the Son also does in like manner."*
> —*John 5:19*

In that vein, I believe God will *show you* what He wants your healing process to look like, so you know how best to position yourself to receive the healing Jesus died for you to have!

---

[47] See Matt. 8:5, Matt. 9:28, Matt. 15:30, Matt. 17:14, Matt. 21:14, Mk. 1:40, Mk. 1:45, Mk. 2:3

[48] "When the sun was setting, all those who had any that were sick with various diseases brought them to Him; and He laid His hands on every one of them and healed them." —Lk. 4:40; more on this in Chapter 15, "Whom Does God Heal?"

Copycat Healings

Sometimes your healing will look exactly like someone else's. Don't let the term "copycat healing" trick you. If your healing looks like someone else's, that is certainly not a bad thing!

We see an example of God replicating a particular sequence of events in the healing process for different people in Matthew's gospel. First, we see a "woman who had a flow of blood for twelve years" approach Jesus, desperate for her healing:

> *And suddenly, a woman who had a flow of blood for twelve years came from behind and touched the hem of His garment. For she said to herself, "If only I may touch His garment, I shall be made well." But Jesus turned around, and when He saw her He said, "Be of good cheer, daughter; your faith has made you well." And the woman was made well from that hour.*
> *—Matthew 9:20-22*

There is much to be said on this passage.[49] This woman had exhausted every other path to healing of which she was aware. Nothing had worked, so, out of desperation, she turned to Jesus. There is faith in action here. There is insistence at play. There is boldness. It was illegal for this "unclean" woman to be in public, and had she been found in public in her condition, she could have been stoned![50]

However, for our purposes in this chapter, all I want you to notice is that once this woman received her healing, others followed suit.

---

[49] We will cover this passage in much greater detail in Chapter 8.

[50] Also notice that one of the enemy's goals in sickness is to get you separated from community. It was "illegal" for this woman to be in community because she was sick. For you, it may not be "illegal," but it very well may be uncomfortable and/or inconvenient.

*When they had crossed over, they came to the land of Gennesaret.
And when the men of that place recognized Him, they sent out into
all that surrounding region, brought to Him all who were sick, and
begged Him that they might only touch the hem of His garment. And
as many as touched it were made perfectly well.*

—Matthew 14:34-36

When other people saw *how* this woman was healed, they went out
and did the same things she did! They begged to "touch the hem of His
garment." And do you know what? It worked! *Everyone* who touched the
hem of Jesus' garment was made "perfectly well" (v. 36).

So, do you know someone who has been healed? Ask them how they
got their healing! Ask them what, if anything, they changed about their
lifestyle. Ask them how they grew their faith! This woman in Matthew 9
paved the way for an entire generation of believers to be healed by her
radical faith. People did as she did, and got the same results! This should
be our starting point.

Sometimes God heals the same way He's healed before. In our
Healing Rooms, we've had multiple instances in a short time frame
of people being healed exactly the same way. One of our volunteers,
Daniela, was miraculously healed of hip and back pain when another
volunteer, Richie, prayed for her and her leg grew out! Here is Daniela's
testimony:

On June 7th, 2019, I volunteered at the Healing Rooms with
great expectation to see healing and deliverance for others. I
interceded through prayer for those that would be touched by
this great ministry. To my surprise, I was called out by Richie.
He had me sit straight up in a chair and asked me to look
towards my feet. He then asked me what I saw.

For the first time, I noticed that my right leg was shorter than my left. Richie laid his hands on my leg and prayed, and to my amazement, the leg began to grow. Finally, it all made sense. I had always felt discomfort on my hip, but never gave it much thought. I was completely healed! ALL GLORY TO MY LORD JESUS CHRIST WHO IS THE SAME YESTERDAY, TODAY, AND FOREVERMORE!   —DA, 6/7/2019

But it didn't stop there! Another one of our volunteers, Mary, watched Daniela's miracle unfold right in front of her eyes. Here is Mary's account of Daniela's healing:

Towards the end of the healing room time, I was in a corner with Daniela. Richie came over—he went straight to Daniela and sat in front of her. He held out his hands and told Daniela to give him her feet, which she did. I was sitting to her right, and I could see clearly that her right leg was shorter than her left leg. Richie asked me what I saw, and I replied that her right leg was shorter. Before my eyes, her right leg grew until it was equal length with her left leg! We were both so happy and overwhelmed at Abba's grace and love.

However, later that evening at home, the events of the day really hit me. I realized I had witnessed a miracle with my own eyes. Between the words spoken over me, and the miracle I witnessed, I was in awe and stunned by the grace and love of our God! Miracles do happen, in New York City, in 2019!
                                        —MB, 6/7/2019

But it gets even better! The next month, someone walked into the Healing Rooms and asked for prayer for hip and back pain. Because our volunteers had just seen the miracle God worked in Daniela, a group of them jumped at the opportunity to pray. They were filled with faith and prayed with all their heart, and guess what? They watched as the client's leg grew out one full inch.

Isn't that beautiful? Our team witnessed Daniela's miracle, and from that moment on they were so full of faith for God to heal the same thing, the same way, that healing happened when they released their faith over someone who needed prayer for the same condition! God will show you how He did it in someone else, so you will have the faith to believe He will do it again.

Wouldn't it be nice and easy if all healings happened like that? But healing doesn't always happen the same way. If you try everything you saw someone else to do get healed, and nothing works, *don't get discouraged*. Using a successful model you have seen before is the best place to start! But more often than not, no two healings are exactly alike.

Your Unique Healing

You are unique. God made you *you* on purpose. And that means, more than likely, your healing process is going to be unique too! So don't get frustrated if you try what worked for someone else and it doesn't work for you! There is a process at play. Sometimes God does it right away, but sometimes He asks you to *lean into His presence* in new ways before your healing comes. Just because it doesn't happen to you the way it happened to someone else doesn't mean God isn't going to do it. It doesn't mean He loves you any less! It simply means you have to return to that step two question: "God, what is my healing going to look like?"

Naaman the Syrian

Naaman was "commander of the army of the king of Syria" (2 Kings 5:1). He was a "great and honorable" man (v 1), feared on the battlefield, and respected by everyone in the nation of Syria. However, Naaman had a not-so-secret problem. He was a leper:

> *Now Naaman, commander of the army of the king of Syria, was a great and honorable man in the eyes of his master, because by him the Lord had given victory to Syria. He was also a mighty man of valor, but a leper.*
> —2 Kings 5:1

Look at how Scripture frames a description of Naaman. He had everything you could ever want! He was successful! But there was one thing missing. He wasn't healthy. He wasn't experiencing the fullness and the goodness of God in his life! So God positioned someone special next to Naaman so he could hear God's heart:

> *And the Syrians had gone out on raids, and had brought back captive a young girl from the land of Israel. She waited on Naaman's wife. Then she said to her mistress, "If only my master were with the prophet who is in Samaria! For he would heal him of his leprosy." And Naaman went in and told his master, saying, "Thus and thus said the girl who is from the land of Israel."* —2 Kings 5:2-4

That was all Naaman needed to hear. Up until that point, he had *no idea* healing was even possible! He thought he would be a leper for the rest of his life. But out of nowhere, God caused a messenger to come forth. A young slave girl shared the news I have been sharing with you: "Did you know that God is the Healer?" So Naaman made a decision. If healing was an option available to him, he was going to pursue it!

Think through this with me. Naaman was a Gentile ruler under the old covenant. He was *not* one of God's people! Yet even in that "lost" state, God wanted to heal him! Even then, God made sure Naaman knew that He is the Healer. If God was willing to do that for a Gentile under the old covenant, how much more is He willing to heal His you and me—His sons and daughters—under the new covenant!

First, God is going to heal you. Then, He is going to give you the same opportunity He gave to this "young girl from the land of Israel" when she was in a foreign land. You get to go out and tell other people that God is the God Who Heals!

As soon as Naaman asked, the king of Syria granted his request:

> Then the king of Syria said, "Go now, and I will send a letter to the king of Israel." So he departed and took with him ten talents of silver, six thousand shekels of gold, and ten changes of clothing. Then he brought the letter to the king of Israel, which said, Now be advised, when this letter comes to you, that I have sent Naaman my servant to you, that you may heal him of his leprosy.
>
> And it happened, when the king of Israel read the letter, that he tore his clothes and said, "Am I God, to kill and make alive, that this man sends a man to me to heal him of his leprosy? Therefore please consider, and see how he seeks a quarrel with me."
>
> —2 Kings 5:5-7

The king of Israel should have rejoiced that Naaman was coming to get his healing! Instead, he panicked. Unfortunately, this is the typical pastoral response when people ask for healing prayer, and the reason we don't hear about physical healing more in church. Too often, pastors and leaders don't talk about healing because they are afraid that if they do, people will come to them and ask for healing![51]

---

[51] More on this in Chapter 10, "The Missing Ingredient."

The king was afraid, because he didn't have confidence that God would heal through him. But there was a man in Israel who didn't have that problem:

> *So it was, when Elisha the man of God heard that the king of Israel had torn his clothes, that he sent to the king, saying, "Why have you torn your clothes? Please let him come to me, and he shall know that there is a prophet in Israel."*   *—2 Kings 5:8*

This should be the church's response! When someone comes to us who is sick and in pain, hurting and in need of healing, we should step up to the challenge with *eager anticipation* for what God is about to do! We shouldn't back away as if we're not sure He's going to do it!

> *Then Naaman went with his horses and chariot, and he stood at the door of Elisha's house. And Elisha sent a messenger to him, saying, "Go and wash in the Jordan seven times, and your flesh shall be restored to you, and you shall be clean." But Naaman became furious, and went away and said, "Indeed, I said to myself, 'He will surely come out to me, and stand and call on the name of the Lord his God, and wave his hand over the place, and heal the leprosy.' Are not the Abanah and the Pharpar, the rivers of Damascus, better than all the waters of Israel? Could I not wash in them and be clean?" So he turned and went away in a rage.*   *—2 Kings 5:9-12*

Take very careful note of what is happening here. This is Naaman failing to complete step two. He had already finished step one! He had a desire to be healed, and he believed God could do it. But he failed to stop and ask the question, "God, what is my healing going to look like?"

51

Naaman had very particular expectations about what his healing *had to* look like. He wanted his healing to be dramatic, as evidenced by his self-reflection: "Indeed, I said to myself, 'He will surely come out to me, and stand and call on the name of the Lord his God, and wave his hand over the place, and heal the leprosy'" (v 11). Naaman wanted a lightning bolt to flash across the sky, and a boom of thunder to shake the ground! Then he would know he had been healed! But when God refused to be bound by Naaman's expectations, Naaman was *furious*.

Are you expecting your healing to look a certain way? Were you hoping to be healed in a public and dramatic way, with the eyes of your church watching? Or maybe you were hoping to be healed in private, so nobody even knew you were sick in the first place? God will do what is necessary to remind you that *your healing is unique*. Our first response is to try and do exactly the same thing someone else has already done! But if that fails, the biblical response is to ask God, "What is my healing supposed to look like?" and wait for an answer.

God humbled Naaman. When Naaman showed up at Elisha's house, the prophet wouldn't even come to the door. The path to healing was simple! All Naaman had to do was dip in the Jordan River seven times, and he would be completely healed. At first, Naaman refused to believe that his healing would be anything less than exceptionally dramatic. But then wise counsel spoke into Naaman's life:

> *And his servants came near and spoke to him, and said, "My father, if the prophet had told you to do something great, would you not have done it? How much more then, when he says to you, 'Wash, and be clean'?"* —2 Kings 5:13

In that moment, Naaman's servants were wiser than their master because their emotions were not tied up in the situation. His servants asked a fair question. If God had given you something *hard* to do, wouldn't you have done it? How much *easier*, then, was it to fulfill the simple request God was making? So Naaman did:

> *So he went down and dipped seven times in the Jordan, according to*
> *the saying of the man of God; and his flesh was restored like the flesh*
> *of a little child, and he was clean.*   —*2 Kings 5:14*

Naaman was healed when he 1) abandoned his expectations of what his healing "should" look like, and 2) did what God asked him to do. Many times, God heals this way. He will give you something 1) insanely simple and 2) seemingly inconsequential to do, because He wants to test your humility. He wants to test your obedience! He wants you to *lean on Him* like never before.

If God gives you something simple to do, will you do it?

The Exploration Process

God has healed me this way several times. The first case is excruciatingly embarrassing, so I'll share it with you so you don't feel so bad about what you're going through. I used to have sweaty hands.[52] I'm not talking about hands that get a little clammy before a sermon or an interview. I mean they were so sweaty, even when I was sitting around and doing *absolutely nothing*, that my hands would drip like I had just stepped out of a *pool!*

Gross, right? You can see how that would be a problem as a pastor. Do you know how embarrassing it was for *years* to finish preaching a message and stand at the back of the sanctuary to shake hands, only to know I was getting everyone soaking wet with my sweaty palms? My

---

[52] The medical term for this is hyperhidrosis.

condition was so bad that I seriously thought about *quitting ministry* altogether, just to avoid being in a situation where I would have to come in contact with other people. And prayer meetings when we would all hold hands? Forget it. I avoided them like the plague.

I cried out to God for my healing, but for whatever reason, He allowed the sweaty hands to persist for over a decade. I did *everything* I could think of to change my body chemistry. I tried antiperspirants. I drank lots of cold water. I even went up to Columbia University and saw a surgeon at the Center for Hyperhidrosis who told me my only option was to get surgery[53] to sever the nerves that connected my brain to the sweat glands in my hands so I wouldn't sweat ever again!

I remember the day I walked out of that appointment. I was tempted to spend the several thousand dollars required for the surgery. But something screamed inside of me, *Don't do it.* So I finally stopped trying to *heal myself* and asked God the step two question we've been talking about: *Lord, is this what my healing is supposed to look like? And if not, what am I supposed to do?*

I got a hard "no" from God on the surgery almost immediately in prayer, so I politely phoned the doctor and informed him I would be pursuing other options. "Good luck!" he chided me sarcastically. But I made the decision to trust God. And over the following weeks, God started to show me ways He wanted me to tweak my lifestyle and my habits.

First, He asked me to give up caffeine. *I know!* Jesus and coffee go so well together, don't they? I wondered if I could still make it through my morning prayer time without my coffee! But I was so desperate I was willing to try *anything.* So, in March 2018, several weeks before our third

---

[53] The medical name for this surgery is endoscopic thoracic sympathectomy (ETS).

baby was born (terrible timing, wasn't it?), I took my last sip of coffee. Adios, cafeína![54]

I immediately felt a difference. I craved coffee for the first few weeks after I quit almost *every moment* of *every day!* But after a while, my desire faded. I was sweating less. It was a start! So I pressed in and asked God for more.

Next, the Holy Spirit told me to start sleeping in hooded sweatshirts. I know it sounds ridiculous, but remember Naaman dipping in the Jordan! I had always loved to feel *cold* while I slept. I loved the feeling of pulling a warm comforter over my body in a freezing cold room before I went to bed![55] But I started to do it. The first few weeks were *miserable*. I would wake up in the middle of the night *soaked* in sweat! But after a while, my body adjusted. I could feel the difference, first at night, and then *all day*. Because I was "disciplining" my body[56] to be acclimated to warmer conditions, I felt cooler whenever I didn't have a hoodie on!

Finally, the Lord reminded me of something I had forgotten. When I was in high school, I had used prescription-strength antiperspirant on my armpits. As a result, my armpits *still* didn't sweat over ten years later, even though I hadn't used the stuff for a decade! The Lord prompted me to ask Him to re-activate those sweat glands in a healthy way to take the strain off the rest of my body. In a few weeks, I started to sweat out of my armpits again (I told you this would be embarrassing!). And once that happened, the sweating in my hands *completely dried up*.

---

[54] What's up with the church's addiction to caffeine anyway? Why do we rely so heavily on a drug that helps us to push the healthy limits of rest and take on workloads that are simply unnatural? I feel another book coming . . .

[55] When I was growing up, I used to leave the window open when I went to bed in the middle of winter just so my room would be cold. My mother still hasn't forgiven me for inflating the heating bill all those years.

[56] "But I discipline my body and bring it into subjection, lest, when I have preached to others, I myself should become disqualified." —1 Cor. 9:27

Today, my hands don't sweat *at all*. Not one drop! Isn't God amazing? He cares about the big things, and He cares just as much about the little things that are seemingly small but huge and important to you.

Do you see how my healing happened? I could have *insisted* that God heal me miraculously! I could have cried out for *years* that God would just heal me overnight, instead of opening my heart to making all these seemingly silly adjustments in my life! But instead, I leaned in, and *did the simple things* He was asking me to do. My hands are dry as a bone to this day as a result. Yes, God!

Several years later, God took me through a similar process: this time with my shoulder. I had pulled a muscle in my shoulder training Brazilian Jiu Jitsu.[57] I also had nerve damage that shot excruciating pain up and down my left arm all the way from my shoulder to my wrist. I spoke to a doctor friend at the gym where I train. He did a quick evaluation and recommended I see a specialist. "You will need surgery," he assured me.

But I had been through something like this before! So before scheduling with the surgeon, I pressed in to God in prayer.

One day, a few weeks later, I was at the gym lifting weights. The Lord showed me a picture[58] of myself doing an exercise I had never done before.[59] I did the exercise, and my shoulder felt immediately better. "Thank You, God," I said. The next time I was at the gym, I felt Him asking me to do that exercise as a warm-up and cool-down every time I was at the gym until the pain in my arm went away. And guess what? About one month later, I had completely regained full strength and mobility in my arm and shoulder, and I no longer had *any pain*.

---

[57] Brazilian Jiu Jitsu, known as the "gentle art," is a self-defense martial art and combat sport based on grappling, ground fighting, and submission holds, with the fundamental goal of using leverage to overcome a larger opponent.
[58] This was an open vision. I was wide awake, but the Lord super-imposed what He wanted me to see on top of my surroundings in my mind's eye.
[59] For anyone familiar with weightlifting, this was a variation of a full-body clean and jerk.

Isn't God awesome? He took me from a grim diagnosis of surgery and extensive rehab to complete and total healing. The solution wasn't rocket science! In fact, it was embarrassingly simple. But just like Naaman, the question I believe God was asking me was, "If I give you something simple to do, will you do it?"

Several months after I shared my healing testimony with our congregation, a young man in our church who is a Broadway dancer came up to speak with me after service. He had been completely sidelined from his training due to debilitating pain in one of his knees. But one day in prayer, he remembered my story. He asked God, "Lord, what is my healing supposed to look like?" God immediately showed him an exercise to add to his stretching routine before and after training. After several weeks, he was completely free from pain and back to full-scale training!

One more testimony. I have a friend who spent several years living on the streets and was diagnosed with Hepatitis C. He was shut out from pursuing medical treatment because, as an undocumented immigrant, he didn't have legal status to be in the country or enroll in our healthcare system.

But when he showed up at a Christian recovery program, someone told him that God heals. He started to have faith that God would heal his Hepatitis C! He and I prayed that it would happen, miraculously and right away. But healing sometimes looks different than you expect it to!

One day, he was randomly connected with the head of an organization that specializes in funding medical care for undocumented immigrants. That connection led to a meeting with a doctor at a medical center who was doing a trial for a new treatment for Hepatitis C. All of a sudden, my friend had an *absolutely free* path to the medical care he needed—without insurance, and without documentation.[60] A few months ago, he called to tell me that he had just gotten his blood work back, and he was *completely healed* of Hepatitis C. There was no longer *any trace* of the disease in his blood!

---

[60] If you work in the healthcare field, you know just how miraculous this is!

For my friend, healing started with a shift in perspective. He refused to believe his Hepatitis C was from God and rejected it as something God didn't want him to have!

Did you know that sometimes God will use the medical process to heal you? Sometimes God will do it overnight; but other times He will send you to the hospital and lead you to healing through treatment! After all, who do you think gives the grace to doctors to heal patients? Who puts cures in the minds of medical researchers? That's right! He is the same God who heals.

Our Awesome God

God is not a God of formula, He is a God of *relationship.* Your healing might look *exactly* like someone else's! Then again, it might look *completely different.* And the only way to tell the difference is by *asking God in prayer.*

Sometimes God takes you through an exploration process where you try a few different things that seem too silly to work, before He finally drops something into your lap that will change your life. Sometimes God asks you to humble yourself and do something ludicrous to get the miraculous![61] And do you know *why* God does it this way? He doesn't just want you to be *healed.* He wants you to be healed *and* have a relationship with Him! He wants you to be *sozo*—saved, healed, and delivered.[62] By making *relationship with Him* and *reliance on Him* the focal points of the healing process, He not only gives you a healed body—He also guarantees you a healed heart.

Healing isn't always easy, and God designed it that way on purpose. He wants a relationship with You! So He will insist that you *seek Him.* You will be healed! But more importantly, you will find God in the process.

---

[61] Thank you to Pastor Bojan Jancic, Lead Pastor at CityLight Church, who coined this phrase.

[62] "For 'whoever calls on the name of the Lord shall be saved.'" —Rom. 10:13

CHAPTER FOUR

DO YOU WANT TO BE HEALED?

Step one in your healing process is cultivating an earnest desire to be healed. We already talked about step two—asking God, "Lord, what is my healing going to look like?" We covered step two first to undo damage some of us might have experienced as we pursued a healing process that might not have been from God. But now let's get to the proper starting point of making sure that we *really want* to be healed.

The Pool of Bethesda

In Scripture we witness a remarkable conversation between Jesus and a man who desperately needs healing at a place known as the Pool of Bethesda:

> *After this there was a feast of the Jews, and Jesus went up to Jerusalem. Now there is in Jerusalem by the Sheep Gate a pool, which is called in Hebrew, Bethesda, having five porches. In these lay a great multitude of sick people, blind, lame, paralyzed, waiting for the moving of the water.* —*John 5:1-3*

Jesus walked into a community of people who were "waiting" for their healing. Their ailments were not restricted to a certain category. There were "sick people, blind, lame, [and] paralyzed" people all waiting for the same thing. Jesus came there to make a proclamation: *Now that I am here, you don't have to wait anymore.*

This, by the way, is the proclamation you and I get to go out and make in His name every single day. You know people in your life—I know you do! —who need a miracle. Some of them have been waiting for years! And we get to be the ones who bring them the best news they have ever received—that Jesus Christ, the God who died for their sin to be removed, also died so their disease would be removed too!

Here is why everyone was waiting around the same pool:

> *For an angel went down at a certain time into the pool and stirred up the water; then whoever stepped in first, after the stirring of the water, was made well of whatever disease he had.* —John 5:4

Notice several things from verse 4. First, God did the stirring. The role of the people who needed healing was not to try and make something happen on their own. It was to wait for God to start stirring, and then choose to participate in heaven's agenda. When we try and "make healing happen," nothing will take place, but if we allow God to show us what He wants our healing to look like, all that is required is that we jump in behind Him as He starts to move.

Second, there was *hunger* required for healing to take place. Whoever stepped in "first" would be healed. Healing requires a sense of urgency! Those who took their time would not receive a miracle. Think of the woman with the issue of blood who "came from behind" and touched Jesus by the hem of His garment.[63] Think of blind Bartimaeus, who in response to being warned not to trouble Jesus as He passed by "cried out

---

[63] "Now a woman, having a flow of blood for twelve years, who had spent all her livelihood on physicians and could not be healed by any, came from behind and touched the border of His garment. And immediately her flow of blood stopped." —Lk. 8:43-44

all the more!"[64] There is something important about coming before God with a sense of urgency and immediacy when you need a miracle.

Too often we approach our Christian life in a reclined posture, waiting for God to drop the miraculous into our lap. We sit back and wait to see what life wants to give us, instead of aggressively pursuing the blessings Jesus died for us to have. These things should not be so! Those who waited for their turn at the Pool of Bethesda didn't get healed. Only those who aggressively ran towards the Holy Spirit's stirring got miraculous results.

Third, notice there were no limits to the type of ailments God healed. Whoever got to the "stirring of the water, was made well of whatever disease he had." There were no exceptions! No diseases or conditions were excluded. That means that whatever you are struggling with, Jesus can handle it!

Finally, we meet the subject of our case study:

Now a certain man was there who had an infirmity thirty-eight years. When Jesus saw him lying there, and knew that he already had been in that condition a long time, He said to him, "Do you want to be made well?" —John 5:5-6, emphasis added

What an *offensive question* for Jesus to ask this poor man! He had been there *thirty-eight years,* after all! And here comes Jesus with the audacity to ask him if he even wants to be made well? If this guy didn't want to be healed anymore, wouldn't he have gone to lie down somewhere else around year eighteen?

Why would Jesus ask that? Whenever you see something in Scripture that doesn't make immediate sense, dig deeper. Ask the Holy Spirit

---

[64] "Then many warned him to be quiet; but he cried out all the more, 'Son of David, have mercy on me!'" —Mk. 10:48

to show you what you're missing, and He will give you the revelation and insight you need. In order to find out *why* Jesus would ask such a seemingly silly and downright insensitive question to this man who had been patiently waiting, we need to keep reading:

> The sick man answered Him, "Sir, I have no man to put me into the pool when the water is stirred up; but while I am coming, another steps down before me." —John 5:7

Here we see the condition of this man's heart. He knew healing was *possible*, but he had yet to experience it himself. Notice that He didn't even answer Jesus' question! He didn't reply to Jesus with an emphatic, "Yes!" He offered up an explanation as to why his healing had never come.

This man knew healing was possible. Yet for *years* he had been watching as other people, one by one, got their healing before him. I would like to suggest that this man, though he had seen God heal others with his very eyes, never really thought his time would come. He had been waiting so long that he was tired, frustrated, and confused. His temptation was to rationalize why his healing was taking so long, and maybe even to wonder if healing was still God's will for him at all.

I wonder how many of us fall into that category? What dreams do you have from God that are still outstanding? Did God promise you a promotion at work, only for you to watch other people step in and get promoted ahead of you? Did God promise you an awesome husband, only for you to watch your closest friends get married earlier than you? Did God tell you that you would be healed, only for you to watch other people receive healing, while you continue to struggle with doubt and unbelief?

This man knew God could do it for someone else. But I believe he lost hold of his conviction that God would ever really do it for him.

The enemy can never steal the promises God has spoken over your life. He can, however, convince you to give them up. Satan can make you so tired and confused that you lose hope. He can discourage you so much that you end up letting your guard down. You allow him to *take* what God promised was yours so many years ago as though it never belonged to you. Are you in the same place as the man at the Pool of Bethesda?

Yet even in the face of doubt, watch the divine response:

> *Jesus said to him, "Rise, take up your bed and walk." And immediately the man was made well, took up his bed, and walked.* —John 5:8-9

Jesus commanded, and the man did what He said. And "immediately" the healing he had been anticipating for *thirty-eight years* took place.

Immediately Healed

Verse 9 says that this man was "immediately" healed. We see this often throughout Scripture. Almost every single person Jesus prayed for was healed instantly, the *first time* Jesus prayed.[65] Yet verse 5 tells us that this man had an infirmity for "thirty-eight years." So was the healing immediate, or did it take thirty-eight years?

Yes! Though his healing was immediate, God still had him in a process that had taken some time. We see this same tension with the woman with the issue of blood in Luke 8. She had a flow of blood for "twelve years" (v 43), yet when she met Jesus, "immediately her flow of blood stopped" (v 44). So was this an immediate miracle? Yes! Was there also a *twelve-year process* behind her miracle! Yes!

The point is, we should never get discouraged if our "immediately" doesn't happen right away. What would have happened if this man at

---

[65] Mark 5:29-30 and Matt. 8:3, among others

the Pool of Bethesda had gotten frustrated and asked someone to carry him off? He never would have been healed.

If your healing still hasn't arrived, don't get angry! Don't allow your heart to get hard and bitter towards God. Don't allow the enemy to convince you that a miracle is no longer coming! Will you have the audacious faith to believe God will *still do* everything He promised to do?

The People Respond

When this man was miraculously healed, you would think everyone around him would start celebrating, right? But that was not the case:

> *The Jews therefore said to him who was cured, "It is the Sabbath; it is not lawful for you to carry your bed."* —*John 5:10*

Be wary of people who use your breakthrough as an opportunity to put you back in check. Be careful around people who use your freedom as an opportunity to remind you of what you *cannot* do! Instead of celebrating what Jesus had done, the religious leaders condemned this man for carrying his bed on the Sabbath. He hadn't carried *anything* in thirty-eight years! Yet the Jewish leaders were more concerned about *the traditions of man* than the glory of God.

> *He answered them, "He who made me well said to me, 'Take up your bed and walk.' " Then they asked him, "Who is the Man who said to you, 'Take up your bed and walk'?" But the one who was healed did not know who it was, for Jesus had withdrawn, a multitude being in that place.* —*John 5:11-13*

You don't need perfect theology to be healed! This man didn't even know *who Jesus was*, yet an encounter with the King of Kings and Lord of Lords was still enough. What does that mean for you? You don't have to go to Bible school and seminary to know how to receive your healing. God will meet you right where you are and heal you on terms you can understand!

Healing As a Witness

This man didn't know who Jesus was when he was healed, but he would soon find out:

> *Afterward Jesus found him in the temple, and said to him, "See, you have been made well. Sin no more, lest a worse thing come upon you." The man departed and told the Jews that it was Jesus who had made him well.*   —*John 5:14-15*

I love that verse 14 tells us that in response to being healed, this man went to a house of worship. As you and I encounter people and demonstrate the miracle-working power of God as we pray, something will *awaken inside of them* that sparks a fire to know God. You won't even have to invite them to church. In fact, you won't be able to keep them out of church! If we do our job of showing people that God heals when we lay hands on them,[66] we won't have to worry about inviting people to church! They will just come. And when they arrive, do you know Who will be waiting for them? *Jesus.*

This man might not have known who Jesus was when he got healed, but Jesus made sure he had another encounter as he went to worship!

---

[66] "... they will take up serpents; and if they drink anything deadly, it will by no means hurt them; they will lay hands on the sick, and they will recover." —Mk. 16:18

When we pray, God will show up, and when He shows up, the hearts of the lost will awaken to reconnect with the God Who Heals.

Sin No More

Now let's talk about these three words from verse 14: "Sin no more." For the record, not all sickness is the result of sin. In fact, there is a story in Scripture where the disciples assume that someone's sickness is the result of sin, and Jesus has to correct their assumption.[67] God is creative, not destructive. He doesn't need to cause you physical pain to get your attention and remind you that you shouldn't be living in sin.

If you got in a car crash, it doesn't mean God is mad at you. It means that we live in a fallen world where people like to text message instead of keeping their eyes on the road. So we don't do any favors to people who are sick by adding insult to injury, and assuming that sickness is always the result of sin.

However, in this particular case, Jesus tells us that sin was involved. Now before you jump to conclusions about what this man might have been up to, remember that he *could not move* for thirty-eight years. That means his sin was probably not behavioral.

However, I am sure that thirty-eight years of watching other people get healed did something to this man's psyche. Maybe he got so *bitter* after watching God do it for others and never for him that he refused to have faith in God at all. Perhaps he wasn't careful in the way he used his words, and started speaking death instead of life over himself.[68] If his sin was not behavioral, it had to be related to his faith! Waiting can

---

[67] "Now as Jesus passed by, He saw a man who was blind from birth. And His disciples asked Him, saying, 'Rabbi, who sinned, this man or his parents, that he was born blind?' Jesus answered, 'Neither this man nor his parents sinned, but that the works of God should be revealed in him.'" —Jn. 9:1-3
[68] "Death and life are in the power of the tongue, and those who love it will eat its fruit." —Prov. 18:21

have a corrosive the effect on our internal dialogue. Perhaps over time, "God is going to heal me," turned into, "Is God going to heal me?" which eventually became, "If I'm not healed, does God really exist?"

David Entwistle explains that theologians use the phrase *the noetic effects of sin* to describe the way in which sin distorts our thinking. Sin, Entwistle notes, has a "tremendous ability to skew our thinking about our relationship to God and how we ought to live." [69] Do you see the unhealthy cycle that must have been at work here? We sin because we don't understand God, and then we fail to understand God even more because of our sin! This was where the man at the Pool of Bethesda found himself. Yet Jesus met him in the middle of his erroneous thinking to show him just how badly God wanted him to be healed.

Your thoughts are important. We should never allow the *length* of our healing process to impact how we feel about God, and how we believe He feels about us. This is why it is so incredibly important to come back to His Word again and again. Remind yourself how much He loves you. Remind yourself that He is the God who heals! He will cleanse you "with the washing of water by the word" (Eph. 5:26) and restore your faith in His willingness to heal.

For me, the bottom line is this. There was some form of sin that had *separated* this man from God, and the blockage had to be removed for his healing to take place. But aren't you so glad that for every ounce of sin that ever creeps into our lives, God has already provided a Savior?

Communication Restored

Look at the exact moment this man was healed:

---

[69] David Entwistle, *Integrative Approaches to Psychology and Christianity* (Eugene, OR: Cascade Books, 2015), pg. 95.

When Jesus saw him lying there, and knew that he already had been in that condition a long time, He said to him, "Do you want to be made well?" The sick man answered Him, "Sir, I have no man to put me into the pool when the water is stirred up; but while I am coming, another steps down before me." Jesus said to him, "Rise, take up your bed and walk." And immediately the man was made well, took up his bed, and walked.   —*John 5:6-9*

Jesus asked a question, and the man answered. God called, and the man responded. All that needed to take place for healing to happen was *restored communication with God.* When he started *talking to Jesus again,* when lost communication was restored, this man's thirty-eight year process came to an immediate end.

There is a difference between thinking about God and talking to Him. The man at the Pool of Bethesda might have been thinking about healing for years! But he wasn't actively engaged in conversation with the Healer. As soon as the lines of communication between him and heaven were opened again, healing washed over his body like a wave crashing on the shore.

Jesus is calling. He's asking you something as you read this chapter and believe for your healing: "Do you want to be made well?" Are you willing to cling to His promise for healing, no matter how long it takes? Are you willing to let go of any bitterness over how long your healing has taken, and believe that God wants you healed again? Are you willing to live a life where you cling to His Word with reckless abandon, and refuse to accept anything less than full restoration over your body and your life?

Healing happens when God gives an invitation, and we make the choice to *respond.*

Why Not You?

So why not you? Why not today? Maybe there's been something separating you from God. But God knows what you're going through. He sees you, and He knows you. He's willing to meet you where you are! All He's asking is that you would *talk to Him again.*

Maybe you've been waiting *years* for your healing to happen. But I'm here to tell you it can happen *in a moment.* God has made His presence known. His presence is in the room where you are reading right now! So how will you respond?

> *And the power of the Lord was present to heal them.*
>
> —*Luke 5:17*

Healing Testimony

One of the most amazing healings I've ever seen happened at our church's Healing Rooms in 2015. A young woman named Amanda was visiting New York City from Pennsylvania for the weekend, volunteering at a local feeding ministry called The Father's Heart. She had never even heard of the Healing Rooms, much less made an appointment to come and receive prayer.

Yet when she got to the Father's Heart to volunteer, she met one of our Healing Rooms volunteers. They started a conversation, and Amanda disclosed that she had been struggling with something in her body for a very long time. Our volunteer asked her what she was doing later in the day, and invited her to come for prayer at the Healing Rooms. This is the supernatural result, written in her own words:

> I have literally hit the ground running. I can't shut up telling everyone about my miracle. I can't get out of bed fast enough saying, "Who can I tell today? Who can I show today?"

I just wanted to give you some background on me so you know where I came from to where I am today. PRAISE GOD! When my parents were pregnant with me, my mom's placenta tore loose at eleven weeks and she was placed on bed rest for the duration of the pregnancy. I was born at twenty-six weeks, or three months early. I had a severe head bleed that affected the whole left side of my body, my left lung had collapsed, and my left arm is what I call my "chicken wing" —it does not straighten and I can't move my left hand well. My left leg was shorter than my right because the femur grew incorrectly, and I had no control of my left foot.

Growing up I learned to play softball catching with my right hand, taking my glove off and tucking it under my left arm, and throwing the ball back with my right just as fast as someone would the "normal" way. I made similar adjustments to play basketball and field hockey—and even learned how to type with one hand.

When I came to the Healing Rooms, the team prayed for my left leg to grow, and for full restoration for the entire left side of my body. As they prayed, we watched the leg grow!

I tested the results last Monday morning. I went to my doctor and asked him to measure my length of my leg, without telling him what had happened. My legs are EVEN—he even aligned my hips to make sure because my left hip has always been higher than my right. He was in shock! I am so excited to see the day when I realize my "chicken wing" is straight and my hand and foot work!!!

I am speaking at our church on Sunday morning and sharing my testimony. I even bought new shoes today that don't have an extra lift in them. Right now it feels awkward, like I don't have my "land legs" yet, but I realize I've been like that for twenty-eight years and it will take some time.

THANK YOU HEALING ROOMS TEAM for everything that you did! I can't THANK you enough for being sensitive to the Spirit!

When Amanda walked into the Healing Rooms for prayer, it was immediately apparent that her left leg was almost six inches shorter than her right leg. And all of us watched in awe as Jesus caused supernatural growth to happen instantly.

Notice that, much like the man who *didn't even know who Jesus was* in John 5, Amanda didn't expect to be healed that Saturday morning as she drove to New York City. Maybe she wondered after so many years of struggling if God still wanted to heal her at all. Yet all it took was *one encounter* with someone who had *seen God heal* to change her life *forever*.

Are you willing to go out and be that person to someone else? Are you willing to spread the good news that Jesus heals, so that an entire generation can receive the fullness of everything Jesus died for His people to have?

CHAPTER FIVE

AUTHORITY TO HEAL

T here were many teachers in Jesus' day, but there was only one Jesus. There were many religious leaders who knew Scripture like the back of their hand;[70] but there was only One who taught with authority.

> *Then they went into Capernaum, and immediately on the Sabbath*
> *He entered the synagogue and taught. And they were astonished at*
> *His teaching, for He taught them as one having authority, and not as*
> *the scribes.* —Mark 1:21-22

There was *something special* about Jesus that differentiated His words from the rest of the teaching that was available in His day. What was it? He taught with *authority.*

When the "scribes" taught, nothing happened. But when Jesus taught *with authority,* there was always a manifestation that followed:

> *Now there was a man in their synagogue with an unclean spirit. And*
> *he cried out, saying, "Let us alone! What have we to do with You,*

---

[70] Scripture memorization was and is of paramount importance to the pious Jewish community. The verb *zakhar* (to remember) appears one hundred and sixty-nine times in the Hebrew Bible [Yosef Hayim Yerushalmi, *Zakhor, Jewish History and Jewish Memory*, (Seattle and London: University of Washington Press), 5]. Many Jewish pupils in Jesus' day memorized the Torah by age twelve. They would then go on to memorize the Law and the Prophets, Psalms, and Proverbs.

Jesus of Nazareth? Did You come to destroy us? I know who You are—the Holy One of God!"

But Jesus rebuked him, saying, "Be quiet, and come out of him!" And when the unclean spirit had convulsed him and cried out with a loud voice, he came out of him. Then they were all amazed, so that they questioned among themselves, saying, "What is this? What new doctrine is this? For with authority He commands even the unclean spirits, and they obey Him." And immediately His fame spread throughout all the region around Galilee. —Mark 1:23-28

Jesus not only *spoke* about the power of God—He *demonstrated* the power of God. His was a ministry not just of words, but also of action!

Show and Tell

Jesus didn't have to tell anyone who He was. Because of the authority in which He walked, He was able to simply show them:

Then the disciples of John reported to him concerning all these things. And John, calling two of his disciples to him, sent them to Jesus, saying, "Are You the Coming One, or do we look for another?"

When the men had come to Him, they said, "John the Baptist has sent us to You, saying, 'Are You the Coming One, or do we look for another?'" And that very hour He cured many of infirmities, afflictions, and evil spirits; and to many blind He gave sight.

Jesus answered and said to them, "Go and tell John the things you have seen and heard: that the blind see, the lame walk, the lepers are cleansed, the deaf hear, the dead are raised, the poor have the gospel preached to them." —Luke 7:18-22

It's important to know why you believe what you believe. It's imperative that you develop the ability to explain your faith to other people with a rational, intellectual argument that will encourage them to seek Jesus for themselves. At the same time, I believe God's will is for you to walk with such power and authority that sometimes you won't even have to *say anything* at all—you simply pray, and the miracle-working presence of God floods the room!

This is why healing is so important as a demonstration of the goodness of God. It does a certain amount of good to *talk* about how powerful God is. But it does a whole world of good to *show* people His goodness. Healing is a testimony to God's power that the whole world needs to see! And this is why we need to move and operate in the authority of Jesus Christ. He is the head and we are the body, and it is our job to carry out His agenda on this earth.

Authority Changes Everything

My stance is this. If we are filled with the same Holy Spirit as Jesus,[71] then we should be able to go out and pray the same prayers He prayed and expect exactly the same results. If Jesus didn't want us to believe miracles would happen when we pray, why would He have told us this:

> *"Most assuredly, I say to you, he who believes in Me, the works that I do he will do also; and greater works than these he will do, because I go to My Father. And whatever you ask in My name, that I will do, that the Father may be glorified in the Son. If you ask anything in My name, I will do it".* —*John 14:12-14*

---

[71] "But if the Spirit of Him who raised Jesus from the dead dwells in you, He who raised Christ from the dead will also give life to your mortal bodies through His Spirit who dwells in you." —Rom. 8:11

Jesus doesn't give us vain hope! He gives us perfect confidence. But here is the rub: If you want to see the miracles Jesus saw, you have to walk with the same authority He carried!

Authority (in Mk. 1:22 above) is the Greek word *exousia,* which means "the power of rule or government (the power of him whose will and commands must be submitted to by others and obeyed)." [72] When Jesus taught, the reign of heaven entered the room. Sin, sickness, and disease all submitted to His every command. When He arrived, all of creation responded to His decree.

Did you know that authority is different from power? "Power" as presented in the New Testament[73] is the Greek word *dunamis,* which means the "inherent strength of ability . . . residing in a thing by virtue of its nature."[74] This is the *substance* to perform miracles. But authority is the *character* that supports the substance! Power is the "what"—the stuff that gets miracles done. But authority is the "why"—the foundation that gives you the legal (Scripturally defensible) right to expect miracles in the first place!

Why is that important to understand? The enemy—Satan, the bringer of sickness and disease—is powerful too. Scripture says that he is the "prince of the power of the air" (Eph. 2:2) and holds dominion over the fallen (natural) world. But authority trumps power. So Satan may be the

---

[72] "G1849 - exousia - Strong's Greek Lexicon (KJV)." Blue Letter Bible. Accessed 11 Aug, 2020. https://www.blueletterbible.org//lang/lexicon/lexicon.cfm?Strongs=G1849&t=KJV

[73] "[H]ow God anointed Jesus of Nazareth with the Holy Spirit and with power, who went about doing good and healing all who were oppressed by the devil, for God was with Him." —Acts 10:38

[74] "G1411 - dynamis - Strong's Greek Lexicon (KJV)." Blue Letter Bible. Accessed 11 Aug, 2020. https://www.blueletterbible.org//lang/lexicon/lexicon.cfm?Strongs=G1411&t=KJV

"prince of the power of the air" and the "god of this age,"[75] but you have the authority of the Son of God: the King of Heaven!

When You Say Stop

Have you ever been stopped by a traffic cop? I have. There are many Sunday mornings when we'll get off the Manhattan Bridge on the way to church, only to encounter some kind of traffic stop because of an event going on in the city. If you're not from New York City, you have to understand that the traffic cops here wear special gloves. There is something about those little, tiny gloves that make you slam on the brakes and bring your vehicle to a screeching halt! When you see that glove come out and the traffic cop extend his or her hand, you know you have to stop!

But why should I stop? What is it about a tiny, one-hundred-fifty-pound police officer that causes me to slam on the brakes of my Jeep instead of just plowing right through? Is that cop more powerful than my car? Of course not! However, the cop has something that takes precedence over power: *authority.*

If I decide to ignore that glove and plow right through that officer of the law, I'm not just ignoring that individual's authority. That cop has the backing of the City of New York. And the city has the backing of the State of New York. And the State of New York has the backing of the federal government of the United States of America. So if I were to run down that cop, I might as well just run over the President of the United States!

The same way I always have to respect that cop's authority, Satan has to respect your authority. That's right—you have authority. You're not

---

[75] ". . . whose minds the god of this age has blinded, who do not believe, lest the light of the gospel of the glory of Christ, who is the image of God, should shine on them." — 2 Cor. 4:4

perfect! But you still have authority. Even if you've *never seen a miracle in your life,* you still have the authority of Jesus Christ, King of kings, and Lord of lords. And whenever Satan tries to overrun your life with sickness and disease, you get to exercise that authority, and Satan has to respond the same way he would respond to Jesus Christ Himself. Satan has to respect your authority because you have the full backing of heaven as a guarantee that nothing and no one can mow you down.

Did you know that Satan can never *take* anything from you?[76] The best he can do is convince you that you don't carry authority, to the point where you let your guard down and allow him to walk into your life. When we don't understand our authority in Christ, that is *exactly* what we are doing! We are allowing ourselves to be *run over,* when we should be standing proud and free, victorious in Jesus Christ!

So next time Satan tries to wriggle his way into your life with sickness and disease, hold that hand out. Put on your glove! Tell him he has no access into your life. He needs to change his route, in Jesus' name!

Jesus Has All Authority

Now I recognize when I say you have the same authority as Jesus Christ Himself, you may not believe me. So allow me to prove it to you with Scripture. A biblical proof is a straightforward argument that clearly and logically illuminates truth as demonstrated in Scripture. Did you know that, as a believer, you have *authority* to heal the sick? You have something to offer every time you pray—no matter the recipient, and no matter their physical condition! And I can prove it to you.

---

[76] "My Father, who has given them to Me, is greater than all; and no one is able to snatch them out of My Father's hand. I and My Father are one." — John 10:29-30

1) Jesus starts with all authority.

> *Then the eleven disciples went away into Galilee, to the mountain which Jesus had appointed for them. When they saw Him, they worshiped Him; but some doubted.*
>
> *And Jesus came and spoke to them, saying, "All authority has been given to Me in heaven and on earth. Go therefore and make disciples of all the nations, baptizing them in the name of the Father and of the Son and of the Holy Spirit, teaching them to observe all things that I have commanded you; and lo, I am with you always, even to the end of the age." Amen.*   —*Matthew 28:16-20, emphasis added*

In Matthew's account of the Great Commission, Jesus had a message for His disciples. "All authority" belongs to Jesus! God gave it to Him. That implies a regime change. Whereas Satan was once the "prince of the power of the air" (Eph 2:2) and the "god of this age" (2 Cor. 4:4), Jesus asserts that, because of the Resurrection, He has been given all authority "in heaven and on earth" (v 18). That means your life should *look different* on this side of the cross! Where Satan once had authority to afflict you with sickness and disease, your belief in Jesus Christ means Satan no longer has any room to operate in your body, or in your life!

After Jesus asserts His authority, He communicates an expectation to His disciples. "Go therefore," He says (v 19). Because Jesus has all authority, our job is therefore to go! The disciples were expected to *do something* with the authority Jesus had given them! Jesus expected them to baptize new believers and teach them to receive the radical grace of the gospel. As the disciples did that, His promise was to *always* be with them.

Notice two more things from this passage. First, there is no limit to Jesus' authority. He has "all authority . . . in heaven and on earth" (v 18).

That encompasses anywhere we are in the present, as well as anywhere we will ever be in the future! No matter where you go, you should walk in His authority.

Second, there is no expiration date to Jesus' authority. His authority is good "always, even to the end of the age" (v 20). Jesus will never leave you or forsake you![77] He will never retract His authority over your life.

Jesus has *all authority*. And do you know what He wants to do with it? He wants to give it to you because you believe in Him so you can go out and use it in His name!

2) Jesus gives His authority to the twelve disciples.

Jesus didn't want to keep His authority all to Himself! He wanted to *pass it on* to the people who followed Him:

> *Then He called His twelve disciples together and gave them power and authority over all demons, and to cure diseases. He sent them to preach the kingdom of God and to heal the sick.* —*Luke 9:1-2*

Jesus gave His followers power and authority. He blessed them with the resources of heaven that they would require to carry out deliverance ("over all demons") and healing ("and to cure diseases).

Isn't it comforting to know that God will *equip you* to do what He has called you to do? He never calls you out into the unknown, only to leave you hanging and wondering if what He has promised will come to pass. He gives you the power and authority you need to do His work in His name!

---

[77] "Be strong and of good courage, do not fear nor be afraid of them; for the Lord your God, He is the One who goes with you. He will not leave you nor forsake you." —Deut. 31:6

Notice the pattern into which Jesus called His disciples. "He sent them to preach the kingdom of God and to heal the sick" (v 2). Step one is preach! Step two is heal. When we faithfully fulfill our mandate to "preach the kingdom of God," the miraculous will follow in our midst. When we release the Word, signs, miracles, and wonders will follow!

If you've been in church for some time, you may have heard a version of this popular phrase: "Preach the gospel at all times. When necessary, use words."[78] And while it is true that your *lifestyle*—the way you treat and care for people—should be a demonstration of the good news, there is no getting around the clear mandate from Jesus Christ that we are to open our mouths and preach! If we don't declare the Word of God, we have no guarantee that healing will follow. But when we "preach" (v 2), the scriptural guarantee is that God's Holy Spirit will confirm His Word.

The twelve disciples took Jesus at His word:

> *So they departed and went through the towns, preaching the gospel and healing everywhere.* —Luke 9:6

When they did what Jesus told them to do, they got the results He promised they would see!

I preached a version of this message recently on a church mission trip to Nebaj, Guatemala. Nebaj has a rich cultural history, but also a history of pagan worship that spans many generations into the present. Many of the people in that region of Guatemala have never even heard the gospel. As you can imagine with an audience of people who have barely heard of Jesus, when I stepped up to the pulpit and started declaring that they

---

[78] This quote is often mistakenly attributed to Saint Francis of Assisi when in reality it is not contained in any of his writings. In fact, Saint Francis was quite the preacher [see Mark Galli, *Francis of Assissi and His World* (Downers Grove, IL: IVP Books, 2002)].

had the *authority* to heal in Jesus' name, I was met with looks of shock and awe.

So I shook things up a bit. I asked for twelve volunteers to come up to the front of the sanctuary. Twelve people came forward, albeit very reluctantly. I asked them to stand in a circle around me. I then told them that I was *giving them* the authority to heal. After all, I have seen countless miraculous healings with my own eyes! And Jesus told us to freely give what we have freely received.[79]

One of the volunteers was a girl who served on the dance ministry at the church where I was preaching. She was dressed to the nines, because her dance troupe had performed at the start of the service. When I said, "You have authority to heal," I saw a look of shock on her face. She lifted her arm up and down, as if she were testing something that hadn't worked in a while. She smiled, and then she started to cry.

I interviewed her as everyone went back to their seats, and then asked her to testify before the congregation. She had been living with crippling pain in her shoulder for several months. It had gotten so bad that she considered quitting the dance group because she couldn't take the pain of movement anymore. But when I told her, "You have authority to heal," she felt a wave of electricity run through her body. She lifted her arm high above her head for the whole church to see. "Before today, I couldn't do this," she said in Spanish. "But now I feel no pain at all."

Do you see how powerful it can be to receive the revelation that you have the *authority* of Jesus Christ? You don't have to settle for a body filled with sickness, disease and pain! Jesus gave His authority to His twelve disciples on purpose. But Jesus didn't stop with the twelve!

---

[79] "Heal the sick, cleanse the lepers, raise the dead, cast out demons. Freely you have received, freely give." —Matt. 10:8

3) Jesus gives His authority to even more disciples!

In the remainder of Luke 9, Jesus puts on a clinic in the miraculous. He feeds "about five thousand men" (Lk. 9:14), plus women and children, with five loaves of bread and two fish. Then, He is transfigured on the Mount of Olives (Lk. 9:28-36). He casts out a demon from a boy (Lk. 9:42), and encourages His disciples to put their hands to the plow and never look back (Lk. 9:62).

And then Jesus extends the pattern of distributing His authority to His followers:

> *After these things the Lord appointed seventy others also, and sent them two by two before His face into every city and place where He Himself was about to go. Then He said to them, "The harvest truly is great, but the laborers are few; therefore pray the Lord of the harvest to send out laborers into His harvest."* —Luke 10:1-2

What does it mean to "appoint" someone (v. 1)? It means you give them authority![80] From this moment forward, the disciples were empowered and expected to operate in the capacity in which Jesus called them to function. Jesus, the Man with all authority in heaven and on earth, didn't just give His authority to the twelve disciples. In Luke 10:1, He passes it on to "seventy others also."[81]

---

[80] "Appoint" is the Greek *anadeiknumi* (Strong's G322), which means "to proclaim . . . as elected to office, to announce as appointed a king, general, etc., or to lift up . . . on high and exhibit for all to behold." "G322 - anadeiknymi - Strong's Greek Lexicon (KJV)." Blue Letter Bible. Accessed 11 Aug, 2020. https://www.blueletterbible.org//lang/lexicon/lexicon.cfm?Strongs=G322&t=KJV

[81] Note that this discredits the cessationist assumption that miracles stopped after the last apostle died.

Do you see what was happening here? Jesus was *expanding* His circle of trust. He was growing His ministry team. He wasn't just telling more and more people what they *could see* if they made a decision to believe in Him—He was telling them what they *would see* as recipients of His authority.

Then He sent them out *in teams*[82] (v 1 "two by two") to anticipate His movement. Jesus sent the disciples to a new place because He was about to go there too! And do you know what happened when these disciples came back from 1) preaching, and 2) healing the sick?[83]

> *Then the seventy returned with joy, saying, "Lord, even the demons*
> *are subject to us in Your name."*   —*Luke 10:17*

Christian, are you missing *joy* in your life? Well, are you walking in the miraculous lifestyle to which Jesus has called you? If you don't understand you've already been given authority, you will never move in authority as God has called you to do! The path to joy is the miraculous, and you don't want to miss out on the best God has for you!

Jesus was happy that the disciples were full of joy, but He needed them to know there was *more* He wanted them to see and expected them to do! So He reiterated just how serious He was about the disciples carrying His authority:

> *And He said to them, "I saw Satan fall like lightning from heaven.*
> *Behold, I give you the authority to trample on serpents and scorpions,*
> *and over all the power of the enemy, and nothing shall by any means*

---

[82] While not a focus of this chapter, this point is important. There is power in spiritual agreement. In the Healing Rooms, our volunteers pray in teams so agreement can take place as they pray. See Matt. 18:18-20.

[83] "And heal the sick there, and say to them, 'The kingdom of God has come near to you.'" —Lk. 10:9

hurt you. Nevertheless do not rejoice in this, that the spirits are subject to you, but rather rejoice because your names are written in heaven."   *—Luke 10:18-20*

Think about verse 19 with me for just one moment. Jesus gave His followers authority, not just to trample on serpents and scorpions (demonic entities), but over "all the power of the enemy." If you study out that word "all" in the Greek, do you know what it means? *All!* All means all! And "nothing shall by any means hurt you." Nothing means nothing!

You don't just have authority over "some" of the enemy's power. Jesus didn't even stop after giving you authority over "most" of the enemy's power! He has given you authority over *all* the power of the enemy. That is the highest level of authority you could ever expect to have! And there is *nothing* the enemy can do to steal what God has given you.

4) Jesus gives His authority to all believers.

This is the grand finale, and the conclusion to our biblical proof. So far we've seen that Jesus started with all authority. We saw Him give His authority to the twelve disciples. Then He passed it on to another "seventy others also" (Lk. 10:1). But as the final step in this authority distribution process, Jesus made His trusted circle of representatives exponentially wider:

Later He appeared to the eleven as they sat at the table; and He rebuked their unbelief and hardness of heart, because they did not believe those who had seen Him after He had risen. And He said to them, "Go into all the world and preach the gospel to every creature.

He who believes and is baptized will be saved; but he who does not believe will be condemned. And these signs will follow those who believe . . ."   —*Mark 16:14-17a, emphasis added*

Do you "believe?" Then Jesus says "these signs" will follow you:

"In My name they will cast out demons; they will speak with new tongues; they will take up serpents; and if they drink anything deadly, it will by no means hurt them; they will lay hands on the sick, and they will recover."   —*Mark 16:17b-18*

Did you know that you are called to deliverance? Were you aware that you have been mandated to speak in tongues? Did you have any idea that you are *immune* to the work of the enemy? And of course by now you *must* realize that when you lay hands on the sick, they *will*—not might, and not could—recover!

Jesus, the Man with all authority, made a deliberate example of His disciples by passing His authority on to them. Then He widened His circle of trusted representatives to "another seventy also" to show that the miracle-working power of Jesus Christ was never meant to be boxed up and confined to a small group of privileged individuals (i.e., pastors and preachers). And finally, He made perhaps the most significant endorsement for the way we are supposed to live our lives by challenging *every believer* to walk in the same level of authority as Jesus Himself, with signs, miracles, and wonders following everywhere we go!

It's Up to You

You have a choice as you're reading this. Will you believe this is really for you? Will you open your heart and receive the fullness of everything Jesus died for you to have—including His authority

86

and His power? I urge you not to continue living cognitively aware that miracles are possible, yet experientially distant from the New Testament lifestyle you were created to live. Grab hold of this truth and begin living with a practical understanding that Jesus has given you His authority. When you know you have authority, it changes everything!

The disciples made the choice I am encouraging you to make. They took Jesus at His word. They believed that what He told them was true! And the result was *immediately* manifested in their lives:

> *So then, after the Lord had spoken to them, He was received up into heaven, and sat down at the right hand of God. And they went out and preached everywhere, the Lord working with them and confirming the word through the accompanying signs. Amen. —Mark 16:19-20*

As you *preach*, God will work with you, confirming His Word through the accompanying signs. If you will simply preach His Word, God will make sure to back up your speech with a divine response. And as you take God at His Word, everything around you will change.

Your life will change. You church will change! Your city will change.[84] And this world will change, all for the glory of God.

People will have proof that God is real, because you have accepted the authority Jesus died for you to have.

---

[84] "At evening, when the sun had set, they brought to Him all who were sick and those who were demon-possessed. And the whole city was gathered together at the door. Then He healed many who were sick with various diseases, and cast out many demons; and He did not allow the demons to speak, because they knew Him." —Mark 1:32-34

CHAPTER SIX

FAITH TO HEAL

Mark 5 is one of my favorite chapters of Scripture. I love it so much because of the picture it paints of how Jesus lived His daily life—and, by extension, how we can live our daily lives in and through Him.

My son, Clive, who is five years old at the time of this writing, has Mark 5 fully memorized. To make a long story short, we learned Clive has a memorization gift when he started reciting an audio story (Disney's *Brave*) after listening to the thirteen-minute CD several times. So, given his passion for toys and our desire to sanctify his memory gift, we offered him a brand new Transformer™ toy if he memorized Mark 5. It took him two days.

Mark 5 is a lesson on the *faith* required for healing to take place. Make no mistake about it—faith is essential to your healing process. It is essential to the healing ministry God will birth in you after your personal healing takes place. So note that this message on the importance of faith has two applications—1) for you, and 2) for others. If you want to be healed in your own body, you have to have faith! And if you want to see others healed as you pray for them, you have to have faith!

A Woman of Faith

Mark 5 details three miracles. First, a demon-possessed man is delivered (vv 1-20). Then, a woman with a medical condition causing relentless bleeding is healed (vv 25-34). Finally, the daughter of a ruler of the synagogue, a man named Jairus, is raised from the dead (vv 21-24, 35-

43). In this chapter we are going to focus on the second miracle. This is the story commonly known as the healing of the woman with the issue of blood:

> *Now when Jesus had crossed over again by boat to the other side, a great multitude gathered to Him; and He was by the sea. And behold, one of the rulers of the synagogue came, Jairus by name. And when he saw Him, he fell at His feet and begged Him earnestly, saying, "My little daughter lies at the point of death. Come and lay Your hands on her, that she may be healed, and she will live." So Jesus went with him, and a great multitude followed Him and thronged Him.*
> —Mark 5:21-24

Verses 21-24 contain the prelude to our story, which truly begins in verse 25. However, they are important to include if we are to have the proper context. As Jesus traveled, there were people all around Jesus pressing into Him and touching Him. When Scripture says that a great multitude "thronged" Jesus, the word employed in the original Greek text means "to press on all sides."[85] This will be important as we move forward in our discussion of faith.

> *Now a certain woman had a flow of blood for twelve years, and had suffered many things from many physicians. She had spent all that she had and was no better, but rather grew worse. When she heard about Jesus . . .*
> —Mark 5:25-27a

---

[85] Strong's G4918 *sunthlibo*: to press together; to press on all sides. "G4918 - synthlibō - Strong's Greek Lexicon (KJV)." Blue Letter Bible. Accessed 11 Aug, 2020. https://www.blueletterbible.org//lang/lexicon/lexicon.cfm?Strongs=G4918&t=KJV

Notice that this woman had been in pain for quite some time. She visited the best medical specialists of her day, but could find no relief. To pay for her treatment, she "spent all that she had." Not only was she still sick—she was worse and flat broke!

But then someone *told her about Jesus*. This is another important precondition for the healing we are about to witness. Someone told this woman about Jesus, and hope was revived. Someone told her about Jesus, and the possibility of healing was restored! Do you see that we have a responsibility, every single one of us who call ourselves Christians, to open our mouths and share the gospel?[86]

When this woman heard about Jesus, she was filled with a bold faith that she never had before. How do I know? Because, according to Jewish law, it was *illegal* for this woman to be in a crowd of people.[87] Had she been found out by the religious leaders, she would have been stoned, killed at the hands of the very throng of people she was pressing through! This woman *risked her very life* to get close to Jesus. Why? Because she knew that if she could only get close to Him, she would be completely healed.

It is biblical for you to pursue your healing. There is no holiness in persisting with a condition God doesn't want you to have! There is no reason to be proud of wearing a stain from the enemy that God wants to cleanse from your life. If Jesus made healing a priority, we should make it a priority too!

So what did this woman do that was so powerful?

---

[86] "How then shall they call on Him in whom they have not believed? And how shall they believe in Him of whom they have not heard? And how shall they hear without a preacher?" —Rom. 10:14

[87] "If a woman has a discharge of blood for many days, other than at the time of her customary impurity, or if it runs beyond her usual time of impurity, all the days of her unclean discharge shall be as the days of her customary impurity. She shall be unclean." —Lev. 15:25

When she heard about Jesus she came behind Him in the crowd and touched His garment. For she said, "If only I may touch His clothes, I shall be made well."   *—Mark 5:27-28*

She pressed through. Look at her boldness. Look at her faith! This woman didn't even *know* Jesus, but she knew that if she could so much as grab the edge of His clothes, something would happen that would change her life forever. And as she exercised her faith, she received her reward: "Immediately the fountain of her blood was dried up, and she felt in her body that she was healed of the affliction" (Mk. 5:29).

Notice the words "she felt." Healing *feels* like something! Seeking Jesus for healing is not an intellectual exercise! It is not a checklist you have to follow, where as soon as you do everything God has prescribed, you will be healed. Healing is a process in which you have to *feel out* what the Holy Spirit wants you to do. The good news is that when your healing happens, you are going to feel it! You are going to know it!

Kenneth Hagin said that whenever he prayed for someone to be healed, he knew in that moment whether the person would be healed or not.[88] How did he know? Because he would *feel* it. When this woman with persistent bleeding was healed, she felt it! And Jesus felt something too:

And Jesus, immediately knowing in Himself that power had gone out of Him, turned around in the crowd and said, "Who touched My clothes?" But His disciples said to Him, "You see the multitude thronging You, and You say, 'Who touched Me?' "   *—Mark 5:30-31*

---

[88] Rev. Kenneth E. Hagin. "God's Healing Anointing." YouTube video, accessed 1 Sep. 2020. https://www.youtube.com/watch?v=n3YXRnkObMw

Healing happened. The woman felt it. Jesus felt it! There was "power" (v. 30) that had gone out of Jesus and into that woman. "Power" is the Greek *dunamis,*[89] which means "the inherent power residing in a thing by virtue of its nature." Remember that Jesus *is* the God Who Heals (Ex. 15:26). Healing is not just something He *does*— it is who He is! The very substance of Jesus came out of Him. He knew it, and the woman felt it.

Many people in the multitude that "thronged" Jesus touched Him, but only one woman got healed. What does that tell us? There was something different about that woman's touch. There was something she brought to Jesus that nobody else did. What was it?

And He looked around to see her who had done this thing. But the woman, fearing and trembling, knowing what had happened to her, came and fell down before Him and told Him the whole truth. And He said to her, "Daughter, your faith has made you well. Go in peace, and be healed of your affliction." —Mark 5:32-34

It was her *faith!* Her *faith* had made her well. This woman's touch was not just a casual encounter. It had *faith* attached to it. This woman knew that if she *expected* a miracle from Jesus and positioned herself accordingly,[90] she would get one.

Notice one more thing in verses 32-34. Jesus rewarded this woman's faith with a face-to-face encounter. Jesus asked His disciples, "Who touched My clothes?" (v 30). He was not seeking punitive action against

---

[89] "G1411 - dynamis - Strong's Greek Lexicon (KJV)." Blue Letter Bible. Accessed 11 Aug, 2020. https://www.blueletterbible.org//lang/lexicon/lexicon.cfm?Strongs=G1411&t=KJV

[90] Charles Finney notes that our prayers are not answered when we do not "comply with the revealed conditions upon which God [has] promised to answer prayer," namely that we *expect* God to give us the things for which we ask (Charles Finney, *Memoirs*, Kindle loc. 251).

a person who had stolen something from Him—He was seeking to look her in her eyes and *say more.* Jesus wanted a relationship with this woman because of her faith! The woman was scared, but Jesus was thrilled. Did you know that Jesus *loves* when we reach out and touch Him with faith?![91]

You Have a Role to Play!

So, here is my question for you: What was it that healed this woman? Was it the power of God? Or was it her faith? The answer to *both questions* is *yes.*

God is the One who heals. But can't you see that there is something required of us? He cannot heal the way He wants to heal unless we reach out in faith! You might ask, "But can't God do anything He wants to do?" In response, I would point you to Jesus' visit to Nazareth, where Jesus "could do no mighty work there, except that He laid His hands on a few sick people and healed them. And He marveled because of their unbelief" (Mark 6:5-6). Lack of faith constrains the power of God, but great faith releases it!

I can tell you the Bible makes provision for physical healing until I'm blue in the face, but at some point you have to take hold of what the Word of God says and pair your faith with God's command.

The writer of Hebrews tells us that *faith makes a difference:*

> *Therefore, since a promise remains of entering His rest, let us fear lest any of you seem to have come short of it. For indeed the gospel was preached to us as well as to them; but the word which they heard did not profit them, not being mixed with faith in those who heard it. For we who have believed do enter that rest . . .* —Hebrews 4:1-3a

---

[91] "When Jesus heard these things, He marveled at him, and turned around and said to the crowd that followed Him, 'I say to you, I have not found such great faith, not even in Israel!'" —Lk. 7:9

Are you mixing God's Word with your faith? The Word of God will not "profit" you (v 2) unless you *mix it* with faith! This is often the difference between people who get healed and those who do not. This is often the difference between churches that move in healing and those that do not. When you mix faith with the presence of God (proximity to Jesus), a supernatural spark is lit that results in healing. Do you want to see a supernatural reaction in your life? Exercise this divine formula! Mix your faith with the Word of God, and watch what happens in Jesus' name!

At our church, we have a ministry team that comes up for prayer at the end of every service. Our anointed—and awesome!—volunteers line up at the front of the sanctuary, and everyone who needs prayer for anything at all is invited to come forward. Our volunteers lay their hands on them, release the Word of God over them, and believe for the impossible.

When some people come up for prayer, they fly backwards through the air and fall down on the ground. Others start to shake under the power of God. Some cry, and some laugh. But sometimes, *nothing happens.* Do you know why some people are touched by God, and others aren't? It actually has very little to do with the person praying! Some people bring *faith* with them when they come up for prayer, and others do not.

Without Faith

What happens if you don't have faith? First, it will be "impossible" to please God. I know that sounds harsh! But don't take my word for it. Take God's Word for it:

> *But without faith it is impossible to please Him, for he who comes to God must believe that He is, and that He is a rewarder of those who diligently seek Him.*　　　　　—Hebrews 11:6

God is not impressed by your pious behavior. Yes, piety is a good thing! But no, it doesn't improve your standing with God. Do you know what really excites God? Your faith! In fact, Scripture tells us that when we seek God with faith, we will find a *reward!*

Scripture does not speak highly of men and women who are devoid of faith:

> *But let him ask in faith, with no doubting, for he who doubts is like a wave of the sea driven and tossed by the wind. For let not that man suppose that he will receive anything from the Lord; he is a double-minded man, unstable in all his ways.* —James 1:6-8

If you ask in faith, you will "have the petitions" that you ask of God.[92] But according to James, if there is doubt present in your prayers, you are "double-minded" and "unstable" not just in your prayers, but in "all your ways!" Yikes! If we go to God without faith, verse 7 (above) cautions us not to expect that we will receive "anything" from God!

Notice that James invokes a two-pronged definition of faith. In a proactive sense, faith means accepting the Word of God and believing it for your life. Yet faith also means, in a reactive sense, rejecting doubt and unbelief (v. 6). Not only do you have to receive the truth, you also have to reject the lie!

We often miss this second element of faith in the church. We love to hear uplifting sermons about all the positive things God wants to do in our lives! Yet we hesitate to accept the reality that we must *actively reject*

---

[92] "Now this is the confidence that we have in Him, that if we ask anything according to His will, He hears us. And if we know that He hears us, whatever we ask, we know that we have the petitions that we have asked of Him." —1 Jn. 5:14-15

the un-heavenly plans and purposes that the enemy wants to push on us if we want to see healing come to pass.

When you're contending for healing, you have to listen to the right things. You have to listen to the Word of God! But you also have to avoid listening to the wrong things. Philippians 4:8 states it this way:

> *Finally, brethren, whatever things are true, whatever things are noble, whatever things are just, whatever things are pure, whatever things are lovely, whatever things are of good report, if there is any virtue and if there is anything praiseworthy—meditate on these things.*

To "meditate" means to "take into account" or to "include in your calculations."[93] If you want to have faith, you have to "meditate" on the good things of God! But that also means that you have to *avoid meditating* on anything not mentioned in Philippians 4:8! Don't waste time thinking about things that aren't true, noble, just, pure, lovely, of good report, virtuous, or praiseworthy!

When you get a bad report from the doctor that doesn't line up with the expectations dictated by your faith, don't dwell on it! Go back to the Word of God! Meditate on what He says instead of allowing fear to infiltrate your mindset. Don't allow your mind to go into the dark places filled with questions about "what if." *What if my healing doesn't come? What if I have to spend the rest of my life like this? What if healing stopped when the last apostle died?*

Don't go there! The one and only thing you should "include in your calculations" is the faithfulness of God, and the truth of His Word. Leave the rest alone!

---

[93] "G3049 - logizomai - Strong's Greek Lexicon (KJV)." Blue Letter Bible. Accessed 11 Aug, 2020. https://www.blueletterbible.org//lang/lexicon/lexicon.cfm?Strongs=G3049&t=KJV

When Abraham needed a miracle baby, he had to *block out* everything that did not line up with God's plan for his life:

> *And not being weak in faith, he did not consider his own body, already*
> *dead (since he was about a hundred years old), and the deadness of*
> *Sarah's womb. He did not waver at the promise of God through*
> *unbelief, but was strengthened in faith, giving glory to God, and*
> *being fully convinced that what He had promised He was also able to*
> *perform. And therefore "it was accounted to him for righteousness."*
> —*Romans 4:19-22*

Abraham might have been weak in his body, but he certainly was not weak in his faith! To "consider" is the Greek *katanoeo*,[94] which means "to fix your eyes upon." Abraham had obstacles in front of him, but he refused to fix his eyes upon them! Instead, he was "strengthened in faith." Do you know what that means? He kept *talking to God*. He went back to God as many times as necessary to ensure that he was full of miracle-working faith.

Abraham had plenty of opportunities to give up and decide that maybe God had changed His mind about giving him a son. Instead, he persevered. He became "fully convinced" (v 21) that God would come through. And *then and only then* was it "accounted to him for righteousness" (v 22).

Faith is built in times of trial. If you're not going through something difficult and believing for something impossible, you don't need faith! But trials require faith. It means nothing to say you have faith when faith

---

[94] "G2657 - katanoeō - Strong's Greek Lexicon (KJV)." Blue Letter Bible. Accessed 11 Aug, 2020. https://www.blueletterbible.org//lang/lexicon/lexicon.cfm?Strongs=G2657&t=KJV

is not required. But it means *everything* to keep your faith when things don't go your way!

How Can I Get Some Faith?

So what should you do if you don't have the faith required to pray for your healing? Here are my Seventeen Kingdom Keys to increasing your faith. Just kidding! Aren't you glad it's *so much easier* than that?! If you need more faith, *just ask God.*

When the disciples didn't have the faith they knew they needed, they simply asked Jesus for more:

And the apostles said to the Lord, "Increase our faith." —Luke 17:5

Do you see how simple that is? Do you need more faith? You don't have to beg for it. In fact, you don't have to do anything except ask!

Needing more faith is not a *bad thing.* I remember being in a church service once where a guest minister invited anyone who needed healing to come forward. A precious woman came forward using a cane. Something was clearly wrong with her leg, and she was walking with a limp. The guest minister prayed for her, and nothing happened. So what did he do? He berated her in front of the congregation for her lack of faith. Out loud into the microphone he told her, "You need to go home and get some more faith!"

Do you think that woman left encouraged? Do you think she left that service empowered to seek more of God? Absolutely not! We do our brothers and sisters in Christ a disservice when we heap guilt, shame, and condemnation on people who don't feel like they have enough faith to believe for miracle. This woman probably already knew she needed more faith! But perhaps she didn't know *how to get it.* She had no idea that she didn't have to go home and *work* for more faith. All she needed to do was ask.

If you don't regularly find yourself in situations that require more faith than you currently have, I don't believe you're taking enough risk. You're not asking big enough! You're not stepping out on the water[95] and trusting God to do miraculous things! We should constantly be asking God for things that are *so big* that we need more faith to properly pray for them.

Mark 9 tells the story of a father who asks Jesus to heal his son. The father wanted to have more faith! But he knew he simply didn't have what he needed. Look at the tension in the father's plea to Jesus:

> *Jesus said to him, "If you can believe, all things are possible to him who believes." Immediately the father of the child cried out and said with tears, "Lord, I believe; help my unbelief!"*   —Mark 9:23-24

"Lord, I believe; help my unbelief!" So desperate! So honest! The father wanted to believe! He knew that he *needed faith* to see a miracle! But he was also acutely aware of his own shortcomings. He knew that he had trouble believing. But notice that instead of going home sad and ashamed, He asked Jesus to "help" his unbelief! And Jesus rewarded this man by showing him a miracle that would forever cement his faith in the power of God:

> *When Jesus saw that the people came running together, He rebuked the unclean spirit, saying to it, "Deaf and dumb spirit, I command you, come out of him and enter him no more!" Then the spirit cried out, convulsed him greatly, and came out of him. And he became as*

---

[95] "And Peter answered Him and said, 'Lord, if it is You, command me to come to You on the water.' So He said, 'Come.' And when Peter had come down out of the boat, he walked on the water to go to Jesus." —Matt. 14:28-29

one dead, so that many said, "He is dead." But Jesus took him by the
hand and lifted him up, and he arose.   —*Mark 9:25-27*

When you ask, Jesus will answer. Do you need more faith? Ask and trust
that God will give it to you.

Great Faith

Years ago, we had a young woman in our church who was seriously
injured and had to be rushed to the emergency room. Our worship team
was having a gathering at our worship leader's home in Brooklyn. He
lived on the third floor, and his building had a nice rooftop overlooking
part of the city, so the worship team was going back and forth between
the third floor and the rooftop, bringing food and drinks up to the top of
the building.

This young woman, Callie, was on a trip back downstairs and stopped
to talk to someone. She wasn't paying attention to where she put her
hands, and left her finger on the doorframe to the entrance of the roof.
One of her friends closed the door, not knowing her finger was there.
It was a big, heavy fire door that automatically slammed shut right on
Callie's left ring finger and chopped off the top inch of it.[96] The severed
part dropped to the ground, and soon blood was everywhere.

Some of the worship team members immediately wrapped a towel
around Callie's hand to control the bleeding. Another friend with a
strong stomach grabbed the tip of her finger off the ground and put it in
a Ziploc bag full of ice. The plan was to get Callie to the emergency room
so doctors could sew her finger back on as soon as possible.

But when Callie arrived at the emergency room, doctors told her
they couldn't re-attach her finger. They told her she would never have

---

[96] Callie happened to be young, single, and waiting for her husband. I saw
this event as a symbolic attack on her hope.

a fingertip or a fingernail again. The finger would grow new skin, they said, but would never be as long as it once was.

In the midst of the absolute chaos, Callie was calm, almost smiling. She had faith that her finger was going to grow back out, no matter what the doctors said.

The doctors recommended a procedure that involved cutting an incision in the palm of her hand and curling the tip of her finger inside the incision. That environment, they said, would give her finger the best chance of healing well. But Callie refused. She felt peace from the Holy Spirit to simply bandage the wound, and trust that God would grow that finger back.

When church members visited Callie in the hospital, she was bright-eyed and full of faith. Her mind was made up. Losing the tip of her finger was not even a possibility. Instead of meditating on the worst-possible outcomes, she became "fully convinced that what [God] had promised He was also able to perform" (Rom. 4:21).

God responded to Callie's faith. Over the next several weeks, the tip of her finger *grew back completely.* We have the photos to prove it! The nail grew back, and you *cannot even tell* that anything ever happened to her finger.

When an accident happened, adrenaline told Callie to panic! But faith told her to remain calm, and trust that God would fulfill His Word.

Faith for Others

I pray that you would ask God for the faith you need to believe for your own healing. But this chapter would be incomplete unless I told you your faith is not just for you. It's also for others.

As Jesus was teaching in Luke 5, a group of men brought "a man who was paralyzed," to Jesus (v 18). Because they couldn't get into the house where Jesus was teaching, "[T]hey went up on the housetop and let [the paralyzed man] down with his bed through the tiling into the midst before Jesus" (v 19). These men were willing to do *whatever it took* to get their friend in the presence of Jesus so he could be healed. And watch how Jesus responded: "When He saw their faith, He said to him, 'Man, your sins are forgiven you'"(Lk. 5:20).

Did Jesus see the paralyzed man's faith? No! How could a paralyzed man possibly demonstrate his faith in a visible way? But Jesus saw "their faith." He saw the faith of this man's friends! And that was enough:

> *But that you may know that the Son of Man has power on earth to forgive sins" —He said to the man who was paralyzed, "I say to you, arise, take up your bed, and go to your house."*
>
> *Immediately he rose up before them, took up what he had been lying on, and departed to his own house, glorifying God. And they were all amazed, and they glorified God and were filled with fear, saying, "We have seen strange things today!"*   —Luke 5:24-26

This paralyzed man didn't have the means to put his faith into action on his own, so his friends stepped in and stood in the gap. You and I are called to do exactly the same thing for others.

You know people in your life who may not have a personal relationship with Jesus. Or maybe they're saved, but they don't know what God's Word says about healing. Guess what? You have the immense privilege of bringing them to Jesus, and setting them in His midst. As you bring other people to God *in prayer*, Jesus will respond to *your faith*, even if the person you are praying for may not have their own. As long as *someone* believes, it will be enough.

Take heart. As much as you want to increase your faith, God wants to increase it all the more.

CHAPTER SEVEN

ANOINTED TO HEAL

Inf you call yourself a disciple of Jesus, it is your job to heal the sick:

> *And as you go, preach, saying, "The kingdom of heaven is at hand."*
> *Heal the sick, cleanse the lepers, raise the dead, cast out demons.*
> *Freely you have received, freely give.* —*Matthew 10:7-8*

Look at verse 8 for a moment. "Heal the sick, cleanse the lepers, raise the dead, cast out demons." Let it sink in. Now ask yourself this question: Does my life look like that verse? When I pray, are people healed? When I go to a funeral, are the dead raised? Do breakthrough and deliverance happen everywhere I go?

If not, don't panic. I believe verses like the ones above are intentionally designed to encourage healthy self-reflection. We should look at those verses and think, *That sounds impossible.* And then we get to return to the Word of God and remind ourselves that "with God nothing will be impossible" (Lk 1:37).

Healing Like Jesus

If you want to heal like Jesus, you have to know how Jesus healed! Jesus healed *by the anointing:*

> *[H]ow God anointed Jesus of Nazareth with the Holy Spirit and with power, who went about doing good and healing all who were oppressed by the devil, for God was with Him.* —*Acts 10:38*

Jesus was anointed! This verse tells us two things we already knew: Jesus 1) did good and 2) healed people. But what you may not know is that Jesus was *anointed* to do these things. God anointed Him with 1) the Holy Spirit and 2) power. It wasn't until the anointing took place that the healing could be accomplished!

Don't try to run out and do what God has called you to do without being anointed first! When God calls you to do something that seems impossible, don't try to do it alone. Wait on God for the anointing to get it done.

The anointing is the manifest presence of God's Holy Spirit. For an illustration, let's look at the moment David was chosen to be king:

> *Then Samuel took the horn of oil and anointed him in the midst of his brothers; and the Spirit of the Lord came upon David from that day forward. So Samuel arose and went to Ramah.* —1 Samuel 16:13

Once David was anointed, the "Spirit of the Lord came upon" David to do what God had called him to do!

In Acts 10:38, "anointed" is the Greek word *chrio*,[97] which means, "Enduing Christians with the gifts of the Holy Spirit." To "anoint" someone means to consecrate him (to make him holy or separate) by the presence of the Holy Spirit. The anointing in noun form, then, is the consecrating presence of the Holy Spirit. When the Holy Spirit wants to do something *through you,* He will come and settle *on you.*

Since the Holy Spirit is the Spirit of Jesus,[98] the anointing is the *substance* of Jesus. When you have it, you can go out and pray the same prayers Jesus prayed, and expect exactly the same results!

---

[97] "G5548 - chriō - Strong's Greek Lexicon (KJV)." Blue Letter Bible. Accessed 11 Aug, 2020. https://www.blueletterbible.org//lang/lexicon/lexicon.cfm?Strongs=G5548&t=KJV

[98] "But you are not in the flesh but in the Spirit, if indeed the Spirit of God dwells in you. Now if anyone does not have the Spirit of Christ, he is not

Now let's put two and two together. How did Jesus heal? By the anointing! So if Jesus asks you to heal in His name, do you know how He expects that healing to happen? You guessed it! *By the anointing.*

But if you're like me, there are days and seasons in your life where you just don't *feel* very anointed. You feel unqualified, not up to the task! So what do you do if you don't *feel* like you're anointed?

How to Increase in the Anointing

In 2 Timothy 1:6, the apostle Paul outlines two ways to increase in the anointing:

> *Therefore I remind you to stir up the gift of God which is in you through the laying on of my hands.* —2 Timothy 1:6

First of all, we see that Timothy, to whom Paul is writing, already had an *experience* with the Holy Spirit. The apostle Paul laid hands on him, and a "gift of God" was deposited in Timothy. This is the first way to increase in the anointing. Ask God to touch you in a mighty way! He will anoint you, either as someone who is anointed lays hands on you, or as you cry out to Him in prayer. Ask God to give you an *encounter* with Him!

I love *encounters* with God. Charles Finney, a great man of God used in revival meetings all over the United States in the 1800s, described his initial encounter with the presence of Jesus in his memoirs. He had this to say about encountering (i.e. experiencing) the presence of God:

> But as I returned and was about to take a seat by the fire, I received a mighty baptism of the Holy Ghost. Without

---

His." – Rom. 8:9
"Now the Lord is the Spirit; and where the Spirit of the Lord is, there is liberty." – 2 Cor. 3:17

expecting it, without ever having the thought in my mind that there was any such thing for me, without any recollection that I had ever heard the thing mentioned by any person in the world, at a moment entirely unexpected by me, the Holy Spirit descended upon me in a manner that seemed to go through me, body and soul. I could feel the impression, like a wave of electricity, going through and through me. Indeed it seemed to come in waves, and waves of liquid love—for I could not express it in any other way. And yet it did not seem like water, but rather as the breath of God. I can recollect distinctly that it seemed to fan me like immense wings; and it seemed to me, as these waves passed over me, that they literally moved my hair like a passing breeze.

No words can express the wonderful love that was shed abroad in my heart. It seemed to me that I should burst. I wept aloud with joy and love, and I do not know but I should say I literally bellowed out the unutterable gushings of my heart. These waves came over me, and over me, and over me one after the other, until I recollect I cried out, "I shall die if these waves continue to pass over me." I said to the Lord, "Lord, I cannot bear any more." Yet I had no fear of death. [99]

I don't know about you, but I want God to touch me like that! Prior to this encounter with Jesus, Finney was a Christian in ritual only. He was a successful lawyer who attended church but had no *relationship* with Jesus. In fact, Finney was so far from God that another man in his

---

[99] Charles Finney, *The Original Memoirs of Charles G. Finney* (Grand Rapids, MI: Zondervan, 2002), Kindle Edition, loc. 384 of 8226.

town remarked, "If you Christians can convert Finney, I will believe in religion."[100]

Yet after this anointing by the Holy Spirit—this "baptism of the Holy Ghost"—Finney was most sure of his salvation, and determined to be used by God. He remarked that Jesus became so all-consuming that everything else had lost its flavor. He "had no disposition to make money" and no "hungering and thirsting after worldly pleasures or amusements in any direction."[101] The cares and concerns of this world had lost their hold on him. The morning after his first encounter with Jesus, a client came to see Finney to see if he was ready to defend him in court. Finney replied, "Deacon Barney, I have a retainer from the Lord Jesus Christ to plead His cause, and I cannot plead yours."[102]

Dr. Randy Clark has a similar story. In 1989 he had an encounter with Jesus where he felt waves of electricity running through his body. Leading up to that experience, he had been praying that God would touch him the way God touched Charles Finney. And God delivered! Dr. Clark recounted that the presence of God coursing through his body was so strong that he thought he was going to die. It felt like he had grabbed an electric fence and couldn't let go.[103]

Finney and Clark were marked by their encounters with God. After their experiences with God, they were used mightily by God in massive revivals that impacted the world.[104] I hope you have a powerful encounter with God! It will forever mark you for use in God's kingdom, and change your life from that moment on!

---

[100] Finney, *Memoirs*, loc. 496.

[101] Finney, *Memoirs*, loc. 473.

[102] Finney, *Memoirs*, loc. 448.

[103] Personal communication, 11/6/2019.

[104] Finney held meetings from Rhode Island to Ohio from 1821 to 1875. Clark was used as a catalyst for the Toronto Blessing starting in 1994 and has traveled the world sparking revival ever since.

If you've never had a life-changing *encounter* with God, find someone who has! Ask him or her to lay hands on you, the same way the apostle Paul laid hands on Timothy. Believe that as they lay their hands on you, you are going to receive the same anointing they carry! Believe that their testimony will be your testimony, and cry out for God to touch you in a powerful way.

But there is another way to increase in the anointing. Remember what the apostle Paul told Timothy:

> *Therefore I remind you to stir up the gift of God which is in you through the laying on of my hands.*   —2 Timothy 1:6

There was already something *in* Timothy. He had already had an encounter with the presence of God! But it was Timothy's job to "stir [it] up."

The second way to increase in the anointing is to "stir up" the anointing that God has already deposited in you—that is, to internalize the revelation that *you are already anointed*. I pray you've had a powerful encounter with the presence of God that has marked you forever. But once you have, it's time to stir it up. And here is how to do exactly that.

Stirring Up the Gift

1) Understand that you are anointed.

First, you have to understand that you are anointed. Maybe you've never been stuck to the floor with waves of electricity coursing through your body like Charles Finney or Dr. Randy Clark. But if you've received Jesus as Lord, you've already been anointed:

But if the Spirit of Him who raised Jesus from the dead dwells in you,
He who raised Christ from the dead will also give life to your mortal
bodies through His Spirit who dwells in you. —*Romans 8:11*

When you gave your life to Jesus, the Holy Spirit made a home inside you. And that means that you have His manifest presence—the *anointing*—already!

Now He who establishes us with you in Christ and has anointed us
is God, who also has sealed us and given us the Spirit in our hearts
as a guarantee. —*2 Corinthians 1:21-22*

God has already anointed you, and the proof—the "guarantee" —is the indwelling presence of His Holy Spirit!

Here is why this is so important. Yes, you can *increase* in the anointing by having a fresh experience. But you can increase the anointing on your life *just as much (if not more!)* as you simply 1) understand and 2) remind yourself that God has already anointed you! When you have an encounter with God, you are anointed by God from the *outside in*. But when you truly understand the revelation that you have already been anointed by God, the presence of His Holy Spirit will increase on your life from the *inside out!*

Jesus tells everyone who believes in Him that He expects us to do great things in His name:

"Most assuredly, I say to you, he who believes in Me, the works that
I do he will do also; and greater works than these he will do, because
I go to My Father. And whatever you ask in My name, that I will do,
that the Father may be glorified in the Son. If you ask anything in
My name, I will do it." —*John 14:12-14*

You will do the same works Jesus did. In fact, you are called to "greater works" than these. And if Jesus healed because He was anointed (Acts 10:38), do you know how you and I are going to do "greater works?" That's right—only *by the anointing.*

If Jesus hadn't already anointed His disciples, He wouldn't have promised they would do "greater works." Do you see it? Jesus didn't need His disciples to have a new experience or an encounter at a Christian conference; He simply needed them to get the revelation that they were already anointed.

Maybe you've forgotten just how anointed you are over the years. The first thing that will happen after God anoints you powerfully is this: The enemy will come and lie to you, tempting you to *doubt* the anointing on your life. Jesus knew that, even before He sent His disciples out. Remember what He told them before their ministry trip:

> *"And as you go, preach, saying, 'The kingdom of heaven is at hand.'*
> *Heal the sick, cleanse the lepers, raise the dead, cast out demons.*
> *Freely you have received, freely give."* —Matthew 10:7-8

Why would Jesus have said "freely you have received" unless He knew the disciples would doubt their anointing as soon as they needed it? Jesus took the time to *remind them* that they *already had something to offer.* He had already given it to them, whether they knew it or not! And now it was time for the disciples to share their anointing with someone else.

If you want to see the anointing *come out,* first you have to believe that it has *gone in.*

2) Declare that you are anointed.

Once you understand that you are anointed, you have to start declaring it. I've gotten in the habit of declaring Isaiah 61:1[105] over my life every

---

[105] "The Spirit of the Lord God is upon Me, because the Lord has anointed Me

single morning. Let me tell you, it has made an *amazing* difference in the way I start my day!

What is your declaration over yourself first thing every morning? Do you look at yourself in the mirror and declare you are powerfully anointed? Or do you look at yourself with pity and self-doubt and wonder if God is ever really going to use you?

Even Jesus had to *declare* that He was anointed! When He came to His hometown, He had a very specific message for the people who had seen Him grow up:

> *So He came to Nazareth, where He had been brought up. And as His custom was, He went into the synagogue on the Sabbath day, and stood up to read. And He was handed the book of the prophet Isaiah. And when He had opened the book, He found the place where it was written: "The Spirit of the Lord is upon Me, because He has anointed Me to preach the gospel to the poor; He has sent Me to heal the brokenhearted, to proclaim liberty to the captives and recovery of sight to the blind, to set at liberty those who are oppressed; to proclaim the acceptable year of the Lord."*
>
> *Then He closed the book, and gave it back to the attendant and sat down. And the eyes of all who were in the synagogue were fixed on Him. And He began to say to them, "Today this Scripture is fulfilled in your hearing." So all bore witness to Him, and marveled at the gracious words which proceeded out of His mouth. And they said, "Is this not Joseph's son?"* —Luke 4:16-22

---

to preach good tidings to the poor; He has sent Me to heal the brokenhearted, to proclaim liberty to the captives, and the opening of the prison to those who are bound…" —Is. 61:1

Starting in verse 18, Jesus was quoting Isaiah 61: the same passage I am encouraging you to declare over yourself every morning. He was announcing to the world that He had been anointed. He was declaring that He had had an *encounter* with the Holy Spirit,[106] and from that moment forward, everything would change!

Notice two things. First, not everyone believed Jesus when He declared He was anointed. In verse 22, His listeners gently began to question if Jesus was really capable of doing the things He promised. By verse 28, His listeners were downright angry:

> *So all those in the synagogue, when they heard these things, were filled with wrath, and rose up and thrust Him out of the city; and they led Him to the brow of the hill on which their city was built, that they might throw Him down over the cliff.*   —Luke 4:28-29

You will have people in your life who don't believe in your anointing. You have an enemy named Satan who will come and lie to you, whispering in your ear that you aren't as anointed as God says you are! But your response should be to let it go, just like Jesus did: "Then passing through the midst of them, He went His way" (Lk. 4:30).

Second, Jesus' anointing was not followed by immediate breakthrough. It was actually followed by *demonic resistance.*

In Luke 3 as Jesus was baptized, the Holy Spirit "descended in bodily form like a dove upon Him" (Lk. 3:22). It would be nice if Jesus had come up out of the water and immediately started healing people! But that wasn't how events unfolded. This is how Luke 4 starts:

---

[106] "When all the people were baptized, it came to pass that Jesus also was baptized; and while He prayed, the heaven was opened. And the Holy Spirit descended in bodily form like a dove upon Him, and a voice came from heaven which said, 'You are My beloved Son; in You I am well pleased.'" —Lk. 3:21-22

Then Jesus, being filled with the Holy Spirit, returned from the Jordan and was led by the Spirit into the wilderness, being tempted for forty days by the devil. And in those days He ate nothing, and afterward, when they had ended, He was hungry. —Luke 4:1-2

Jesus had an encounter in which He was powerfully anointed by God, but the enemy responded by *tempting Him.* The times God touches us the strongest are often followed by the times the enemy attacks us the most! But notice how Jesus responded.

First, in that moment as the enemy tempted Him, Jesus responded 1) out loud and 2) with Scripture![107] You cannot *think* the enemy away with your own thoughts! The only way to fight the lies of the enemy is by declaring the Word of God *out loud* over your life.

Second, after the temptation ended, Jesus started declaring that He was anointed! His temptation was followed by His declaration starting in Luke 4:18 that we read above.

Now that you know you have been anointed, your job is to declare it over yourself every single day! Expect that as you do, heaven is going to *add* to your anointing, and hell is going to *bow* to your anointing, in Jesus' name!

3) Lay hands on people.

Once you know you're anointed and have declared that you are anointed, it's time to *do something* with your anointing! Notice the wording in the verses from Isaiah 61 that Jesus declared in the synagogue:

The Spirit of the Lord God is upon Me,
Because the Lord has anointed Me
To preach good tidings to the poor . . .

—Isaiah 61:1a

---

[107] See Lk 4:1-13

The anointing comes *to do something*. I'm all for enjoying the presence of God without restriction or reservation! I love to laugh and marinate in the joy of the Lord. But when His presence comes, we should *do something* with it. It's good to enjoy the anointing at a powerful service on Sunday! But we're not doing our job if we don't *do something* with that anointing from Monday through Saturday.

Once you know you are anointed, it's time to start praying for people. Ask God to show you whom He wants you to pray for. Jesus said He did "nothing of Himself, but what He sees the Father do" (Jn. 5:19). When God shows you what He wants you to do with the anointing, and over *whom* He wants you to pray, make a list! Write it down, and start every day by believing it's going to happen. Believe that God has not only anointed you, but that He will also create opportunities for you to utilize that anointing every day so the people around you will know that Jesus is Lord.

Then, when you're in a situation where God has told you to act, it's time to *move*. Jesus promised *every believer* that when we lay hands, the sick will recover:

> *"And these signs will follow those who believe: In My name they will cast out demons; they will speak with new tongues; they will take up serpents; and if they drink anything deadly, it will by no means hurt them; they will lay hands on the sick, and they will recover."*   —Mark 16:17-18

The only question is, do you believe Him?

> *So then, after the Lord had spoken to them, He was received up into heaven, and sat down at the right hand of God. And they went out and*

preached everywhere, the Lord working with them and confirming
the word through the accompanying signs. Amen.

—Mark 16:19-20

Because when you take God at His Word, there is no limit to what His
Holy Spirit can do through you.

All That Matters

Aimee Semple McPherson was a woman who lived a full life of faith
in Jesus Christ. Her favorite Bible verse was Romans 13:8: "Jesus Christ
is the same yesterday, today, and forever." Her stance was that if Jesus
healed when He walked the earth, then He still heals today!

Healing testimonies from her crusades numbered in the tens
of thousands. Daniel Epstein remarks, "The healings [people saw
in Semple McPherson's meetings] present a monstrous obstacle to
scientific historiography. If events transpired as newspapers, letters,
and testimonials say they did, then Aimee Semple McPherson's healing
ministry was miraculous." He explains that "very sick people came to
Sister Aimee by the tens of thousands, blind deaf, paralyzed. Many were
healed, some temporarily, some forever. She would point to heaven, to
Christ the Great Healer, and would take no credit for the results."[108]

But Aimee Semple McPherson's call to ministry was as unlikely
as they come. Before she was known around the world as a powerful
preacher and faith healer, Aimee Semple McPherson came from humble
beginnings. She was born near Ingersoll, Ontario, Canada, on October 9th,
1890. Her parents raised her in what one biographer called the "desolate
Canadian countryside, where she learned self-reliance and toughness."[109]

---

[108] Daniel Epstein, *Sister Aimee: The Life of Aimee Semple McPherson*, (New
York: Harvest, 1993), 111.

[109] M.A. Sutton, *Aimee Semple McPherson and the Resurrection of Christian*

She didn't have access to the best schools. She didn't plan to change the way an entire nation worshipped Jesus!

Though religion occupied a central place in her household and her mother worked for the Salvation Army, Semple McPherson had a crisis of faith in high school. She learned about Darwin's theory of evolution, and "began quizzing local pastors about the relation between faith and science."[110] She was far from secure in her belief in Jesus, and a life in ministry was not part of her plan.

But one day, God anointed her. The anointing of the Lord put her crisis of faith to bed. Semple McPherson describes that when she was seventeen years old, God spoke these words from the Book of Jeremiah "plainly into [her] startled ears" [111] as she was alone praying in her bedroom one day:

> *"Before I formed you in the womb I knew you;*
> *Before you were born I sanctified you;*
> *I ordained you a prophet to the nations."*

> *Then said I:*

> *"Ah, Lord God!*
> *Behold, I cannot speak, for I am a youth."*

> *But the Lord said to me:*

> *"Do not say, 'I am a youth,'*

America (Cambridge, MA: Harvard University Press, 2007), 9.

[110] Sutton, *Aimee Semple McPherson and the Resurrection of Christian America*, 10.

[111] Aimee Semple McPherson, *This Is That: Personal Experiences, Sermons and Writings* (Jawbone Digital, 2015), Kindle loc. 36.

For you shall go to all to whom I send you,
And whatever I command you, you shall speak.
Do not be afraid of their faces,
For I am with you to deliver you," says the Lord.

Then the Lord put forth His hand and touched my mouth, and the
Lord said to me:

"Behold, I have put My words in your mouth." — *Jer. 1:4-9*

She heard the words, but couldn't believe they were true, even as God spoke them over her:

At first it seemed too astounding and impossible to be true that the Lord would ever call such a simple, unworthy little country girl as I to go out and preach the Gospel but the call and ordination were so real that, although later set apart and ordained by the saints of God, the memory of my little bedroom, flooded with the glory of God as He spoke those words, has always been to me my real ordination.[112]

It seemed impossible! But Aimee Semple McPherson had been *anointed* by the Lord. She had an *experience* with Jesus! And from that day forward, her life was never the same.

You see, God anoints whom He chooses. Remember what God told the prophet Samuel when he went to anoint a new king over Israel:

---

[112] Aimee Semple McPherson, *This Is That: Personal Experiences, Sermons, and Writings of Aimee Semple McPherson, Evangelist,* 2nd rev. ed. (Los Angeles: Foursquare Publications, 1923), 13.

But the Lord said to Samuel, "Do not look at his appearance or at his physical stature, because I have refused him. For the Lord does not see as man sees; for man looks at the outward appearance, but the Lord looks at the heart."   *—1 Samuel 16:7*

God doesn't see like you see. He looks at the *heart*. So don't ever allow someone else to tell you you're not anointed when God has told you that you are! And don't ever allow the enemy to convince you you're not anointed when Jesus has put His hand on you and changed you forever!

Aimee saw herself as "simple" and "unworthy," too humble for the call God was putting on her life! But she would learn firsthand that God knows what He is doing, and that His calling is irrevocable.[113] Once she had been anointed by God, there was no turning back. Because the anointing is all that matters.

So, are you "simple?" Are you "unworthy?" Are you under-educated and under-qualified? Unsure if you will ever accomplish anything for God? Then rejoice! Because God uses the simple to confound the wise.[114] Your education and background can be helpful and relevant, but at the end of the day, the only qualifier you need to be used by God is having been *anointed by Him.*

---

[113] "For the gifts and the calling of God are irrevocable." — Rom. 11:29

[114] But God has chosen the foolish things of the world to put to shame the wise, and God has chosen the weak things of the world to put to shame the things which are mighty..." — 1 Cor. 1:27

CHAPTER EIGHT

POWER TO HEAL

God anointed Jesus of Nazareth with two things, 1) the Holy Spirit, and 2) power:

> *God anointed Jesus of Nazareth with the Holy Spirit and with power, who went about doing good and healing all who were oppressed by the devil, for God was with Him.* — Acts 10:38

We already covered #1. The anointing is the manifest presence of God's Holy Spirit. So now let's cover #2. Jesus "went about doing good and healing all who were oppressed by the devil." But He could only do that because He moved in power. So if we want to move like Jesus, we have to know how to carry and utilize the power He carried!

Jesus Moved In Power

In Mark 5, Jesus encountered the woman with a "flow of blood":

> *Now a certain woman had a flow of blood for twelve years, and had suffered many things from many physicians. She had spent all that she had and was no better, but rather grew worse. When she heard about Jesus, she came behind Him in the crowd and touched His garment. For she said, "If only I may touch His clothes, I shall be made well."* —Mark 5:25-28

We've already talked about this woman's faith.[115] There were many people touching Jesus (Mark 5:24 says a multitude "thronged Him"), but there was something different about this woman's touch because of her faith. If we want to be healed, and if we want to see healing, we have to go to God with faith!

But what I want to highlight now is the *physical exchange* between this woman and Jesus. When this woman touched Jesus, she "felt" something:

> *Immediately the fountain of her blood was dried up, and she felt in*
> *her body that she was healed of the affliction.* —Mark 5:29

When you are drawing on the power of God, you will know it. You will *feel it.* As a general principle, we should not be led by our feelings. We should be led by the Holy Spirit,[116] and He is not a feeling, He is God! You can trust the Holy Spirit, and you can't always trust your feelings.

But in this instance, we *have to acknowledge* that as this woman was healed, she "felt" something. In verse 29, "felt" is the Greek *ginosko,*[117] which means to gain intimate knowledge through perception or touch.

When this woman touched Jesus, she immediately knew she was healed. This was not an intellectual knowing supported by a theological proof, but an intimate understanding that an exchange had just taken place that would forever change her life. She knew she was healed because she "felt" it.

But she wasn't the only one who felt it!

---

[115] See Chapter 6, "Faith to Heal."

[116] "For as many as are led by the Spirit of God, these are sons of God." — Rom. 8:14

[117] "G1097 - ginōskō - Strong's Greek Lexicon (KJV)." Blue Letter Bible. Accessed 11 Aug, 2020. https://www.blueletterbible.org//lang/lexicon/lexicon.cfm?Strongs=G1097&t=KJV

And Jesus, immediately knowing in Himself that power had gone out of Him, turned around in the crowd and said, "Who touched My clothes?" —Mark 5:30

"Knowing" is the Greek *epiginosko*[118], which has the same root as the woman who "felt" (or *ginosko)* that she was healed. Jesus recognized, through sensory perception, that something had happened. He immediately knew that something had gone out of Him. She felt it, and He felt it! She knew it, and He knew it! Something powerful had just taken place. So what was it?

There was a *transfer of power.* When this woman drew on the anointing of Jesus with her faith, *power* went out of Jesus. Power is the Greek *dunamis*,[119] which means the strength, power, or ability residing in something or someone "by virtue of its nature." The King James Version reads,

And Jesus, immediately knowing in himself that virtue had gone out of him, turned him about in the press, and said, Who touched my clothes? —Mark 5:30 KJV

What flowed out of Jesus was the strength, power, and ability to heal residing in Him by virtue of His nature. The power that flowed out of Jesus was the *substance* of Jesus! As this woman approached Him in faith, the virtue of Jesus flowed out of Him, and into her body. Sickness had no choice but to flee. The woman was instantly healed.[120]

---

[118] "G1921 - epiginōskō - Strong's Greek Lexicon (KJV)." Blue Letter Bible. Accessed 11 Aug, 2020. https://www.blueletterbible.org//lang/lexicon/lexicon.cfm?Strongs=G1921&t=KJV

[119] "G1411 - dynamis - Strong's Greek Lexicon (KJV)." Blue Letter Bible. Accessed 11 Aug, 2020. https://www.blueletterbible.org//lang/lexicon/lexicon.cfm?Strongs=G1411&t=KJV

[120] "And He said to her, 'Daughter, your faith has made you well. Go in peace,

What I want to highlight is that the *power* residing in Jesus was a function of the "virtue of His nature," or His identity. In other words, this power was not a function of what He had done, but of *who He is*. Jesus had, and has, *power* because He is the Son of God! So if you want to 1) be filled with and 2) move in that same power, you have to know that it does not depend on your resume and what you've done—it depends on *who you are!*

So, who are you?

1) You are a child of God:

> *Behold what manner of love the Father has bestowed on us, that we should be called children of God!* —1 John 3:1

2) You are a new creation:

> *Therefore, if anyone is in Christ, he is a new creation; old things have passed away; behold, all things have become new.* —2 Corinthians 5:17

3) You are the righteousness of Christ!

> *For He made Him who knew no sin to be sin for us, that we might become the righteousness of God in Him.* —2 Corinthians 5:21

When you received Jesus as Lord, His Holy Spirit transformed you. You are no longer the old you—you are a new, resurrected you. Now the Holy Spirit lives inside of you, and He is "quickening you" every single day:

---

and be healed of your affliction.'" —Mk. 5:34

> *But if the Spirit of him that raised up Jesus from the dead dwell in you,*
> *he that raised up Christ from the dead shall also quicken your mortal*
> *bodies by his Spirit that dwelleth in you.* —*Romans 8:11 KJV*

To "quicken" is the Greek *zoopoieo*,[121] which means to be "endued with new and greater powers of life." Do you see it? Because you have Jesus, nothing about you is the same. Your very substance has changed. Your DNA now reflects the DNA of Jesus Himself! And that means there are "greater powers of life" active in you that were not active before.

You see, God has made you something new—a new breed that the world has never seen before! You are a "new man which was created according to God, in true righteousness and holiness" (Eph. 4:24). And now that you are new, the very substance and nature of the new you can come out of you *every time* you pray for others.

When you go to Jesus for healing, you should *feel* a difference in your body and your life. And from this moment forward when someone comes to you for prayer, there is *power* that should come out of you! They should *feel* transformation taking place as you speak the Word of God over them.

You should move in *Holy Spirit power* every day of your life. The very substance and nature of Jesus Christ should flow through you! You are a resurrected vessel, and the power of Jesus should come out of you as you lay hands on others!

Why This Matters

If you want to move in power, you have to know that you have power. Wielding the power of God starts with the recognition that God has given you something you can use to impact others with heaven's agenda. If

---

[121] "G2227 - zōopoieō - Strong's Greek Lexicon (KJV)." Blue Letter Bible. Accessed 11 Aug, 2020. https://www.blueletterbible.org//lang/lexicon/lexicon.cfm?Strongs=G2227&t=KJV

you don't believe it in private, you won't see it in public! Powerful prayer starts with the revelation that God has filled you with the same power Jesus carried, because you have been made in His image.

In the summer of 2019, I was offered a sabbatical for the first time in my ministry career. After six years of full-time ministry, eight years of marriage, and the births of our three wonderful children, my wife and I were tired. So we took two months off to recharge our batteries and seek the Lord for strength.

One morning in prayer during our time off, God convicted me.[122] He asked me this question:

Do you want to be known for wisdom or for power?

I didn't know it, but I had a pride problem that was interfering with my ministry. I prized my intellect. I went to an Ivy League school, and I often patted myself on the back for being well-educated and articulate. I love Scripture, and that is a healthy thing! But I could rarely listen to someone else speak without critically evaluating their knowledge of God's Word. It was messy. It was ugly! And I needed to change.

So I started laying down my pride in prayer. I started laying down my need for people to think I was *smart*. Wisdom is a good thing! But for me, it had become an idol. So I started asking God to move through me with *power*. Wisdom will change someone's mind, but only the power of God can change someone's heart! From that point forward, I decided my ministry would no longer be measured by what people thought when I spoke, but instead by what they felt when I prayed! And nothing has been the same since.

---

[122] Conviction is healthy and holy! This was not condemnation from God that paralyzed me—it was Holy Spirit conviction that revitalized me!

126

That fall, I preached on the power of God one of the first Sundays I was back in service. I invited anyone who needed a miracle to come forward. One of our worship team members limped forward, wincing in pain. She told me she had fallen and hit her left knee on concrete over the summer. Several weeks after the initial injury, she fell *again* and hit her knee in exactly the same spot. Every time she took a step, pain shot up and down the left side of her body. She told me she could actually feel small crunchy pieces of bone, like broken glass, whenever she touched her knee. She and I prayed. We expected God to move! I'll let her finish the story in her own words:

> [CityLight] started a series on healing and last Sunday left time for an altar call, following an incredible message about faith and healing.
>
> I went up for prayer. Even though I was believing for healing, I was still in shock when Pastor Mike ended the prayer to ask me how my knee felt and realized the pain was fully gone. I no longer feel the crunchy bits and I can touch my knee without any pain at all. God is so good. Thank you, Lord!
>
> —PG, 10/6/2019

When you pray to move in *power*, God is faithful to answer your prayers! I had spent much of my summer repenting for pursuing the wrong things in prayer, and God met me with His power in response.

I've had members and attenders at our church approach me after service and tell me that we shouldn't focus so much on miracles. The focus should be Jesus, not miracles! I couldn't agree more. But if you don't have *miracles, it's not Jesus.* If you don't show people the *power* of the gospel, they won't want to hear the message of the gospel! When we work with the Holy Spirit instead of resisting Him and ask Him to show us miracles when we pray, people who have never even considered believing in Jesus will be forced to reconcile what they just saw with what they believe.[123]

The shift in focus I experienced is just a microcosm of what the church in the United States needs to experience in our services. We see so much content in our services, but so little power! The church needs to regain the *power* of God. We spend so much time planning clever messages (with props and whole stage setup teams!), but so little time being powerfully impacted in the presence of God. We spend time doing marketing and promotion and advertising (which is not, in and of itself, a bad thing!) to try and get people to come to church. Yet Scripture says that if we would simply put the *power of God* on display, we would have no problem filling our sanctuaries on Sunday:

> *At evening, when the sun had set, they brought to Him all who were sick and those who were demon-possessed. And the whole city was gathered together at the door. Then He healed many who were sick with various diseases, and cast out many demons; and He did not allow the demons to speak, because they knew Him.*
>
> *—Mark 1:32-34*

If you and I would pursue the power of God so we had something to offer other people when we pray, the "whole city" would be gathered together at the door of the church. We would have extended revival *overnight* if we simply started to move the way Jesus calls us to move. Every Christian should be moving in power everywhere we go! Why? Because the Spirit of Jesus lives in us, and wherever He goes, His "power" is present for miracles to take place.

---

[123] Read more on this in Chapter 14, "Why God Heals."

Luke 5 tells a powerful story of a paralyzed man being brought to Jesus on a mat by his friends. The man was miraculously healed. He rose up before them "took up what he had been lying on, and departed to his own house, glorifying God" (Lk. 5:25).

But before the healing happened, the atmosphere had to change:

> *Now it happened on a certain day, as He was teaching, that there were Pharisees and teachers of the law sitting by, who had come out of every town of Galilee, Judea, and Jerusalem. And the power of the Lord was present to heal them.* —*Luke 5:17*

Jesus was in a room full of *skeptics!* The Pharisees and teachers of the Law did not believe He was the Son of God. In other words, this was not a room full of faithful disciples who readily believed that Jesus was able to heal and came ready to draw the anointing out of Jesus like our friend in Mark 5!

But *the attitude of the audience didn't matter.* "The power of the Lord was present to heal." Because Jesus was in the building, the atmosphere completely changed! There was nothing inherently special or unique about the physical construction of the house where Jesus was teaching. But the atmosphere *changed* because Jesus was there. There was *power* in Jesus that was ready to come out!

And everywhere you go, the atmosphere should change too! Why? Because "Christ is in you."[124]

How to Move in Power

If you want to move in power, you have to know you have power. Hopefully I've already convinced you of that. But the *most critical thing* you can do to move in *power* when you pray for other people is incredibly simple.

---

[124] "And if Christ is in you, the body is dead because of sin, but the Spirit is life because of righteousness." —Rom. 8:10

You can't *buy* the power of Jesus.[125] You certainly can't *fake* the power of Jesus! The only way you can move in the power of Jesus is by *spending time with Jesus.*

Intimacy with Jesus is everything. With great power comes great responsibility! Power can easily become an idol. We must never seek Jesus to *get something* that we want for ourselves from Him. We must only seek Jesus for the sake of being with Him!

Jesus is not the means to an end—He is "the Beginning and the End" (Rev. 22:13)! God will not give you more power than your character can support. God won't give you His power unless you have a relationship with Jesus, because absent from relationship, the power of God will destroy you.

You need to seek Jesus if you want to *move* in power. But once you start moving in power, beware. You will never need Jesus *less* than you did before you started experiencing the power of God—you will always only need Him *more.*

They Had Been With Jesus

The disciples spent every day with Jesus. They saw Him perform miracle after miracle. They witnessed the supernatural power of God firsthand! But after Jesus was raised from the dead, it was time for them to step out with boldness and do what they had seen Jesus do.

In Acts 3, we see Peter and John do exactly that:

---

[125] We see a man named Simon try to buy the power of God in Acts 8: "And when Simon saw that through the laying on of the apostles' hands the Holy Spirit was given, he offered them money, saying, 'Give me this power also, that anyone on whom I lay hands may receive the Holy Spirit.' But Peter said to him, 'Your money perish with you, because you thought that the gift of God could be purchased with money!'" —Acts 8:18-20

Now Peter and John went up together to the temple at the hour of prayer, the ninth hour. And a certain man lame from his mother's womb was carried, whom they laid daily at the gate of the temple which is called Beautiful, to ask alms from those who entered the temple; who, seeing Peter and John about to go into the temple, asked for alms. And fixing his eyes on him, with John, Peter said, "Look at us." So he gave them his attention, expecting to receive something from them. —Acts 3:1-5

Here was a man begging at the entrance to the temple. Peter and John showed up for an afternoon prayer meeting, and the man asked them for money. But Peter and John were ready to give him something *so much better:*

Then Peter said, "Silver and gold I do not have, but what I do have I give you: In the name of Jesus Christ of Nazareth, rise up and walk." —Acts 3:6

Peter and John didn't have any pocket change, but they had the *power of God!* They were filled with the same miracle-working power as Jesus Christ Himself. The same Spirit who raised Jesus from the dead lived in them! And it showed:

And [Peter] took him by the right hand and lifted him up, and immediately his feet and ankle bones received strength. So he, leaping up, stood and walked and entered the temple with them—walking, leaping, and praising God. And all the people saw him walking and praising God. Then they knew that it was he who sat begging alms at the Beautiful Gate of the temple; and they were filled with wonder and amazement at what had happened to him. —Acts 3:7-10

Don't you see that if we do our job properly, we won't even have to invite people to church? This man didn't need to wait for an invitation from Peter and John to come into the temple! Once he experienced the power of God, he was going, whether Peter and John were going with him or not.

This man went from beggar to evangelist because of one encounter with the power of God. He started "walking, leaping, and praising God" (v 8), so much so that the entire synagogue took notice! Everyone around this man was "filled with wonder and amazement at what had happened to him" (v 10).

The best way to tell people about Jesus is to *show them* what He is capable of by putting His power on display! If we walk in the *power* of Jesus, people—not only in our churches, but *around us every day*—will take note and want to know how those miracles are possible! And we will get to tell them: *Jesus heals.*

So *how* did Peter and John get filled with so much power?

> *And it came to pass, on the next day, that their rulers, elders, and scribes, as well as Annas the high priest, Caiaphas, John, and Alexander, and as many as were of the family of the high priest, were gathered together at Jerusalem. And when they had set them in the midst, they asked, "By what power or by what name have you done this?"* —Acts 4:5-7

Notice that even the skeptics—the religious leaders—could not deny that a miracle had taken place. They didn't want to believe it! But they had no choice. So Peter told them how the healing happened:

> *Then Peter, filled with the Holy Spirit, said to them, "Rulers of the people and elders of Israel: If we this day are judged for a good deed done to a helpless man, by what means he has been made well, let it be known to you all, and to all the people of Israel, that by the name of Jesus Christ of Nazareth, whom you crucified, whom God raised*

from the dead, by Him this man stands here before you whole. This is the 'stone which was rejected by you builders, which has become the chief cornerstone.' Nor is there salvation in any other, for there is no other name under heaven given among men by which we must be saved." — Acts 4:8-12

Peter *refused* to take any of the credit for the miracle himself. It wasn't Peter's ministry that had healed this man! It was the ministry of Jesus. Peter didn't do anything! But Jesus did something *mighty* through Peter. So Peter pointed his listeners straight to Jesus and urged them to be saved. And as Peter spoke, they listened, because he showed them Jesus' *power* before he tried to preach them a message.

Now when they saw the boldness of Peter and John, and perceived that they were uneducated and untrained men, they marveled. And they realized that they had been with Jesus. And seeing the man who had been healed standing with them, they could say nothing against it. — Acts 4:13-14

What was so striking about this miracle to the religious leaders is that Peter and John were "uneducated and untrained men." The scribes and the Pharisees weren't seeing any miracles as they prayed! Yet here came Peter and John, healing definitively because they had spent several years with Jesus. The word "uneducated" in the original translation is the Greek word *idiotes*,[126] which is where we get the English word "idiots!" In other words, Peter and John weren't winning anyone to Jesus with an intellectual argument.

---

[126] "G2399 - idiōtēs - Strong's Greek Lexicon (KJV)." Blue Letter Bible. Accessed 11 Aug, 2020. https://www.blueletterbible.org//lang/lexicon/lexicon.cfm?Strongs=G2399&t=KJV

But they had something better than a theological proof. They had the *power of God*. There was no denying they had been with Jesus! How do you want people to remember you? Do you want to be remembered for your head knowledge? Or do you want to be remembered as someone who saw miracles when you prayed?

Do you want to move in power? Do what Peter and John did! Be with Jesus. Drop everything and follow Him! Sit at His feet. Spend hours in His presence every day—as much time as you can afford! When you have His presence, you have *everything* you could ever need.

But I've Never Been With Jesus . . .

You may read Acts 3 and 4 and think, "Well that's great for Peter and John because they were with Jesus every day! But I've never been with Jesus." If that's you, I have a story for you.

Do you remember Thomas?

> *Now Thomas, called the Twin, one of the twelve, was not with them when Jesus came. The other disciples therefore said to him, "We have seen the Lord." So he said to them, "Unless I see in His hands the print of the nails, and put my finger into the print of the nails, and put my hand into His side, I will not believe."* —John 20:24-25

After He was resurrected, Jesus showed Himself to the disciples. But Thomas wasn't there. So Thomas drew a hard line. His stance was, "I'm not going to believe that what Jesus promised is possible until I see Him for myself."

But days later, Jesus came to Thomas. He gave Thomas what Thomas thought he needed to believe. He met Thomas right where he was, in the midst of his doubt and unbelief:

And after eight days His disciples were again inside, and Thomas with them. Jesus came, the doors being shut, and stood in the midst, and said, "Peace to you!" Then He said to Thomas, "Reach your finger here, and look at My hands; and reach your hand here, and put it into My side. Do not be unbelieving, but believing."

—John 20:26-27

But then Jesus gave future generations of believers a strong message:

And Thomas answered and said to Him, "My Lord and my God!" Jesus said to him, "Thomas, because you have seen Me, you have believed. Blessed are those who have not seen and yet have believed."

—John 20:28-29

Peter, John, Thomas, and the other disciples who were alive to witness the cross believed Jesus because they saw Him with their eyes. But, "Blessed are those who have not seen and yet have believed" (v 29). Think about that. Jesus promised successive generations that the level of blessing on their lives would *increase*—not decrease—because they had not physically been with Jesus, yet still made a decision to believe in Him by faith! We should be *more blessed* because we "have not seen" Jesus with our own eyes, not less! Walking in the miraculous is one of the marks of God's blessing. If Peter and John moved in power because they saw Jesus with their eyes, how much more should we move in power because we trust Him by faith?

Don't get stuck wishing you had been alive when Jesus walked the earth. You are alive *now*. This is the moment in history into which God chose to insert you to *change the world*. He didn't do it by accident! All you need is faith. Even if you haven't seen a *single miracle*, blessed are those who "have not seen and yet have believed."

Want to hear a funny story? When my wife and I started the Healing Rooms at our church, we had *never seen a miracle.* Not one healing! No blind eyes opened. No curved spines straightened. No terminal illnesses healed! But we had faith. And since the day the Healing Rooms opened, God has shown us *miracle after miracle* in response to our faith.

Most recently, we had a mother, Jackie, come to the Healing Rooms with her six-month-old daughter, Rose. Rose was having *over one hundred seizures per day.* This had been happening since birth. Think about the agony and torture Jackie must have been going through as a mother! It was tough to watch. Even as we prayed for Rose in the Healing Rooms, she experienced seizures. Jackie would sigh, take Rose up into her arms, and wait until the seizures stopped. It was hopeless and bleak.

But a little faith goes a long way. When Jackie visited us for the first time, we sat with her and Rose, prayed together, and laid hands on Rose. We spoke the Word of God over her, and believed that she would be completely healed. Jackie had never seen a miracle either, but she told us that for some reason she couldn't fully explain, she *just expected* Rose to be healed.

We first prayed for Jackie and Rose in July. Then we saw them again in August. Nothing had changed. Jackie had taken Rose to the hospital to start seizure medication, but there was no improvement. Doctors were cautioning Jackie to temper her faith with what they called "realistic expectation," but Jackie still believed Rose would be miraculously healed.

We stayed in touch with Jackie throughout the rest of August and September. Our promise to her was that we would continue to pray and believe that Rose would be healed until it happened. In late October, my wife got a text message from Jackie: "Rose starts steroids at home today and then we will go to the hospital next Monday for 2-4 days. Please pray that the steroids go directly to the right place and stop spasms and seizures and that there are zero side effects." We believed and agreed according to Jackie's faith.

On November 2nd, we had a water baptism service at our church. As I was standing in the baptismal tub, I looked out at the line of several dozen people waiting to get baptized. Can you guess who was standing at the end of the line? Jackie! I also saw Jackie's husband and older daughter. And there, in her husband's arms, was little baby Rose, peacefully sleeping, with no signs of seizures whatsoever.

When it was Jackie's turn to be baptized, she bounded into the water. We baptized her, and as she came up out of the water, she turned to me. "Thank you," she said, giving me a big hug. "For what?" I asked. She leaned forward and whispered into my ear. "Rose went from over one hundred seizures per day . . . to *zero.*"

Jackie smiled from ear to ear, gave me another hug, and ran up the stairs and out of the baptismal pool. I started weeping, absolutely amazed at God's faithfulness.

It's not that I hadn't seen Him heal before. What moved me was Jackie's faith. She refused to believe anything but the Word of God, even when everyone around her told her to temper her expectations, and God responded to her faith. As a result, her whole family came to church to see her make a public profession of her faith in Jesus Christ. I knew her husband and children wouldn't be far behind.

One year later, I reached out to Jackie and asked her for an update. I also asked her to share the full story of Rose's healing in her own words. Here is her reply:

Hi Pastor Mike,

Thank you so much for reaching out. Today we celebrate. It has been one year since Rose has been seizure free! I haven't shared this story with many. I didn't want anyone to try to take it away from me, but it's our story and I hope it helps others!

Last year, Rose was diagnosed with a severe and fatal seizure disorder that is very resistant to being cured. She tried so many hardcore meds and none of them were working. The meds were so hard on her body, I had to take her to the pediatrician daily to check her vitals. She was having over 100 seizures per day and it was the scariest thing I have ever witnessed. When front line meds didn't work, I tried acupuncture, Chiro, CBD oil, and energy medicine, all to no avail.

We were scheduled to go back to the hospital on October 28th for a 2-week period of trying even more hardcore drugs, until something worked. That meant I would have to be away from [my older daughter] for 2 weeks. That Friday, October 25th, I walked into a Catholic church in Red Hook, Brooklyn. I told God that I wasn't leaving until the love of God released the fear that was SEIZING us. I confessed that doctors were stumped with Rose, but that God was limitless. I stayed all day Friday, Saturday and Sunday, and had some pretty profound experiences (another story). Rose was still having seizures, but I kept the faith.

We went in to [Weill Cornell Medical Center] on that following Monday. My husband packed for multiple days. I packed for one night. I knew the seizures would leave and our family would be together again. That night, with all the wires connected to Rose, I did not sleep. I wrapped her in a shawl that my friend gifted us from Israel and read healing Scriptures over her all night long.

The next day, a whole team of neurologists came to visit my room and told me that to their utter surprise, Rose went from having over 100 seizures a day, to zero. We were free to go home! I sobbed and sobbed and we were able to be united as a family again. We were finally free from this devastation. I still have PTSD from that dark period and we still have a long way to go, but I know we are blessed beyond belief. It's been one year and Rose hasn't had any seizures since. Thank you for being a positive part of this journey with us! Love you all xo

The miracle-working power you want to see in your life is waiting on the other side of your decision to believe with all of your heart that Jesus wants you to walk in His power. Receive the revelation that you have the power of Jesus in you! And never look back, in Jesus' name.

CHAPTER NINE

THE WORD TO HEAL

A ll throughout Scripture, God puts the same pattern on display: Where God's Word goes, healing follows. We see Jesus illustrate this pattern for us:

And the apostles, when they had returned, told Him all that they had done. Then He took them and went aside privately into a deserted place belonging to the city called Bethsaida. But when the multitudes knew it, they followed Him; and He received them and spoke to them about the kingdom of God, and healed those who had need of healing.
—Luke 9:10-11

The multitudes came to Jesus because they needed healing. He didn't have to invite them—they just came! And as they arrived, He "spoke to them." He gave them the Word! And when the Word was delivered, healing followed. Jesus "healed all those who had need of healing." Everyone present was healed of any disease that ailed them!

Then we see Jesus ask His disciples to follow in His footsteps:

These twelve Jesus sent out and commanded them, saying: "Do not go into the way of the Gentiles, and do not enter a city of the Samaritans. But go rather to the lost sheep of the house of Israel. And as you go, preach, saying, 'The kingdom of heaven is at hand.' Heal the sick, cleanse the lepers, raise the dead, cast out demons. Freely you have received, freely give."
—Matthew 10:5-8

Jesus reminded His disciples that they had something to offer. He also reminded them not to forget the pattern He had shown them. They were to "preach" (proclaim the Word) first, and healing would follow![127]

But the disciples weren't the only ones who took hold of this biblical principle. We even see Gentiles recognize the effectiveness of this Word/healing pattern:

Now when Jesus had entered Capernaum, a centurion came to Him, pleading with Him, saying, "Lord, my servant is lying at home paralyzed, dreadfully tormented." And Jesus said to him, "I will come and heal him."

The centurion answered and said, "Lord, I am not worthy that You should come under my roof. But only speak a word, and my servant will be healed." —Matthew 8:5-8

This centurion was a Gentile. He didn't know God through history and experience the way the Jewish people did! But he understood that wherever the Word was spoken, healing followed:

For I also am a man under authority, having soldiers under me. And I say to this one, 'Go,' and he goes; and to another, 'Come,' and he comes; and to my servant, 'Do this,' and he does it." —Matthew 8:9

---

[127] See also Mark 16:19-20: "So then, after the Lord had spoken to them, He was received up into heaven, and sat down at the right hand of God. And they went out and preached everywhere, the Lord working with them and confirming the word through the accompanying signs. Amen."

And as a result, "[H]is servant was healed that same hour" (Matt. 8:13). Are you ready to take hold of this principle in your own life, just like this Gentile centurion did?

The Word Brings Healing

Your faith is important. It is good and right to receive prayer from someone who walks in power! But the *most powerful* ingredient in your healing process—no matter what it looks like—is the Word of God.

Psalm 107 describes a period in Israel's history when God's people were far from Him. They were living *outside* of covenant with God, and didn't know if they had access to His healing power:

> *Fools, because of their transgression, and because of their iniquities, were afflicted. Their soul abhorred all manner of food, and they drew near to the gates of death.* —Psalm 107:17-18

But they decided to give prayer a try. They cried out to God, and He answered. And do you know what He sent as the remedy to everything that ailed them?

> *Then they cried out to the Lord in their trouble, and He saved them out of their distresses. He sent His word and healed them, and delivered them from their destructions.* —Psalm 107:19-20

God sent His word! And His word brought exactly what He designed it to bring: healing, salvation and deliverance.

If you want to see healing in your own body, you need to be *filled up* with the Word of God. If you want to see healing happen when you pray for other people, you need to be *saturated* with the Word of God! If you aren't full of the Word, you won't have any Word come out of you when you pray! But if you are *steeped*[128] in the Word of God, no matter how bad the diagnosis or unpromising the prognosis, the Word of God will come flowing out of you like water, and healing will follow as a result.

But this is bigger than healing. Healing is part of the atonement. But it isn't the only part! And whether you need healing in your body, restoration in your relationships, or breakthrough in your finances, the remedy is always the same: You *need* the Word of God!

Apply this simple truth to your life:

You don't have a _____ problem.
You have a Word problem.

What is your blank? What mountain are you up against that just won't move? What problem are you facing that just won't go away? The answer is *always* the Word of God!

You don't have a sickness problem—you have a Word problem. You don't have a relationship problem—you have a Word problem! You don't have a destiny problem—you have a Word problem. *No matter what* you are up against, the prescription to what ails you is the Word of God.

My Story

My wife and I started the Healing Rooms at our church in 2012. I've already mentioned that we launched them completely by faith, because up until that point in our lives neither of us had seen God heal anybody! But we launched them anyway out of obedience.

---

[128] When tea is "steeped," tea leaves are left in hot water until the water takes on the flavor of the tea. In the same way, when we ingest or "eat" (Jer. 15:16) the Word of God and allow it to be immersed in our hearts, over time we take on the flavor of Jesus, who is His Word (Jn. 1:1)!

Do you know what I did before we *even considered* opening our doors? I got myself *full*—completely saturated—with the Word of God! I had purchased a compilation of all of John G. Lake's[129] teachings on healing the year prior, and his messages had completely changed the way I thought about healing. He had a level of faith for healing that I could only dream of, and he had seen dozens and dozens of people healed. I wanted to know the Scripture he knew, because I knew that was what had given him faith to believe for healing, and I wanted the same level of faith!

So, I pored through that book of sermons on healing and wrote down *every single Scripture* John G. Lake ever used in any one of his messages. And then I wrote them down—all one hundred and sixty-seven of them—on index cards. And I started to study. I memorized all of those Scriptures. I made sure they were part of me. Because when I started praying for the sick, I didn't want anything but the pure, uncorrupted and unadulterated Word of God coming out of my mouth in prayer!

You see, something changes when you have the Word of God. God's Word is true, and His promises are sure. He holds His Word above His name![130] When you speak the Word of God, you are no longer speaking under your own authority. You are speaking with the authority of Jesus Christ, the Word made flesh.

It took a lot of time to internalize those verses. I was working in finance at the time, and I actually built a Microsoft Excel spreadsheet with all the verses so I could memorize them during downtime at work. My

---

[129] Roberts Liardon, *John G. Lake on Healing* (New Kensington, PA: Whitaker House, 2009).

[130] "I will worship toward Your holy temple, and praise Your name for Your lovingkindness and Your truth; for You have magnified Your word above all Your name." —Ps. 138:2

boss (hopefully he doesn't read this!) thought I was crunching numbers, but I was actually getting full of the Word of God!

Why the Word?

If you want to 1) *know* what God has called you to do and 2) *do* what God has called you to do, you have to read His Word. The psalmist explained the importance of God's Word this way:

> *Blessed is the man who walks not in the counsel of the ungodly, nor stands in the path of sinners, nor sits in the seat of the scornful; but his delight is in the law of the Lord, and in His law he meditates day and night. He shall be like a tree planted by the rivers of water, that brings forth its fruit in its season, whose leaf also shall not wither; and whatever he does shall prosper.*
>
> *The ungodly are not so, but are like the chaff which the wind drives away. Therefore the ungodly shall not stand in the judgment, nor sinners in the congregation of the righteous. For the Lord knows the way of the righteous, but the way of the ungodly shall perish.* —Psalm 1:1-6

Do you know who the "ungodly" are (v 4)? People who take advice from other people who don't rely on God's Word! When disaster strikes, where do you turn? Do you hit up YouTube for a self-help message? Do you call your mom for some parental advice? Or do you turn to the Word of God to answer all your questions and concerns?

When you "delight in" the Word of God, you will be blessed! You will be "like a tree" planted by water. You will be fruitful— not just someone who talks about doing stuff for Jesus, but someone who actually bears fruit! Even if drought is all around you, you will never wither. *Everything you do* will proper.

I want to highlight two important self-reflection questions that should have been generated as you read through verse 2:

1) Do you "delight" in God's Word?

If you take an honest self-inventory, do you really delight in what God has to say? Is God's Word the first thing your eyes settle on in the morning? Is His law the last thing your eyes see before you go to bed?

Here's a good litmus test. When I say "Bible," what is the first emotion that comes to mind? Do you think of a life-giving text that is a manifestation of God Himself? Or do you think of *homework?* Do you think of Scripture reading as an activity that you only do because you feel like you have to? Or is it the one thing in life that refreshes you the most?

Reading God's Word should be like drinking a tall glass of ice water on a hot summer day. When you feel tired, you need His Word. When you feel exhausted, you need His Word. When you just need a break, you need His Word!

So if you don't "delight" in God's Word, the remedy is not to pretend you do! The solution is to *ask the Holy Spirit for help.* You may not live for the Word, but the Holy Spirit certainly does! And the same Holy Spirit who inspired men to write God's Word lives in you. So *ask Him* to fill you with delight for His Word!

Do you know another great thing to do if you don't "delight" in the Word? Get it in front of you anyway. You have to start somewhere! There's no better day than today, and no better time than now. In the field of psychology there is a principle called the mere-exposure effect.[131]

---

[131] Zajonc, R.B. "Mere Exposure: A Gateway to the Subliminal," *Current Directions in Psychological Science* 10, no. 6, (2001): 224–228. doi: 10.1111/1467-8721.00154.

The more you are exposed to something, the more your affinity for that thing grows. The more often you see something, the more you like it! This is why the more you see a friend, the more you like him or her. And that means that the first step to *loving* the Word of God is *looking at* the Word of God!

Under the old covenant, God told His people to keep His words "as frontlets between [their] eyes" (Deut. 6:8). That means always right in front of them. But in the modern church, we hardly read His Word at all![132] Do you want to fall in love with your Bible? Make sure you open it every day!

2) What does it mean to "meditate" in God's Word?

Psalm 1:2 tells us that whoever "meditates day and night" in God's Word will be blessed and fruitful. But what does it mean to meditate in God's Word?

"Meditate" is the Hebrew *hagah*,[133] which means to moan, growl, utter, or mutter. In other words, meditating is so much more than just *thinking about* God's Word. If you want to activate the blessing that comes with meditating in His Word, you have to know that "meditating" means speaking God's Word over yourself *out loud* until your life lines up with His Word!

I cannot understate the importance of speaking God's Word *out loud*. I'm all for quiet, contemplative prayer. I'm all for thinking about God! In fact, Scripture even says that our thought life is important![134]

But mountains move when you start to *pray out loud:*

---

[132] A 2019 Lifeway Research study found that only 32% of regular church attenders read the Bible every day. Retrieved from: https://lifewayresearch. com/2019/07/02/few-protestant-churchgoers-read-the-bible-daily/

[133] "H1897 - hagah - Strong's Hebrew Lexicon (KJV)." Blue Letter Bible. Accessed 11 Aug, 2020. https://www.blueletterbible.org//lang/lexicon/ lexicon.cfm?Strongs=H1897&t=KJV

[134] "For as he thinks in his heart, so is he." —Prov. 23:7

"For assuredly, I say to you, whoever says to this mountain, 'Be removed and be cast into the sea,' and does not doubt in his heart, but believes that those things he says will be done, he will have whatever he says."

—*Mark 11:23*

Jesus told His disciples that they would have to *speak to* certain obstacles. You can't defeat the enemy with thoughts! You need words.[135] If you have mountains in your life that *just won't move,* start speaking the Word of God over your life!

Notice in Mark 11 that Jesus didn't just tell His disciples to say whatever they wanted to the mountain. He gave them something specific to say. He gave them His Word, and asked them to repeat it over the mountain! And this is where we often get into trouble.

When you meet a mountain, don't just respond off the cuff. Don't just "follow your heart,"[136] and say whatever you feel! Say what God told you to say. Repeat His Word *out loud* over your life, and watch your situation conform to everything that was spoken!

The Creative Power Formula

There is power in declaring the Word of God over your body. Did you know that every time God creates something in Scripture, the same conditions are met? I call this the Creative Power Formula:

Holy Spirit + God's Word = Creation

Take a look at Genesis 1, which tells the Creation story:

---

[135] See Matthew 4. When Jesus is led by the Holy Spirit into the wilderness to be tempted by the devil, He responds to every single temptation 1) with the Word of God 2) out loud. Our response to darkness should never deviate from Jesus' response.

[136] "The heart is deceitful above all things, and desperately wicked; Who can know it?" —Jer. 17:9

In the beginning God created the heavens and the earth. The earth
was without form, and void; and darkness was on the face of the deep.
And the Spirit of God was hovering over the face of the waters. Then
God said, "Let there be light"; and there was light. And God saw the
light, that it was good . . .   —*Genesis 1:1-4a*

As the Christian narrative begins, we see absolute nothingness. The earth
was "without form, and void" (v. 2). There was darkness everywhere!
But the Holy Spirit was "hovering over the face of the waters" (v. 2). I
wish the church would understand that when the Holy Spirit shows up,
creation happens! Everything can change in an instant simply because
the Spirit of God is present.

When the foundations of our universe were laid, both conditions of
the Creative Power Formula were met. The Holy Spirit was present to
effect change. Then, God spoke His Word into an atmosphere that was
ripe for change:

Then God said, "Let there be light"; and there was light. And God
saw the light, that it was good . . .   —*Genesis 1:3-4a*

Once God spoke, He saw! When He spoke it happened. But this was not
a one-time formula that God meant for us to see in the Book of Genesis
and never use again. When we use it in our daily lives, things are going
to start to line up with God's will!

Here is what you have to understand. If you believe in Jesus, you
are filled with His Holy Spirit. That means that wherever you go, the
first condition to the Creative Power Formula is already satisfied.
The Holy Spirit is *in you* to effect change. So all that's left for you
is to declare the Word of God wherever you go, and watch creation
take shape!

What is there in your life that is "without form" and "void?" Is your body crippled? Is your heart empty? Is there physical and emotional healing that needs to take place because part of your life is refusing to line up with God's Word? Then *proclaim the Word of God* over yourself! As you do, creation will take shape, the same way it did in Genesis 1. There will be a tangible manifestation of God-breathed change so that you can step back, observe and declare, "This is good," just as God did in Genesis 1 after He spoke the world into existence.

Declaring the Word

Our church recently took a team on a missions trip to Guatemala. We've been visiting the Mayan people in the region surrounding Nebaj, Guatemala, for over a decade now. The Maya are a beautifully diverse people with generations of tradition and diverse faith backgrounds.

The first night of our most recent trip to Nebaj, we hosted a healing service in one of the biggest churches in the area. There were almost 1,500 people in the sanctuary thanks to several weeks of radio advertisements leading up to our arrival. Our entire team was expectant and excited to see what God was going to do. Some of us had experience laying hands on other people and seeing them healed, while others did not. But we were about to learn the immense power of declaring God's Word and watching what He does with it.

We preached on healing, and then after the message, the pastor of the host church called our team forward to pray. We were overwhelmed by the response. Family after family came forward because someone under their roof needed healing. We watched in awe as God healed fractured skulls, opened blind eyes,[137] and straightened crooked bones. After about

---

[137] Read this full testimony in Chapter 15.

twenty minutes of prayer, the host pastor invited anyone who had been healed to come testify into the microphone.

After several people had shared, I heard a loud crash at the back of the sanctuary. We all swiveled around to see what was happening. A frantic woman had flung the doors into the church wide open. She was running as fast as she could to the altar, a sea of mesmerized people parting in front of her as she moved.

The woman vaulted up the stairs to the stage and asked if she could share her testimony. She had been at home cooking dinner for her family and had flipped on her kitchen radio. Our service was being broadcast to the entire town, and it was the only thing she could find as she scanned the channels. So she listened. And as we preached on healing, she was absolutely overcome by the power of God, right there in her kitchen. She had been to church, but she never knew that Jesus heals. She had heard Scripture read in church service, but she had never heard this living, breathing Word of God that was being preached!

For many months, her leg had been so sore that she could barely walk. But as she listened to God's healing Word, she felt the presence of God wash over her entire body. She crumpled to the floor in her kitchen. She started sobbing. Then she rose up and started to jump up and down as she felt a wave of electricity pass through her body. She put all her weight on her left leg. No pain. She put all her weight back on her right leg. Still no pain! So she turned off her stove and ran down to the church to testify as fast as her legs would carry her.

This woman wasn't even in the church! But the Word of God broadcast over a radio channel completely healed her, right where she was. This is what happens when you declare the Word of God over a city. This is what transpires when you release the Word of God over broken bodies that need healing! God gave us His Word to heal, and as we release His Word by faith, healing is going to happen!

Do Something With It!

God gave us His Word on purpose. He expects us to do something with it!

The Holy Spirit issued a challenge to God's people through the Old Testament prophet Isaiah. He challenged us to *do something* with the Word of God. He promised us:

> *"For as the rain comes down, and the snow from heaven, and do not return there, but water the earth, and make it bring forth and bud, that it may give seed to the sower and bread to the eater, so shall My word be that goes forth from My mouth; It shall not return to Me void, But it shall accomplish what I please, and it shall prosper in the thing for which I sent it."* —Isaiah 55:10-11

God has given us His Word! His Word has inherent growth properties. It will cause your life to flourish and grow, as rain gives life to a parched field. God's Word will cause God's purpose to take root and flourish in your life!

But if you want to see His Word work in your life, you have to make it "return" to God (v. 11). He has sent it out! But you have to bring it back to Him, and the way you do that is through prayer. You internalize His Word and pray it back to Him every day. You pick a healing verse[138] and declare it out loud over your body in prayer, and watch what happens! His Word will "accomplish what [He pleases], and it shall prosper in the thing for which [He] sent it" (v. 11).

It's time to activate God's Word over your body. You know what His Word says. You know what His Word can do! But now it's time to get His

---

[138] Please see the Appendix for a complete list of every healing verse that appears in this text.

Word in your mouth and let it come out. Bring God's Word back to Him in prayer, and it will do everything God designed it to do.

> *Death and life are in the power of the tongue, and those who love it will eat its fruit.* —*Proverbs 18:21*

CHAPTER TEN

SAY GOODBYE TO FEAR

I love testimonies. I love that when you preach on God's power to heal, God starts to show up.

Recently, a man who had been coming to our church for several months was completely healed of debilitating pain in his back. About a year prior to coming to our church, he had had a serious accident that resulted in a traumatic brain injury (TBI) and back pain, which made it difficult to walk and intensely painful to lie down. But Jesus had a different plan for him! Here is his story in his own words:

> Well, I was healed last night of this piercing back pain I've had for so long. [The pastor] was about to bring down the Spirit and we were all worshipping and he's saying in the background how [God] wants to do something special because there's people [in the sanctuary] who need healing. Sitting there, I knew I needed healing, but I was just going to stay in my seat. Some people got up but [the pastor] just asked them to stand and wait for prayer.

> Then he says, "Someone's back is on fire and now is the time while to get healed while the anointing is here." When he says this, suddenly my eyes start to pulsate from the inside, kind of like paparazzi cameras flashing but without the flashes, or like rubber bands snapping in rhythm but without hurting. So I'm like, *Okay, I guess I'm the person.* So I get up and go to the stage.

Another lady follows me. We are now both on stage and [the pastor] starts praying.

He put his hands on me and he almost knocked me down. I felt a burst of energy go through my body. This clean energy burst. Next [the pastor] told me I had to forgive if I wanted to see complete healing. He starts saying how someone put a curse on me who hates me and that I had to forgive him and forgive people who owed me money. Then he laid hands on me and I felt the burst of energy again. Then he did it a third time! He almost knocked me down! Immediately I felt my back go numb. Then I felt all the pain disappear.

Walking up to the stage my back had hurt all service prior to that moment. It had been hurting for almost a year. I couldn't believe the relief. I've been testing it and bending over is so much easier. I did my [physical therapy] exercises and it didn't hurt in my back in that area.

Obviously I have more healing to do from my brain injury but God literally healed my sharp back pain that has been a huge discomfort to my life. I woke up the next morning still feeling light. I even genuinely feel forgiveness towards people I needed to forgive. I also slept through most of the night, and waking up I feel so much peace. This is the first time I slept through the night since my accident.

Thinking about it now when that beautiful energy went through me it was like when you see a ghost walk through someone in a film. Well that Holy Spirit washed through me like the ocean against beach sand.   —DC, 12/6/2019

Isn't God amazing?! When we preach His Word, healing follows. When we step out and pray for the conditions His Word tells us He wants to heal, we see the miracles He promised!

The Missing Ingredient

God heals. But what frustrates me is that not every church believes in divine healing. Pastors in pulpits all over the country should be preaching that God is the Healer. After all, if we see Jesus heal in Scripture, and we are filled with the same Holy Spirit,[139] we should go out and heal the way He healed! Why would Jesus call us to do the works that we see Him do, along with "greater works,"[140] if He wasn't going to show up and deliver on His promise?

I believe the primary reason we don't hear divine healing preached more from the pulpit in the United States is *fear*. Pastors are afraid. They are afraid that if they preach that Jesus is the Healer, people will want to be healed. They are afraid that when people in their church come up for prayer, nothing will happen when they pray. So instead of resolving that inconsistency by praying for an increase in anointing, they shut up the message on healing altogether.

Reverend Andrew Murray was an influential pastor in the Dutch Reformed Church of South Africa in the 1800s. At one point in his ministry, Rev. Murray contracted a condition known as "Preacher's

---

[139] "But if the Spirit of Him who raised Jesus from the dead dwells in you, He who raised Christ from the dead will also give life to your mortal bodies through His Spirit who dwells in you." —Rom. 8:11

[140] "Most assuredly, I say to you, he who believes in Me, the works that I do he will do also; and greater works than these he will do, because I go to My Father." —Jn. 14:12

Throat," which made it impossible for him to speak. Obviously this was a problem for a preacher, whose livelihood and mission depended on the ability to proclaim the gospel.

Rev. Murray sought out every medical specialist in South Africa, but no one could help him. Out of desperation, he traveled to London to see the world's leading experts for the condition, but no one could help him there either. With his earthly options exhausted, he threw a "hail Mary" and went to a healing room for prayer.

The Holy Spirit met him there. John G. Lake recounts that, "In despair [Rev. Murray] visited the Bethshan Divine Healing Mission in London, conducted by Dr. Bagster. He knelt at the altar, was prayed for by the elders, and was healed."[141]

Needless to say, Rev. Murray was profoundly impacted by his immediate healing. He returned to South Africa and made it his mission to tell everyone in the Dutch Reformed Church of South Africa that God is the Healer. He wrote a book titled *Divine Healing*, which was extensively circulated throughout the entire denomination.[142] Much of the denomination heard about Rev. Murray's healing, and started to read his book.

You would think that the pastors in the Dutch Reformed Church of Africa would have been thrilled, but they were far from it. Before long, congregants started to approach their pastors for healing prayer. But instead of being *excited,* the pastors were *scared.*

The pastors didn't have faith to pray for healing. They had never seen someone healed through prayer! And instead of allowing their own insufficiency and insecurity to point them to the cross, they recoiled out of fear. Instead of praying for an increased anointing and an increase in

---

[141] Liardon, *John G. Lake on Healing,* 210.

[142] Andrew Murray, *Divine Healing* (Annotated and Updated), (Aneko Press, 2016). https://www.amazon.com/Divine-Healing-sickness-weakness-Classics-ebook/dp/B01CIWDVFS/ref=sr_1_3?keywords=andrew+murray+healing&qid=1576077441&sr=8-3

spiritual gifting,[143] they wrote Rev. Andrew Murray a formal letter and requested he take his book out of circulation. The pastors simply could not stand to have people come and ask for healing prayer because they did not know what to do with that request. After all, what would it mean for them if they prayed for healing and people stayed sick?

Sadly, denominational leadership capitulated and Rev. Murray's book was taken out of circulation. The great healing revival that had begun to sweep through the Dutch Reformed Church of South Africa came to a sudden, screeching halt.

This is a sad but incredibly pertinent example of how we typically react when we see the Holy Spirit moving in a new way through our churches. We don't have the theology to process what's happening, so instead of "searching the Scriptures,"[144] we recoil. We assume that because we haven't seen God move like that before, it must not be Him! It's ignorant and short-sighted. It puts God in a box! And it has to stop if we want to fulfill the mission of Jesus.

The Miracle Gap

Whenever you see a gap between what happens when you pray and what *Scripture says* should happen when you pray, that gap should inspire healthy reflection. I call this the Miracle Gap. Jesus saw healing *every time* He laid hands on someone! For you and me, that might not be our experience. But what are you going to do with the Miracle Gap?

---

[143] "But the manifestation of the Spirit is given to each one for the profit of all: for to one is given the word of wisdom through the Spirit, to another the word of knowledge through the same Spirit, to another faith by the same Spirit, to another gifts of healings by the same Spirit, to another the working of miracles . . ." —1 Cor. 12:7-10a

[144] "These were more fair-minded than those in Thessalonica, in that they received the word with all readiness, and searched the Scriptures daily to find out whether these things were so." —Acts 17:11

The Miracle Gap should force you to spend some time in healthy reflection, talking to God. "God, what am I missing when I pray? Is there a greater level of intimacy with You that I need to experience before miracles start happening in my life?" But instead of reflecting, we often start rejecting. If our life experience doesn't line up with God's Word, we throw out the Word instead of asking God to change our life experience! We bring the Word down to the level of our experience, instead of asking God to raise our level of experience to His Word! And the result is disaster. In the case of the Dutch Reformed Church of South Africa, an entire denomination was robbed of the scriptural truth that Jesus heals, simply because pastors were afraid they wouldn't see miracles when they prayed.

In a letter to the Southern Association of Evangelists (circa 1920), John G. Lake[145] expressed his distaste for the church's reaction to Murray's experience:

> Although the truth of the teaching of Divine Healing, and the personal experience in the healing of Andrew Murray, and hundreds of others through his ministry and the ministry of believers in the Church remained unchallenged, Rev. Andrew Murray was requested not to practice the teaching of Divine Healing in the Dutch Reformed Church of South Africa.
>
> This experience illustrates with clearness, the difficulties surrounding the introduction of a more vital faith in the living God in the Modern Church. Every Church has had, in a greater or lesser degree, a somewhat similar experience. The usual

---

[145] Lake is the founder of the Healing Rooms in Spokane, Washington, which served as the precursor to what has become the International Association of Healing Rooms (IAHR).

custom in the Modern Church is that when a preacher breaks out in a living faith and begins to get extraordinary answers to prayer, he is cautioned by the worldly wise, and if persistent, is eventually made to feel that he is regarded as strange. If he still persists, he is ostracized and actually dismissed by some churches and conferences."[146]

It's been over a hundred years since Lake penned those words, but the attitude in the church still hasn't changed! So the question for you is: Is your ministry driven by faith or by fear? Too often we are driven by the mindset, "What if nothing happens when I pray?" when in fact we should be motivated by the opposite mindset: "What if *something happens* when I pray?" We stop short of grabbing hold of the truth that God heals and putting it into practice because of fear. And we have to nip that in the bud if we want to become the New Testament church that Jesus died for us to be!

Say Goodbye to Fear

If you want to move in healing, you have to say goodbye to fear. There is simply no place for fear in the supernatural lifestyle. You cannot care what anyone else thinks. You cannot give ear to doubt or unbelief. Jesus asks us to be bold.[147] Boldness does not require you to have some unthinkable superhuman level of courage. Boldness simply means you stop caring what other people think, and do what God asks you to do no matter the cost.

---

[146] Liardon, *John G. Lake on Healing*, 211-212.

[147] "Now when they saw the boldness of Peter and John, and perceived that they were uneducated and untrained men, they marveled. And they realized that they had been with Jesus." – Acts 4:13

The apostle Paul reminded the younger Timothy of the pervasive nature of fear:

I thank God, whom I serve with a pure conscience, as my forefathers did, as without ceasing I remember you in my prayers night and day, greatly desiring to see you, being mindful of your tears, that I may be filled with joy, when I call to remembrance the genuine faith that is in you, which dwelt first in your grandmother Lois and your mother Eunice, and I am persuaded is in you also.

Therefore I remind you to stir up the gift of God which is in you through the laying on of my hands. For God has not given us a spirit of fear, but of power and of love and of a sound mind. Therefore do not be ashamed of the testimony of our Lord . . .   *—2 Timothy 1:3-8a*

Timothy had "genuine faith" (v 5). Do you know what genuine faith is? Faith paired with action. Faith that not only *talks about* what God can do, but *shows* God doing it.

Paul reminded Timothy that when he had laid hands on him, a "gift of God" had been deposited in Timothy. God had done the depositing, but it was now Timothy's job to "stir up" the gift. Timothy had to remind himself that miracles were possible every single day! He had to make a determination never to settle for a life of counterfeit faith, a life devoid of healing and miracles. And the way he would stay in the miracle zone was by rejecting fear and embracing bold faith.

Paul identifies fear as a spirit. We are reminded that the spirit of fear is not from God. And if God has not given it to us, we should refuse to keep it! Instead, we should reject the spirit of fear that Satan wants us to wear, and instead take delivery of "power and of love and of a sound mind" (v 7), all with the purpose of preaching the gospel without fear (v 8a).

Power

Power. Love. A sound mind. Do you know what power looks like?

> *Now by this we know that we know Him, if we keep His commandments. He who says, "I know Him," and does not keep His commandments, is a liar, and the truth is not in him. But whoever keeps His word, truly the love of God is perfected in him. By this we know that we are in Him. He who says he abides in Him ought himself also to walk just as He walked.* —1 John 2:3-6

Power means *doing* what God tells you to do. It means "keeping His commandments" (1 Jn. 2:3), one of which is, "Heal the sick, cleanse the lepers, raise the dead, [and] cast out demons" (Matt 1:8a). Power means keeping the Word of God, so that His love can be perfected in us!

Power means not just talking as Jesus talked, but walking as Jesus walked. Jesus saw healing and miracles *everywhere He went!* And I don't think it's too bold or unrealistic to believe that you and I should have the same experience in His name.

Love

Power. Love. A sound mind. Do you know what love looks like?

> *This is love, that we walk according to His commandments.* —2 John 6

Love means walking according to His commandments. In other words, the source of supernatural power and divine love is the same— obedience! When God asks you to pray for the sick, will you do it? When He encourages you to expect a miracle to happen, will you believe it? The ministry of Jesus is not just a fairy tale of unlikely events that took place a long time ago. The Gospels and the Book of Acts are *templates* for how we are supposed to live our daily lives! If God tells us to "heal the sick" (Matt. 10:8), we cannot say we love Him unless we do what He says.

Sound Mind

Power. Love. A sound mind. Do you know what a sound mind looks like?

> For "who has known the mind of the Lord that he may instruct Him?" But we have the mind of Christ.   —1 Corinthians 2:16

You have the mind of Christ. You get to think like Jesus thinks! When you're faced with a bad diagnosis, you get to respond like Jesus would respond. Jesus didn't back down in fear! He declared the Word of God, knowing that His Father would heal whoever was in front of Him!

Jesus was *bold*. Do you remember when Jesus raised Lazarus from the dead? By the time Jesus got to Lazarus' tomb, he had already been dead four days![148] But Jesus didn't care! There is no expiration date on the anointing! He called for Martha and Mary and demanded to know where Lazarus was being kept (v 34). He barged into that funeral where everyone was mourning and weeping and told them to take away the stone. Martha resisted, but Jesus insisted: "Did I not say to you that if you would believe you would see the glory of God?" (v 40).

And then Jesus did what He does best:

> Now when He had said these things, He cried with a loud voice, "Lazarus, come forth!" And he who had died came out bound hand and

---

[148] "So when Jesus came, He found that he had already been in the tomb four days." —Jn. 11:17

foot with graveclothes, and his face was wrapped with a cloth. Jesus said
to them, "Loose him, and let him go."   — *John 11:43-44*

What are you missing out on because you don't believe? All it takes to
see the glory of God is faith! Jesus didn't bow to the fear and crowded
mindsets of the people around Him! He ransacked Lazarus's tomb and
raised him from the dead. And you get to live your life with the same
level of boldness.

Jesus never had to stop and wonder, *If I pray for this person, will (s)he*
be healed? He knew the Father would do what He had promised to do.
And you can have the same confidence, because you have the mind of
Christ!

What Are You So Afraid Of?

God wants you to heal in His name. He doesn't want you to be afraid of
sickness and disease. He wants you to charge into situations where dead
bodies need to be brought back to life, and have faith that He will do
everything He promised to do!

We can learn a lot from Jesus' disciples, especially Simon Peter. We
often give Peter a hard time for denying Jesus and making some big
mistakes. But early on in his walk with Jesus, Peter was the one who
really got it. Peter knew who Jesus was when the rest of the disciples
were still figuring it out.[149] And when Jesus asked the disciples to step
out and walk on the water, Peter was the *only one* who accepted the
invitation:

---

[149] "So they said, 'Some say John the Baptist, some Elijah, and others Jeremiah
or one of the prophets.' He said to them, "But who do you say that I am?'
Simon Peter answered and said, 'You are the Christ, the Son of the living
God.'" —Matt. 16:14-16

And Peter answered Him and said, "Lord, if it is You, command me to come to You on the water." So He said, "Come." And when Peter had come down out of the boat, he walked on the water to go to Jesus. But when he saw that the wind was boisterous, he was afraid; and beginning to sink he cried out, saying, "Lord, save me!"

And immediately Jesus stretched out His hand and caught him, and said to him, "O you of little faith, why did you doubt?"
—Matthew 14:28-31

It is true that Simon Peter started to sink because he doubted. But it is also true that Simon Peter was the only disciple who put himself in a situation where sinking was even possible. Jesus told him to come, and he came. When Jesus tells you to heal, will you heal?

Look at Jesus' response when Peter started to sink. He "immediately . . . stretched out His hand and caught him" (v 31). If you would simply take God at His Word and step out and pray for the sick, you would see a miracle. You would walk on water! You will do things that other people, even other Christians, say are impossible.

And if you ever feel like you're praying for something that seems impossible, *good.* You're in good company. Because anyone who ever did anything worth recording in Scripture trusted God through an impossible situation and watched Him come through! God will not let you sink. He will reach out His hand and show you His glorious power.

You see, Peter's experience was not just about Peter:

And when they got into the boat, the wind ceased. Then those who were in the boat came and worshiped Him, saying, "Truly You are the Son of God."
—Matthew 14:32-33

There was an entire boat full of disciples who needed to be injected with bold faith. When they saw Peter step out, and watched Jesus lift him up, they *finally believed* Jesus was the Son of God.

And in the same way, healing for the sick is not just about you. There are people in your life who will not believe God exists unless they see a miracle. And God has asked *you* to be the one to show them.

CHAPTER ELEVEN

PRESENCE TO HEAL

God is not a God of formula. You can pray the same prayer over two people with the same sickness and one will be healed while the other will stay sick. Why? Because the *presence of God* matters.

I am a big fan of prayer models. Jesus gave us a very effective prayer model in Matthew 6.[150] Prayer models exist for healing,[151] and they are helpful because they help us to focus our prayers. They build on what has worked in the past as a bridge to God's will in the future. But hear me on this. A prayer model without the presence of God is not worth the paper on which it is printed.

You might know *how* to pray. But if you are praying from your flesh, instead of with the Spirit, your prayer is going to fall flat. You might repeat all the right words! But Jesus told us we would not be heard for our many words.[152] Knowing *what* to pray is important! But knowing the God who answers prayer is even more important.

---

[150] "In this manner, therefore, pray: Our Father in heaven, hallowed be Your name. Your kingdom come. Your will be done on earth as it is in heaven. Give us this day our daily bread. And forgive us our debts, as we forgive our debtors. And do not lead us into temptation, but deliver us from the evil one. For Yours is the kingdom and the power and the glory forever. Amen." —Matt. 6:9-13. For a detailed analysis of the Lord's Prayer please see Chapter 7 of my book *Deeper: A Guide to Spirit-Filled Prayer* (New York: Intelligent Charismatic, 2019).

[151] For one of the most effective prayer models for healing, visit the Global Awakening store and find the "Prayer and Deliverance" card. globalawakeningstore.com

[152] "And when you pray, do not use vain repetitions as the heathen do. For they think that they will be heard for their many words." —Matt. 6:7

Scripture shows us that people who tried to pray apart from the presence of God were absolutely ineffective. In Matthew 17, the disciples tried to cure a boy suffering from epilepsy, but they "could not cure him" (v 16). Jesus commented on their faith (v 17), and then went to work. "And Jesus rebuked the demon, and it came out of him; and the child was cured from that very hour" (v 18). Frustrated, the disciples came to Jesus and asked him why they couldn't cure the boy. So Jesus told them, "Because of your unbelief . . . However, this kind does not go out except by prayer and fasting" (vv 20-21).

Jesus has a living relationship with God, because He and the Father are One![153] But the disciples were in a place where they were trying to minister from their own strength. The remedy, according to Jesus, was not a better prayer model! It was more time in the presence of God. It was cultivating a lifestyle of prayer and fasting as a means of staying close to God's heart.

Acts 19 tells us that God "worked unusual miracles by the hands of Paul, so that even handkerchiefs or aprons were brought from his body to the sick, and diseases left them and the evil spirits went out of them" (vv 11-12). But when "some of the . . . Jewish exorcists" (v 13) and the sons of Sceva tried to imitate Paul, an evil spirit "leaped upon them, overpowered them, and prevailed against them" (v 16). Paul had the *presence,* but his imitators only had a *prayer model.* Can you see that while prayer models are a valuable resource, the presence of God is of infinitely more value?

There's No Faking It

What was the difference between Paul and his imposters? Paul had had an *experience* in God's presence, while the other men were faking it!

---

[153] "I and My Father are one." —Jn. 10:30

When I was eighteen years old and a freshman in college, I bought a fake ID. (*I know, I know,* it wasn't right! But you can't spell pastor without "past!") I went to school in Upstate New York. My best friend from home went to a college in rural Pennsylvania. He had a roommate who was from New York City. One day, we convinced his roommate to take us to Saint Mark's Place in the East Village of Manhattan.[154] We dressed up to look older than we were, and we walked into a small store. I scanned my surroundings, thinking I was slick. The store owner looked at me.

"We're here for IDs," I announced.

"*Shh!*" the owner replied, motioning for me to keep my voice down. Then he slunk to the front of the store and bolted the lock. "Follow me," he said, as he opened a trap door into the basement. We took turns kneeling in a hole in the floor as the owner dropped a green screen behind us from the ceiling. Within minutes, we had fake IDs.

I drove back to campus feeling ten feet tall. But when I tried to use my new ID, things didn't quite go as planned. One of my friends drove me to the grocery store in the center of town. He and two other friends stayed in the car while I hurried into the store. I picked up a case of Natural Ice, the classiest beer I could find. I went to the register, my palms moist with anticipation. I gave my ID to the cashier at the register. She looked at me, and then back at the card. Then she pursed her lips and nodded in approval, and handed me back my ID.

I was free! Or so I thought. When I went to grab my beer and leave the store, I noticed the two employees who had been stocking shelves were now blocking the exits. They had locked the door and wouldn't let me leave. I looked out into the parking light and saw red and blue lights flashing in the twilight. The police came and charged me with a misdemeanor, which meant a day in court, a hefty fine, and a suspension

---

[154] Ironically, this would end up being the same neighborhood in Manhattan where I would become a pastor years later. God has a sense of humor!

of my real driver's license. When I finally made it outside, my friends were slouched to the bottom of their seats, waiting and hoping I would come back soon. They had seen the police lights and knew things had taken a turn for the worse.

What went wrong? I tried to claim the *identity* without the *experience*. I wanted to pretend I was more mature than my life experience allowed! My point is this: Years of life experience cannot be faked. And in the same way, *moments* in God's presence cannot be faked! Faith is the currency of heaven. But if you want to have the authority to *use* the identity you have been given, you have to wait until moments in God's presence transform you into the son or daughter He designed you to be.

Listen to me now. When it comes to your healing (and your healing ministry), you don't need a new prayer technique! You don't need a new healing course or certification! It is infinitely more important that you usher in the presence of God like never before. Fall on your face[155] and seek God with reckless abandon. And He will do in a moment what you never could have accomplished in years.

Mountains Melt Like Wax

God's presence melts sickness away. Can I prove it to you?

> *The mountains melt like wax at the presence of the Lord, at the presence of the Lord of the whole earth.*　　　　—Psalm 97:5

Some mountains have to be spoken to.[156] Sometimes God will ask you to *command* sickness and disease to flee! But sometimes God simply wants to melt your mountain away as you soak in His presence.

---

[155] "Then Abram fell on his face, and God talked with him . . ." —Gen. 17:3
[156] "For assuredly, I say to you, whoever says to this mountain, 'Be removed and be cast into the sea,' and does not doubt in his heart, but believes that

So, what mountain are you facing? Do you see how you would be subjecting yourself to unnecessary anger and frustration by telling that mountain to move over and over again if God is simply asking you to come into His presence and let Him take it away?

What if you prized the presence of God to such an extent that *every time you walked into a room*, sickness and disease simply melted away? Whenever I visit a member of our church who is sick, I start our time together in the same way: "Holy Spirit, I welcome Your presence in this room." You don't know who's been in a hospital room before you! The fastest way to healing is to clear out whatever was in that room before you, and invite God's manifest presence to cause whatever ails you to melt away.

Our church starts every year with twenty-one days of prayer and fasting. That means we meet for corporate prayer every night for twenty-one days, and many of our church members fast for all or a portion of that time. Several years ago, we had a young woman named Lucy who came to almost every single prayer meeting at our Manhattan location. We spent the first week or so praying for corporate needs in the church, our city, the nation, and other nations all over the world. But one night, I felt the Lord lead me to have people pray for each other. Lucy teamed up with a group of people and they all laid hands on each other and started to pray. They asked the presence of God to fill their lives like never before.

After prayer was over, Lucy stopped in the restroom. Several moments later, she flung open the door and everyone's heads swiveled to see what was going on. Lucy's eyes were as wide as saucers. Her jaw dropped to the floor and she ran over to talk to me. Lucy told me that ever since she was a little girl, she had struggled with patches of red, itchy skin. The patches covered much of her legs, some of her arms, and

those things he says will be done, he will have whatever he says.'" —Mk. 11:23

even parts of her neck. I had never really noticed it when I said hello to Lucy before or after service, but Lucy quickly explained that she always wore long sleeves and long pants to cover up the blotches on her skin.

"But look at this!" Lucy said. She rolled up one of her pant legs and showed me her ankle. "This was one of the *worst* areas," she said.

"Was?" I asked.

"Well," she continued, "My team just prayed for me and then I went to the bathroom, and as soon as I got into the bathroom I realized I hadn't felt the urge to itch my legs in a while, so I looked and saw *this!*"

I looked closely. The skin on Lucy's ankle looked like the skin of a baby.

Lucy was completely healed that night. She assured me that she had checked out every square inch of her skin in the restroom, and every single blotch was gone. But notice something particularly powerful here. Lucy's prayer partners didn't even know what was going on with her. They didn't know what her mountain was, because Lucy was too embarrassed to tell them! But as they simply welcomed the presence of God into the room, Lucy was completely healed. Do you see how powerful His presence is?

So, finish reading this book. Take a Healing Rooms training course![157] Read everything about healing that you can get your hands on.[158] But never forget to prize the presence of God.

We can get so caught up in pursuing our healing that we forget about our Healer. We can become so focused on a cure that we forget Who redeemed us from the curse! But when you spend time in the presence of Jesus, every mountain you could ever face will melt away.

---

[157] For free training from the NYC Healing Rooms, visit healingrooms.nyc.
[158] I highly recommend *The Healing Breakthrough* and *Power to Heal* by Dr. Randy Clark, *Healing the Sick* by T.L. Osborn, and *Christ the Healer* by F.F. Bosworth.

Moses Loved the Presence of God

There is much to learn by looking at the lives of men and women in Scripture who were powerfully impacted by the presence of God. Moses was one of these people. In Moses, God had a man who *refused* to be distracted from God's presence!

Moses was so committed to hosting the presence of God that He told God point-blank that He would *refuse* to carry out God's mission without God's presence:

> *Then Moses said to the Lord, "See, You say to me, 'Bring up this people.' But You have not let me know whom You will send with me. Yet You have said, 'I know you by name, and you have also found grace in My sight.' Now therefore, I pray, if I have found grace in Your sight, show me now Your way, that I may know You and that I may find grace in Your sight. And consider that this nation is Your people." And He said, "My Presence will go with you, and I will give you rest." Then he said to Him, "If Your Presence does not go with us, do not bring us up from here."* —Exodus 33:12-15

Do you insist on having God's presence with you wherever you go, just like Moses did? Do you *refuse* to step out and try to complete any task, no matter how significant or mundane, without the presence of God? Moses *would not* go anywhere without God's presence, because he knew that if he faced an obstacle on the way, he would have what he needed if he only had the presence of God.

Moses cultivated a lifestyle focused around the presence of God. While Israel was focused on complaining about what they didn't have,[159] Moses focused on prizing what he did have—God's very presence.

---

[159] "Then the whole congregation of the children of Israel complained against Moses and Aaron in the wilderness. And the children of Israel said to them,

Moses took his tent and pitched it outside the camp, far from the camp, and called it the tabernacle of meeting. And it came to pass that everyone who sought the Lord went out to the tabernacle of meeting which was outside the camp. So it was, whenever Moses went out to the tabernacle, that all the people rose, and each man stood at his tent door and watched Moses until he had gone into the tabernacle. And it came to pass, when Moses entered the tabernacle, that the pillar of cloud descended and stood at the door of the tabernacle, and the Lord talked with Moses. All the people saw the pillar of cloud standing at the tabernacle door, and all the people rose and worshiped, each man in his tent door. So the Lord spoke to Moses face to face, as a man speaks to his friend. And he would return to the camp, but his servant Joshua the son of Nun, a young man, did not depart from the tabernacle. —Exodus 33:7-11

Moses pitched his tent outside the camp. He separated himself from anyone who would distract him from the presence of God. He distanced himself from anyone who would seek him out for administrative assistance. And what happened as a result? *God met him.*

Whenever Moses made time for God, God was there. Moses would go into his tent and meet with God, and God's presence would settle on their time together in such a powerful way that all the people of Israel took notice. God "talked with Moses . . . face to face, as a man speaks to his friend" (vv 8, 11). Moses made time to seek God's face! And God honored Moses' investment by giving Moses everything he was looking for.

'Oh, that we had died by the hand of the Lord in the land of Egypt, when we sat by the pots of meat and when we ate bread to the full! For you have brought us out into this wilderness to kill this whole assembly with hunger.'"
—Ex. 16:2-3

God's Presence Changes You

Time in God's presence will change you. Moses learned this firsthand:

> *Now it was so, when Moses came down from Mount Sinai (and the two tablets of the Testimony were in Moses' hand when he came down from the mountain), that Moses did not know that the skin of his face shone while he talked with Him.*   —*Exodus 34:29*

This is how God works. Moses was just doing what God told him to do! And little did he know, he left that encounter completely changed. But everyone else quickly started to notice:

> *So when Aaron and all the children of Israel saw Moses, behold, the skin of his face shone, and they were afraid to come near him. Then Moses called to them, and Aaron and all the rulers of the congregation returned to him; and Moses talked with them. Afterward all the children of Israel came near, and he gave them as commandments all that the Lord had spoken with him on Mount Sinai.*
> —*Exodus 34:30-32*

Notice the chain of command. God spoke to Moses, and Moses spoke to the people. When you are interacting with someone in need of healing, your first priority should be to *hear from God* on their behalf! They may be so impacted by their circumstance that they have lost the ability to objectively hear from God about their situation. They may have received so many bad reports from doctors and nurses that they no longer know what to believe! And that is when you get to tell them, as one who prizes the presence of God, *exactly* what God is asking them to do to be healed.

Notice that Moses was not only spiritually transformed in the presence of God, he was also transformed physically. When Moses went into the presence of God, his cellular composition changed in such a way that from that moment forward, he radiated the glory of God. His biological structure changed to emit light like never before.

"Shone" (v 30) is the Hebrew *qaran*, which means "to send out rays."[160] But notice that Moses had to "enter in" the presence before he could "send out" the glory. God wants to heal through you! He wants the people in your community to see His power on display to such an extent that they turn to Him because they can find no other explanation for the healing that takes place as you lay hands on the sick. But in order to move in power, you have to spend time in His presence.

When you spend time in God's presence, your very composition will change to reflect His glorious light. And darkness cannot stay where light is reflected. That is why Scripture says that when you "[r]esist the devil . . . he will flee" (Jas. 4:8). God longs to send you into places where healing is required! But first you must make a commitment to prize His presence wherever you go.

It is in God's presence that you become who He is.[161] He is the God Who Heals,[162] and He wants to heal through you! He is the light of the world,[163] and He wants *you* to be the light of the world too.[164] And the healing and transformation you are looking for all starts in the same place: His presence.

---

[160] "H7160 - qaran - Strong's Hebrew Lexicon (KJV)." Blue Letter Bible. Accessed 11 Aug, 2020. https://www.blueletterbible.org//lang/lexicon/lexicon.cfm?Strongs=H7160&t=KJV

[161] "But we all, with unveiled face, beholding as in a mirror the glory of the Lord, are being transformed into the same image from glory to glory, just as by the Spirit of the Lord." —2 Cor. 3:18

[162] "For I am the Lord who heals you." —Ex. 15:26b

[163] "Then Jesus spoke to them again, saying, 'I am the light of the world. He who follows Me shall not walk in darkness, but have the light of life.'" —Jn. 18:12

[164] "You are the light of the world. A city that is set on a hill cannot be hidden." —Matt. 5:14

One Thing Is Needed

Mary was someone who valued the presence of God just like Moses. From the moment she met Jesus, she could not be moved from His presence. We see this pattern on full display when Jesus visits Mary and her sister, Martha:

> *Now it happened as they went that He entered a certain village; and a certain woman named Martha welcomed Him into her house. And she had a sister called Mary, who also sat at Jesus' feet and heard His word. But Martha was distracted with much serving, and she approached Him and said, "Lord, do You not care that my sister has left me to serve alone? Therefore tell her to help me."*
>
> *And Jesus answered and said to her, "Martha, Martha, you are worried and troubled about many things. But one thing is needed, and Mary has chosen that good part, which will not be taken away from her."* —Luke 10:38-42

Jesus distills effective ministry into one solitary requirement in verse 42. While Martha was running around trying to serve Jesus as best as she possibly could, Mary did the "one thing" that was needed. She "sat at His feet and heard His word" (v 39).

Are you hearing me? There is only *one thing* you need in this life! Drop everything else, and sit at the feet of Jesus. No more excuses. Do it now! Because it is *there and only there* that you will find what you need.

When you are at the feet of Jesus, your problems will melt away. When you are at the feet of Jesus, your sickness cannot stay! When you are at the feet of Jesus, even the enemy's best laid plans will fall lifeless and flat. So why wouldn't you live your life at His feet?

Are you pursuing healing in your own body? The "one thing" you need most is the presence of Jesus. Your natural body will one day be taken away from you.[165] Your health can be stolen if you don't know the Word of God (and the devil will do his best!). But the presence of Jesus can *never* be taken away.

Are you pursuing healing on behalf of someone else? The presence of Jesus is the "one thing" you need to access the healing power of the cross. If you or someone you know is struggling with sickness or disease, you have a choice. Will you panic and run from doctor to doctor trying to find a solution?[166] Will you run around like a chicken with your head cut off trying to figure out how to get healed? Or will you sit at the feet of Jesus for as long as it takes to receive the healing He died for you to have?

A New Lifestyle

I want to invite you to try something. This may sound counterintuitive and strange. But try it anyway! *Stop asking* for God to heal you. Instead, enter into His presence and don't say a thing. Wait on the Lord and allow Him to renew your strength.[167] He will take away your weakness and fill you with His power. He will take away your sickness and fill you with His health!

Mary lived a lifestyle of sitting at the feet of Jesus! And as a result, she attracted His healing presence. In John 11, Mary's brother Lazarus had become sick:

---

[165] "It is sown a natural body, it is raised a spiritual body." —1 Cor. 15:44

[166] Spoiler alert: this will not work. Just ask the woman with the issue of blood from Mark 5: "Now a certain woman had a flow of blood for twelve years, and had suffered many things from many physicians. She had spent all that she had and was no better, but rather grew worse." —Mk. 5:25-26

[167] "But those who wait on the Lord shall renew their strength; they shall mount up with wings like eagles, they shall run and not be weary, they shall walk and not faint." —Is. 40:31

Now a certain man was sick, Lazarus of Bethany, the town of Mary and her sister Martha. It was that Mary who anointed the Lord with fragrant oil and wiped His feet with her hair, whose brother Lazarus was sick. Therefore the sisters sent to Him, saying, "Lord, behold, he whom You love is sick."   —John 11:1-3

We all know what happened next. Mary and Martha sent for Jesus, and He came, but He took His time.[168] Mary must have been confused about what was taking so long! But even though she had questions, do you know what Mary did when Jesus arrived? She fell at His feet:

Then, when Mary came where Jesus was, and saw Him, she fell down at His feet, saying to Him, "Lord, if You had been here, my brother would not have died."   —John 11:32

Oh, that the church would embrace her calling to sit at the feet of Jesus! Mary didn't see the healing she expected right away! But she knew where to go to find it: Jesus' feet. And as Mary settled at the feet of Jesus and poured out her heart, Jesus responded.

Therefore, when Jesus saw her weeping, and the Jews who came with her weeping, He groaned in the spirit and was troubled. And He said, "Where have you laid him?"   —John 11:33-34

Because Jesus and Mary had a relationship, Jesus made it His mission to bring healing where it was required. He came and met the need for healing in the body of someone Mary loved.

---

[168] "So, when He heard that he was sick, He stayed two more days in the place where He was." —Jn. 11:6

Are you contenting for healing on behalf of a family member or someone close to you? Mary made a deposit at the feet of Jesus so that Lazarus could make a withdrawal. The time you spend in the presence of Jesus will actually pave the way for other people in your life to be healed by Him!

Bringing Heaven to Earth

Our mandate is to usher the presence of God into this earth. Our mission as followers of Jesus is not only to get to heaven! It is to bring heaven down.

In the Old Testament, we see two instances of men getting taken straight up into Heaven. Enoch was first: "And Enoch walked with God; and he was not, for God took him" (Gen. 5:24). Enoch was on such a dedicated mission to get close to God that one day the distance between him and heaven simply collapsed. He walked with God "and he was not, for God took him."

Elijah had a similar experience. Because he lived a life of devotion and service to God, he completely bypassed death:

> Then it happened, as they continued on and talked, that suddenly a chariot of fire appeared with horses of fire, and separated the two of them; and Elijah went up by a whirlwind into heaven.
>
> —2 Kings 2:11

But under the new covenant, our mandate is not to be taken up into heaven to be rescued *from* the world, it is to position ourselves so that, through us, heaven would be poured out *into* the world. God meets us exactly as He met Enoch and Elijah—except instead of bringing us up, His Holy Spirit has been brought down.

Jesus told His disciples to pray this bold prayer:

Your kingdom come.
Your will be done
On earth as it is in heaven.

—*Matthew 6:10*

I don't believe God would have asked us to pray for His kingdom to come it unless He knew it was possible. Our mandate is to enforce the will of Jesus here on this earth, to reclaim territory that rightfully belongs to Jesus from the enemy, and bathe the world in His marvelous light!

There is no sickness in heaven! And as people who have experienced heaven on earth in the form of the presence of Jesus, it is now our mandate to invite more of heaven to come down.

CHAPTER TWELVE

WHERE DOES JESUS HEAL?

God is *everywhere* all at once. The theological term for this reality is *omnipresence*. Bible commentator Matthew Henry notes that God's omnipresence "supposes the infinite and immensity of his being, from which follows the ubiquity of his presence; heaven and earth include the whole creation, and the Creator fills them both."[169] For our purposes, that means that there is *nowhere* God cannot heal. Stated positively instead of negatively, that means that God can heal *everywhere*.

We should never assume God can heal in one place but not the next. We should never assume that God can heal on Sunday morning, but not on Wednesday afternoon! He is the same yesterday, today, and forever (Heb. 13:8). And that means He can heal anytime, anywhere.

So, where do we see God heal in Scripture? And where does that mean you have biblical precedent to expect healing in your everyday life?

1) Jesus heals in the church.

The purpose of church service is to *gather people* to Jesus. I love churches that are evangelistic. Our job is not just to have Christian reunions by ourselves, it is also to invite people who don't know Jesus to get to know Him.

---

[169] Matthew Henry's Commentary on Psalm 25
https://www.biblestudytools.com/commentaries/matthew-henry-complete/psalms/139.html

But notice that Jesus never had to invite anyone to church. Because He healed everywhere He went, people sought Him out:

> *At evening, when the sun had set, they brought to Him all who were sick and those who were demon-possessed. And the whole city was gathered together at the door. Then He healed many who were sick with various diseases, and cast out many demons; and He did not allow the demons to speak, because they knew Him.*
>
> —*Mark 1:32-34*

What if you never had to invite anyone to church again? What if healing happened so often at our Sunday services that "the whole city . . . gathered together at the door"? This is our model! I'm all for evangelism, but if we do our job of allowing Jesus to heal people through us, we should technically never have to invite anyone to service. They will see God's healing touch and *insist* on coming!

When Jesus taught in the synagogue, He gave much more than just a nice message:

> *Now He was teaching in one of the synagogues on the Sabbath. And behold, there was a woman who had a spirit of infirmity eighteen years, and was bent over and could in no way raise herself up. But when Jesus saw her, He called her to Him and said to her, "Woman, you are loosed from your infirmity." And He laid His hands on her, and immediately she was made straight, and glorified God.*
>
> —*Luke 13:10-13*

Yes, Jesus taught the Word of God! But when He noticed a "spirit of infirmity" on someone in service, He was not afraid to cast it out. When He saw someone whose healing was being hindered, He stopped the service and dealt with it right then and there!

The Jewish leaders—i.e., the regular church attenders—didn't think Jesus should heal people during a service:

Now when He had departed . . . He went into their synagogue. And behold, there was a man who had a withered hand. And they asked Him, saying, "Is it lawful to heal on the Sabbath?"—that they might accuse Him.

Then He said to them, "What man is there among you who has one sheep, and if it falls into a pit on the Sabbath, will not lay hold of it and lift it out? Of how much more value then is a man than a sheep? Therefore it is lawful to do good on the Sabbath." Then He said to the man, "Stretch out your hand." And he stretched it out, and it was restored as whole as the other. Then the Pharisees went out and plotted against Him, how they might destroy Him.

—Matthew 12:9-14

But Jesus didn't care what was culturally acceptable! He didn't give a second thought to whether or not it was "appropriate" to heal in the sanctuary. He didn't give a rip if time for healing was allocated in the service order. He simply did what the Father showed Him.[170]

I believe that *every single church* should see healing testimonies all the time. If your pastor doesn't agree with me, give him a copy of this book! Church should be a house of healing and restoration. But I also believe that church *should not be the only place* where people get healed!

---

[170] "Then Jesus answered and said to them, 'Most assuredly, I say to you, the Son can do nothing of Himself, but what He sees the Father do; for whatever He does, the Son also does in like manner. For the Father loves the Son, and shows Him all things that He Himself does; and He will show Him greater works than these, that you may marvel.'" —Jn. 5:19-20

Was Jesus' healing power restricted to the sanctuary? I don't think so! Wherever Jesus went, people "came to Him:"

> *Jesus departed from there, skirted the Sea of Galilee, and went up on the mountain and sat down there. Then great multitudes came to Him, having with them the lame, blind, mute, maimed, and many others; and they laid them down at Jesus' feet, and He healed them. So the multitude marveled when they saw the mute speaking, the maimed made whole, the lame walking, and the blind seeing; and they glorified the God of Israel.* —Matthew 15:29-31

So, yes, your responsibility as a Christian is to invite people to church! But don't be bound by the mistaken notion that, if someone wants healing, they have to come to church to get it.

Please hear my heart here. I am a pastor at a church. I've been in church my whole life (except my "lost" years in high school, college, and a little while after). I love the local church! The local church is the single greatest vehicle for global evangelism that we have. But our responsibility as Christians is not only to heal in the church, it is also to bring healing to people *outside* the church.

When was the last time you personally introduced someone to Jesus so he or she could be healed?

> *When the sun was setting, all those who had any that were sick with various diseases brought them to Him; and He laid His hands on every one of them and healed them. And demons also came out of many, crying out and saying, "You are the Christ, the Son of God!" And He, rebuking them, did not allow them to speak, for they knew that He was the Christ.* —Luke 4:40-41

Jesus may not be around anymore in the flesh, but He is still God. He is still seated at the right hand of the Father in heavenly places! He is still on the throne. And His promise is that when we *bring people to Him*, He will make them whole.

Do you have family members who need healing in their bodies? Do you have friends who need a touch from God in their flesh? Do you have coworkers who might need to experience the healing touch of Jesus before they believe He is real? It is your responsibility to bring them, not just to church, but *to Jesus*.

2) Jesus heals in the workplace.

Is your life compartmentalized? Are you a Jesus follower on Sunday, and then a "regular person" Monday through Saturday? These things should not be so! You should get filled up on Sunday, so you can take the anointing—the manifest presence of God's Holy Spirit—with you into your office on Monday.

This is where it gets exciting. Are you called to the marketplace? Has God blessed you with a business or a mind for management? If so, you are *perfectly positioned* to be used by God to reach people who don't know Jesus. There is no better place for you to be! Just because you don't work in the church doesn't mean you can't expect to see *healing* happen!

Did you know that Jesus healed in the "marketplace"?

When they had crossed over, they came to the land of Gennesaret and anchored there. And when they came out of the boat, immediately the people recognized Him, ran through that whole surrounding region, and began to carry about on beds those who were sick to wherever they heard He was. Wherever He entered, into villages, cities, or the country, they laid the sick in the marketplaces, and begged Him that they might just touch the hem of His garment. And as many as touched Him were made well. —Mark 6:53-56

Too often, we label people who are good at making money as "marketplace ministers," and then assume their primary function is to fund the expansion of a ministry or church. But if you are engaged in the marketplace, you are meant for *so much more.* You are a messenger of the gospel every time you step into your office. You are a vessel of healing every time you meet someone who is sick—even at work!

God has anointed you to be in your office. He has given you authority over that place. And yes, that means you should expect to experience divine favor from a financial and promotion standpoint,[171] but that also means you should expect to command a certain degree of *spiritual* authority over your work environment when you pray!

The word "marketplace" (v. 56) is the Greek word *agora.*[172] It means a "place of assembly . . . for public debating, for elections, for trials, for buying and selling, [and] for all kinds of business." Are you an academic? God wants to invade your workplace. Are you a lawyer? God wants to invade your workplace! Are you a financial adviser or a trader? God wants to invade your workplace. Are you seeing the pattern yet? No matter *what you do* to make money, God wants to invade that place with His miracle-working power.

My prayer is that you would invite Jesus to infiltrate every single area of your life, and *especially* your workplace. You don't have to be a different person with different beliefs and lower expectations when you

[171] "For You, O Lord, will bless the righteous; with favor You will surround him as with a shield." —Ps. 5:12

[172] "G58 - agora - Strong's Greek Lexicon (KJV)." Blue Letter Bible. Accessed 11 Aug, 2020. https://www.blueletterbible.org//lang/lexicon/lexicon.cfm?Strongs=G58&t=KJV

step out of church. You can be the same anointed disciple *everywhere* you go!

Several weeks ago, one of the pastors on our church staff was in a lot of pain. After watching him grimace every time he lifted his hands to type for a few minutes, I asked him what was wrong. He told me he had woken up several days prior with severe back pain. Every time he moved, it hurt. This was major, I-feel-like-a-knife-is-being-twisted-into-my-back type of pain.

So do you know what we did? I didn't just tell him, "I hope you feel better." I didn't give him an empty platitude that I was "sorry he felt that way." I didn't tell him to come to church the following Sunday! We stopped and we prayed, right then and there! We were about to have a staff meeting, so we took the first few minutes of the staff meeting to gather around him, lay our hands on him, and pray.

Halfway through the prayer, a startled look crept across his face. Then he started to smile. One of our staff members who is also a Healing Rooms volunteer asked him to rate the level of pain he felt after prayer on a scale of 1 to 10. He lifted his arms up in the air, and started to laugh. "I don't feel a thing! 10 out of 10!"

Do you see how powerful it is to skip the conversation and get right to prayer? People don't need your intellectual proof demonstrating the existence of Jesus and His willingness to heal. They need to experience the power of God as you pray His Word over them!

Now, you might say, "Well that's a great story, but you work in a church! God would never do that in my workplace." But I haven't always worked in a church! I spent five years as a risk arbitrage trader on Wall Street. I worked in multiple financial advisory and money management offices before that. And do you know what I did when I worked in finance? I *prayed for people*. I talked about Jesus. I went on missions trips and then told my whole desk what God had done. To this day, I constantly meet and pray for people outside of church—in the gym, on the train, or on the street! And do you know what I've found *everywhere I pray?* God is still the Healer.

Jesus wants to invade the place where you work with His miracle-working power. He wants to show your co-workers just how much He loves them! He wants to take over the places where you have coffee and lunch. As Jesus walked the earth, healing happened "wherever He entered" (Mk. 6:56). If you invite Him, He is willing to go! And once He arrives in your place of business, whomever He touches will be made whole.

One of our deacons, Mauricio, makes Italian pastries for a living. His specialty is *cannoli*, and I can tell you from personal experience that they are *delicious*.[173] One day he was in his workspace mixing *cannoli* filling. He saw another business owner, Carl, who uses a portion of the space for his own food service business, doubled over in pain. One of Carl's employees rushed over to see what was wrong, but Carl was in so much pain that he let a string of angry expletives fly out in response.

So what did Mauricio do? He marched over to Carl and told him about Jesus. He asked Carl if he could pray for him! Carl was so impacted by the tangible power and presence of God that he staggered backwards several feet. Immediately the pain lifted. A look of surprise crept across Carl's face. And in that moment, Mauricio got to tell Carl about Jesus. He got to give Carl a Bible and invite him to church. God had just worked a profound miracle: right there on a concrete floor, in the middle of mixing filling for *cannoli*.

There doesn't need to be a division in your life between the sacred and the secular! God wants to make your secular more sacred. He will send you about His business at your place of business! He wants to invade your workplace—whether you're blue collar, white collar, or don't even have a collar! —with the miracle-working power of His Holy Spirit.

---

[173] Look up "Heavenly Cannoli" on Facebook.

"Well, how can God heal in my workplace if there's no faith? Don't people have to believe first?" I've heard a lot of pastors and preachers say that Jesus can only heal where there's faith. But that simply is not true. Yes, faith is incredibly important! Without faith, it is impossible to please God.[174] As you pursue healing in your own body, the first thing you should work on developing is your faith.[175]

But even when Jesus went into faithless places and ministered to faithless people, *He still healed:*

> *Then He went out from there and came to His own country, and His disciples followed Him. And when the Sabbath had come, He began to teach in the synagogue. And many hearing Him were astonished, saying, "Where did this Man get these things? And what wisdom is this which is given to Him, that such mighty works are performed by His hands! Is this not the carpenter, the Son of Mary, and brother of James, Joses, Judas, and Simon? And are not His sisters here with us?" So they were offended at Him.*
>
> *But Jesus said to them, "A prophet is not without honor except in his own country, among his own relatives, and in his own house." Now He could do no mighty work there, except that He laid His hands on a few sick people and healed them. And He marveled because of their unbelief. Then He went about the villages in a circuit, teaching.*
>
> —Mark 6:1-6

---

[174] "But without faith it is impossible to please Him, for he who comes to God must believe that He is, and that He is a rewarder of those who diligently seek Him." —Heb. 11:6

[175] We've already covered this in Chapter 6, "Faith to Heal."

When Jesus returned to the town where He was raised, people didn't believe in Him. They were too familiar with Him. They thought there was no way He could be the Son of God because they had known Him as a child!

Jesus "could do no mighty work there" (v. 5) because of the faith and unbelief of the people present. Most sermons stop there. Pastors often use this verse to self-rationalize and make themselves feel better when nothing miraculous happens in a service. *Well, the people must not have brought their faith,* we say! But look what Scripture says next. "Now He could do no mighty work there, *except* that He laid His hands on a few sick people and healed them" (v 5, *emphasis added*).

Thank God for the "except!" You see, even when Jesus was in an environment totally devoid of faith, He still healed. Even when He could do "no mighty work," He still healed![176] Don't you get it? Healing is not a *big deal* to God. It is *who He is.*[177] So, please do not talk yourself out a miracle by saying you don't have enough faith. And please do not talk someone else out a miracle by assuming they don't have enough faith! Wherever Jesus goes, healing happens!

Do people get offended when you talk about Jesus in your office? Good. Are people downright *combative* when you tell them Jesus heals? Good! Jesus has experience in that department. Even when people didn't *accept* what He had to offer, He was still there with His *except!*

If healing doesn't happen *right where you are*, don't blame someone else for their lack of faith. Ask God, "Lord, what am I missing that is preventing healing from happening here?" Maybe you need to

---

[176] "Mighty work" is *dunamis* (Strong's G1411): the inherent power in Jesus to perform miracles. "Healed" is the Greek *therapeuo* (Strong's G2323). It takes faith to activate the dunamis! But even where there is no *dunamis, therapeuo* can still happen. What we want to avoid here is the mistaken notion that just because you can't "feel" God in the room, He doesn't want to do anything. He is the Healer (Ex. 15:26), and you are made in His image (Gen. 1:27), so healing should happen everywhere you go because you are there!
[177] "For I am the Lord who heals you." —Ex. 15:26

declare His Word over the person you are praying for before healing happens. Maybe all you need is a moment to listen to God's voice and see what He wants to do before you assume you know His will! Don't feel *guilty*—get over it! And continue to press in for healing everywhere you go.

If healing is not happening in your workplace when you pray, don't get discouraged. Ramp up your prayers for miracles to happen *in* your office while you're *outside* the office. Ask people in your church home group to help you pray! If healing isn't automatic, it doesn't mean there's something wrong with you—it simply means *there is more* that Jesus wants you to experience.

3) Jesus heals at home.

I love church. Have I told you that yet? But did you know that in addition to showing up to service on Sunday, Jesus also makes house calls?

The gospel of Luke tells us a story of Jesus coming out of church after a great service:

> *Now He arose from the synagogue and entered Simon's house. But Simon's wife's mother was sick with a high fever, and they made request of Him concerning her. So He stood over her and rebuked the fever, and it left her. And immediately she arose and served them.*
> —Luke 4:38-40

Church was done! But Jesus was not done healing. Simon Peter's mother in law was sick. So Peter and his family "made a request of [Jesus] concerning her" (v 38).

Jesus didn't *balk* at Simon Peter's after-hours request. He didn't tell him to come back the following Sunday! Church was over! But He *healed her* right then and there. He rebuked the fever, and it left her. And her response? "She arose and served them" (v. 40).

This is what can happen when you "make a request of Jesus" concerning your family members. Even if they can't make it to church—or even if they're not interested!—He will meet them where they are and heal them. And after they have seen His power, they will have no problem serving Him anymore.

Peter learned his lesson. Once he knew Jesus' healing power wasn't constrained to the synagogue, he expected to see healing everywhere he went:

> *Now it came to pass, as Peter went through all parts of the country, that he also came down to the saints who dwelt in Lydda. There he found a certain man named Aeneas, who had been bedridden eight years and was paralyzed. And Peter said to him, "Aeneas, Jesus the Christ heals you. Arise and make your bed." Then he arose immediately. So all who dwelt at Lydda and Sharon saw him and turned to the Lord.*   *—Acts 9:32-35*

Aeneas was paralyzed! He hadn't left his bed for eight years. Can you see how it would be hard for someone like him to get to church?[178] Peter didn't invite Aeneas to come to a healing meeting to meet Jesus—he brought Jesus to meet Aeneas right in his bed. Peter declared God's Word with boldness over Aeneas, and he was supernaturally healed. But the miracle didn't stop there. Everyone who lived there took note and decided they wanted to meet Jesus too!

Are you praying for friends, family members and co-workers to meet Jesus? What better way to show them He is real than by showing them He

---

[178] This is a major area for growth in church. How are we reaching out to those for whom Sunday service is inaccessible?

heals! Declare His will to heal over their bodies, and watch them come back to life. You won't even have to invite them to church anymore; they will just be there. You won't have to figure out how to bring Jesus up in conversation anymore; they won't be able to stop talking about how good He is!

Jesus Heals "There"

We've seen three specific areas where Jesus heals in Scripture: the church (the "synagogue"), the marketplace, and the home. But by now you're probably starting to notice a pattern. Jesus doesn't just heal in *some places*, He heals in *all* places.

When people followed Jesus, He healed them "there":

> *Now it came to pass, when Jesus had finished these sayings, that He departed from Galilee and came to the region of Judea beyond the Jordan. And great multitudes followed Him, and He healed them there.* —Matthew 19:1-2

Where is "there?" Wherever people are willing to follow Jesus! Wherever you are, He is. He is omnipresent, remember? And better still, if you're a believer, Scripture says that Jesus isn't just *around* you, but that His Holy Spirit is within you![179]

So wherever you are, both in terms of physical location, and in terms of the level of your faith, Jesus can meet you and heal you "there."

Jesus Responds to Invitations

Jesus' healing does not depend on your location, it depends on your *invitation.* God is omnipresent. He is everywhere all at once! He can heal you *where you are!* All that matters is this: Have you given Him

---

[179] "For indeed, the kingdom of God is within you." —Lk. 17:21

an invitation to come into your life—into your church, workplace, and home—and heal?

Jesus responds to invitations. He comes where He is invited:

> *Now when Jesus had entered Capernaum, a centurion came to Him, pleading with Him, saying, "Lord, my servant is lying at home paralyzed, dreadfully tormented." And Jesus said to him, "I will come and heal him."* —Matthew 8:5-7

Jesus was never put off by a request. Whenever someone came to Him with a desire to be healed, His response was always, "I will come!"

You have an amazing opportunity in front of you. Everywhere you go, you can invite Jesus. His promise is that He will come with you. He will show up in places and situations where you need Him most. And He will not come emptyhanded! He will bring the healing that you and people close to you need to see to know that God is real.[180]

From this moment forward, you have scriptural permission to change your thinking. Sickness is not a cause for mourning, but an opportunity for healing! So no matter where you are, when someone tells you they're sick, ask if you can pray. Invite Jesus to come! And He will show up with His healing power.

---

[180] "'But that you may know that the Son of Man has power on earth to forgive sins'—He said to the paralytic, 'I say to you, arise, take up your bed, and go to your house.' Immediately he arose, took up the bed, and went out in the presence of them all, so that all were amazed and glorified God, saying, 'We never saw anything like this!'" —Mk. 2:10-12

CHAPTER THIRTEEN

UNUSUAL MIRACLES

Paul was not one of Jesus' twelve original disciples. But that didn't mean he hadn't *met Jesus* face to face. Prior to an encounter with Jesus, Paul was known as Saul, and Saul was definitely not an asset to the church:

> *Then Saul, still breathing threats and murder against the disciples of the Lord, went to the high priest and asked letters from him to the synagogues of Damascus, so that if he found any who were of the Way, whether men or women, he might bring them bound to Jerusalem.* —Acts 9:1

Paul was on a mission to capture and imprison Christians. But on the way to do his best to decimate the early church, Jesus met Saul:

> *As he journeyed he came near Damascus, and suddenly a light shone around him from heaven. Then he fell to the ground, and heard a voice saying to him, "Saul, Saul, why are you persecuting Me?"*
>
> *And he said, "Who are You, Lord?"*
>
> *Then the Lord said, "I am Jesus, whom you are persecuting. It is hard for you to kick against the goads."*
>
> *So he, trembling and astonished, said, "Lord, what do You want me to do?"* —Acts 9:3-6

From that point forward, Saul was a new man. God gave him a new name. God redeemed his past and gave him a new future!

God is often a fan of picking the people we think are *least likely* to work for Him, and making them His most valuable employees. And Paul was such a man.

The Purpose of An Encounter

Jesus wants to encounter you. I believe that with all my heart. If you look at the lives of great men and women who have been used by God—Heidi Baker, Randy Clark, Charles Finney, John and Charles Wesley—their ministries started with a distinct encounter with God.

We know John Wesley as one of the founders of the Methodist denomination. He was a pillar in the First Great Awakening, a powerful revival that swept through England and the North American colonies in the 1730s and 1740s. But did you know that before John Wesley had an *encounter* with Jesus, he considered himself a failure?

In October 1735, in response to an invitation from General James Oglethorpe, John Wesley left England for the colony of Georgia as an Anglican missionary. But his trip didn't go as planned. The North American colonists didn't appreciate his preaching. He and his brother, Charles, had hoped to serve as missionaries to Native Americans, but opportunities never materialized. John and Charles both returned to England defeated.[181]

But then both brothers had an *encounter* with Jesus. Charles was first. It was Pentecost Sunday, May 21ˢᵗ, 1738. Charles was extremely sick and afraid he might die. But then he had an encounter with the Holy Spirit. "In his journal entry for that day, [he reported] experiencing 'a strange

---

[181] Mark Noll, *The Rise of Evangelicalism: The Age of Edwards, Whitefield and the Wesleys* (Downers Grove, IL: InterVarsity Press, 2018).

palpitation of heart' that caused him to exclaim, 'I believe, I believe!'" [182] For the first time ever, he was sure of his salvation.

John was up next. Three days later, on May 24th, 1738, he had what he calls his "Aldersgate experience." After making contact with the Moravians in North America, John went to a Moravian society meeting at Aldersgate Street in London. The leader of the meeting was reading Martin Luther's preface to the Epistle to the Romans, and John was touched by the Holy Spirit like never before. He wrote the following in his journal to describe the experience:

> In the evening I went very unwillingly to a society in Aldersgate Street, where one was reading [Martin] Luther's preface to the Epistle to the Romans. About a quarter before nine, while he was describing the change which God works in the heart through faith in Christ, I felt my heart strangely warmed. I felt I did trust in Christ, Christ alone, for salvation; and an assurance was given me that He had taken away my sins, even mine, and saved me from the law of sin and death.[183]

Prior to their encounters with the Holy Spirit, Charles and John Wesley weren't even sure of their own salvation! They were trying to convince other people that Jesus was real when they didn't even believe it themselves! But from that May onward, John and Charles Wesley were *convinced* God was real. They had met Him face to face, and there was no turning back.

---

[182] Joe Iovino, "Holy Spirit moments: Learning from Wesley at Aldersgate." The United Methodist Church. Published May 18, 2017. Retrieved from https://www.umc.org/en/content/holy-spirit-moments-learning-from-wesley-at-aldersgate. Accessed 9 Sep. 2020.
[183] Iovino, "Holy Spirit moments."

In the years that followed, both men were used mightily by God. Less than a year after his powerful encounter with the Holy Spirit, John Wesley was open-air preaching to thousands of people. With the fresh anointing that had been supplied by the Lord, he went out and "proclaimed in the highways the glad tidings of salvation."[184]

What is the purpose of an encounter? When you encounter Jesus, He will *change you*. He will purify your heart and mind. He will fill you with power to be a "witness" (Acts 1:8) for Him! In one moment, He will show you His glory and His beauty in such a way that everything else in this world loses its flavor and you become willing to drop everything and follow Him.

We see this throughout the ministry of Jesus:

And Jesus, walking by the Sea of Galilee, saw two brothers, Simon called Peter, and Andrew his brother, casting a net into the sea; for they were fishermen. Then He said to them, "Follow Me, and I will make you fishers of men." They immediately left their nets and followed Him.

Going on from there, He saw two other brothers, James the son of Zebedee, and John his brother, in the boat with Zebedee their father, mending their nets. He called them, and immediately they left the boat and their father, and followed Him. —Matthew 4:18-22

Whoever *met* Jesus wanted to follow Him![185] And Paul was no exception. When he met Jesus, he changed. He dropped his personal agenda (in his

---

[184] Journal of John Wesley: April 2nd, 1739. Retrieved from https://www.ccel.org/ccel/wesley/journal.vi.iii.i.html

[185] This is reminiscent of Elijah calling Elisha. See 1 Kings 19:19-21.

case, persecuting the church). The only question he wanted answered from that moment forward was, "Lord, what do You want me to do?"

An encounter with Jesus also provides a clear designation that you have been chosen for something specific by God. In Paul's case, God told Ananias:

> *"Go, for he is a chosen vessel of Mine to bear My name before Gentiles, kings, and the children of Israel. For I will show him how many things he must suffer for My name's sake."* —*Acts 9:15-16*

What a call! Paul was God's "chosen vessel." He would preach and declare the gospel, even before royalty! But where great calls are issued, great sacrifice is required. Paul would suffer "many things" for Jesus.

But what I want to show you in this chapter is that Paul's ministry was not limited to preaching. Scripture says that God worked "unusual miracles" by the hands of Paul:

> *Now God worked unusual miracles by the hands of Paul, so that even handkerchiefs or aprons were brought from his body to the sick, and the diseases left them and the evil spirits went out of them.*
> —*Acts 19:11-12*

The implication is that, in the years following the resurrection of Jesus, there was such a thing as a "usual" miracle. Why else would Scripture have specified that Paul's miracles were "unusual?" In other words, healing at the hands of the disciples who had been with Jesus had become so common that it was *expected*. Contrast that with the current state of the church, in which most of the church is afraid to pray for healing, and much of the church is confused as to whether or not God even heals!

Paul was doing things *no one had ever seen before*. He had been so profoundly impacted in the presence of Jesus, both through his initial Acts 9 encounter, as well as through subsequent time in prayer,[186] that God was doing a *new thing* through Paul. I believe this was the manifestation of what Jesus told His disciples in John 14:12: "Most assuredly, I say to you, he who believes in Me, the works that I do he will do also; and greater works than these he will do, because I go to My Father." So while these miracles absolutely agreed with the nature and character of Jesus and the precedent He had set, they took a form that was different from anything the world had ever seen.

That tells me there is no such thing as a *formula* for healing. As you pursue your own healing, God will do something unique in you.[187] And as you start to pray that other people would be healed, you should never be locked into a formula. God might do it in ways you've seen before! Or, He might do something completely new.

Because of the time he had spent, and made a habit of spending, with Jesus, Paul was anointed. And his anointing was so strong that even the things he *touched* dripped with the miracle-working power of God. Jesus healed a woman who touched the hem of His garment (Mk. 5), but here was Paul healing people by *sending* his garments to them. As the cloth that had touched Paul's flesh arrived in the hands of people seeking healing, they had such a profound effect that disease left their bodies and demons left their souls.

Recently a woman named Jennifer came up to me for prayer after one of our Sunday morning services in Manhattan. She had a condition in her eyes called myopic degeneration. She was incredibly short-sighted and required thick prescription glasses. Over time, myopic degeneration typically leads to a loss of central vision. People with the disease usually

---

[186] "[P]ray without ceasing..." —1 Thess. 5:17
[187] See Chapter 3, "Your Healing Is Unique."

retain their peripheral vision, but their ability to focus in on a specific object is severely compromised. She was scared she would eventually lose her sight, along with the ability to carry out normal responsibilities.

We prayed. I felt the anointing leave my body and enter hers. But no physical evidence came in that moment. I asked her to test her eyesight. It was unchanged. So I made the promise I typically do in those situations: "I am going to keep praying until you have perfect vision." Jennifer smiled and nodded, clearly discouraged that her healing hadn't been instantaneous. I reassured her that God was a fan of "unusual" miracles that come at times and in places you won't expect.

Several weeks later, Jennifer ran up to me after service with her teenage daughter. She had gone to put her contacts into her left eye that morning and her vision was blurry. *Oh no*, she had thought. *What's wrong with my eyes* now? She thought her worst fears had been realized. She thought she had experienced a rapid deterioration in her vision overnight!

So she took out the contact. And she could see *clearly* from her left eye. She didn't need the contact anymore! I asked her what her vision was like in her left eye previously, and she said, "Minus nine." Now she sees *perfectly* in her left eye. She tested it out and showed me. She admitted she still saw a spot in front of her eyes when she used both eyes together. But God had clearly worked a miracle in her left eye, so we agreed to pray that Jesus would heal her right eye in exactly the same way!

The reaction of Jennifer's teenage daughter to the whole spectacle was absolutely priceless. Jennifer's daughter was a pre-med student. She was in shock. "This doesn't happen!" she kept exclaiming as Jennifer told me exactly what was going on. I love that God establishes His promises![188] And I love that He always allows witnesses to see it.

---

[188] "Now, O Lord God, let Your promise to David my father be

Raise Your Level of Expectation

What is the most "unusual" miracle you have ever seen? When was the last time you saw a miracle in Sunday service? Have you ever prayed for someone at your job and seen them miraculously healed in a way you could have never predicted, and with a plan you could have never known to expect?

I believe it's time we raise our *level of expectation* for healing and miracles in the church. Paul's miracles were "unusual." Again, the implication is that "usual" miracles were happening all the time! When people went to church, they got healed. When people met a disciple, they got healed! What would happen if we carried that radical attitude with us all the time—not only at Sunday service, but *everywhere we go*—so that whenever we met someone struggling with sickness and disease, we would expect God to show us that He loves to move in "unusual" ways!

Jesus Worked Unusual Miracles

Jesus worked unusual miracles too. Did you know that Jesus healed a blind man by spitting in his eyes?

> *When He had said these things, He spat on the ground and made clay with the saliva; and He anointed the eyes of the blind man with the clay. And He said to him, "Go, wash in the pool of Siloam" (which is translated, Sent). So he went and washed, and came back seeing.* —John 9:6-7

established..." —2 Chron. 1:9

That was unusual! The world had never seen healing happen like that before! But Jesus was simply listening to the Holy Spirit and doing what His Father had shown Him to do.[189]

This miracle was so "unusual" that, in 2018, as film producers were filming the movie *Mary Magdalene,* the actor who played Jesus, Joaquin Phoenix, flat-out *refused* to re-enact the John 9:6-7 healing scene according to the biblical narrative. He relayed his exact reaction to spitting in someone's eyes to news outlet CNN:

> "I knew about that scene from the Bible, but I guess I had never really considered it," Phoenix told CNN. "When I got there, I thought, 'I'm not going to rub dirt in her eyes. Who the [expletive] would do that?' "[190]

Jesus moved in ways that make you scratch your head! He did things that make re-enactors *uncomfortable.* Paul did too, and as you follow the Holy Spirit, *so will you.* And that is not a bad thing—it is a sign that God is calling you to do a new thing and be used by Him in new ways.

The appropriate disclaimer here is that God will *never* ask you to do something that disagrees with His Word. But there is no law against spitting in dirt and rubbing it in someone's eyes. There is no rule against rubbing your anointing on a towel and sending it to someone who needs to be healed! There are even instances in Scripture of a disciple healing

---

[189] "Then Jesus answered and said to them, 'Most assuredly, I say to you, the Son can do nothing of Himself, but what He sees the Father do; for whatever He does, the Son also does in like manner.' " —John 5:19

[190] Caleb Park, "Joaquin Phoenix is playing Jesus in new film but refused to do one thing: 'Who the f--- would do that?'" FoxNews.Com, April 15, 2019, https://www.foxnews.com/entertainment/joaquin-phoenix-jesus-mary-magdalene-miracle

with his shadow.[191] And the sooner we ask God to show us "unusual miracles," the sooner He will meet our request.

The cry of your heart every day should be, "Lord, show me something I've never seen before!" As you get accustomed to the sound of His voice and listen to the leading of His Holy Spirit, you will see miracles like never before!

A New Kind of Life

The apostle Paul shows us what it looks like to live a life *fully yielded* to God. Paul was able to do things nobody had ever seen before because He followed Jesus with a devotion no one had ever known before.

Paul had the best education. He was "brought up in [Jerusalem] at the feet of Gamaliel,[192] taught according to the strictness of [his spiritual] fathers' law, and was zealous toward God" (Acts 22:3). He had a specific agenda! He truly believed God had called him to wipe out the early church in a zealous frenzy to preserve a reverential respect for the Word of God!

But then Paul met Jesus. Everything changed in an instant! Paul didn't put up a fight. He didn't give notice at his job, or consider his options. He dropped *everything* and followed Jesus.

This is important because the pattern I typically see in the lives of Christians who have a powerful *experience* usually goes something like this:

1. Seek Jesus
2. Have an encounter with Jesus

---

[191] "And believers were increasingly added to the Lord, multitudes of both men and women, so that they brought the sick out into the streets and laid them on beds and couches, that at least the shadow of Peter passing by might fall on some of them." —Acts 5:14-15

[192] Gamaliel was one of the most renowned rabbinical teachers at the time.

3. Live a changed life *for a time*
4. Eventually settle back into lukewarm faith, settling for the false narrative that God "touched you" once but will never do it again

What a lie from the pit of hell! When you have an encounter with Jesus, it is the *first of many*, not the *last thing* God will ever do in your life! Your initial encounter with Jesus is like turning on a sink. Something is going to come out that will clean you and refresh you! But what many Christians don't realize is that whether the sink stays on or turns off is *up to you.*

Paul nourished his prayer life. He prayed "without ceasing" (1 Thess. 5:17). He made time throughout his day to hear from God.[193] He didn't shy away from visions and trances.[194] And that is why God not only *started* using him, but also why He *never stopped!*

Paul had an encounter with Jesus. And then he *dropped everything* to serve Him. How could he know such love and then go back to his old life?[195] How could He see the glory of God and simply go about his business?[196]

---

[193] Richard Foster refers to this method of always leaving time in your daily routine to hear from God as "holy leisure." Richard J. Foster, *Celebration of Discipline: The Path to Spiritual Growth* (New York, NY: Harper Collins, 1998), 27.

[194] "It is doubtless not profitable for me to boast. I will come to visions and revelations of the Lord: I know a man in Christ who fourteen years ago— whether in the body I do not know, or whether out of the body I do not know, God knows—such a one was caught up to the third heaven." —2 Cor. 12:1-2

[195] "Again, the kingdom of heaven is like treasure hidden in a field, which a man found and hid; and for joy over it he goes and sells all that he has and buys that field." —Matt. 13:44

[196] "Again, the kingdom of heaven is like a merchant seeking beautiful pearls, who, when he had found one pearl of great price, went and sold all that he had and bought it." —Matt. 13:45-46

What do you do after an encounter? Is your attitude "Oh, that was nice"? Or do you cry out to God, "Lord, I want to serve You like never before"? Paul dropped *everything* to passionately pursue Jesus. Will you?

You Are Just Like Paul

You are just like Paul. I'm not saying you will write thirteen out of twenty-seven books of the New Testament! But there is *no reason* your *daily existence* shouldn't be filled with "unusual miracles!"

What made Paul's ministry so powerful was not just his religious education[197] but his fierce devotion to Jesus. It was that he allowed God to do something new in him, instead of simply attempting to replicate things he had seen before.

In Acts 19, as God was working "unusual miracles" by the hands of Paul, a group of onlookers took notice. They tried to replicate what they were seeing *without* first cultivating a relationship with Jesus:

> *Then some of the itinerant Jewish exorcists took it upon themselves to call the name of the Lord Jesus over those who had evil spirits, saying, "We exorcise you by the Jesus whom Paul preaches." Also there were seven sons of Sceva, a Jewish chief priest, who did so.*
>
> *And the evil spirit answered and said, "Jesus I know, and Paul I know; but who are you?"*
>
> *Then the man in whom the evil spirit was leaped on them, overpowered them, and prevailed against them, so that they fled out of that house naked and wounded. This became known both to all Jews and Greeks*

---

[197] I passionately advocate for Bible study and theological education. But it must be paired with a genuine *relationship* with Jesus.

dwelling in Ephesus; and fear fell on them all, and the name of the
Lord Jesus was magnified.   —*Acts 19:13-17*

Whom you know matters! Your ability to heal in the name of Jesus rests not only on your knowledge of Scripture, but also on your *relationship* with Jesus. These exorcists were surely well trained. The sons of Sceva grew up in the house of a chief priest! But none of that made any difference in practical application of God's power. They didn't *know Jesus,* so they were overpowered by the forces of darkness.

When it comes to divine healing, the name of the game is not imitating miracles we see other people perform. It is not reciting a lifeless prayer model you've seen work for someone else![198] It is hearing from God at any given moment and asking Him, "Lord, how exactly is this healing process going to work?"

You are filled with the same Holy Spirit as the apostle Paul.[199] You can have the same *depth of relationship* with Jesus as the apostle Paul! Why wouldn't you expect Jesus to use you for "unusual miracles" just like He did the apostle Paul? But it all starts with dropping whatever interferes with a *constant focus* on Jesus. As you sit at the feet of Jesus and gaze into the glory of our King, the same Spirit who empowered Paul for his earthly ministry will supercharge you for yours!

How to Increase

The first and most important aspect of increasing in the "unusual miracles" anointing is living a life of devotion and prayer to Jesus. Spend

---

[198] As with religious education, prayer models are useful, but only when paired with a genuine relationship with Jesus.

[199] "But if the Spirit of Him who raised Jesus from the dead dwells in you, He who raised Christ from the dead will also give life to your mortal bodies through His Spirit who dwells in you." —Rom. 8:11

time with Jesus like never before. Pursue Him in His Word! Seek His face.

But I don't think it's a coincidence that the first prophetic word spoken over the apostle Paul's life included an acknowledgement of "how many things he must suffer for [Jesus'] sake."[200]

Paul's suffering was all-encompassing. He was physically abused for preaching Jesus.[201] He experienced constant resistance to the message of Jesus, even from the early church. But all of that had an effect on him. The New King James Version says that God "worked" unusual miracles by the hands of Paul. But the King James Version says those miracles were "wrought."

"Wrought" means to be "beaten out or shaped by hammering."[202] That means that when Paul went through some *painful stuff*, miracles came out! As Paul went through persecution and suffering but *clung to Jesus*, his anointing increased. God was wringing something out of him! God certainly didn't *cause* Paul's suffering, but He certainly refused to let it go to waste!

The suffering you experience for Jesus may not be physical like Paul's. But you will get some funny looks when you tell people you believe God can heal them with all your heart. I've visited church members in the hospital and encouraged them to believe for healing, only to have their

---

[200] Then Ananias answered, "Lord, I have heard from many about this man, how much harm he has done to Your saints in Jerusalem. And here he has authority from the chief priests to bind all who call on Your name." But the Lord said to him, "Go, for he is a chosen vessel of Mine to bear My name before Gentiles, kings, and the children of Israel. For I will show him how many things he must suffer for My name's sake." —Acts 9:13-16

[201] "From the Jews five times I received forty stripes minus one. Three times I was beaten with rods; once I was stoned; three times I was shipwrecked; a night and a day I have been in the deep..." —2 Cor. 11:24-25

[202] s.v. "wrought," *Oxford English Dictionary*. 2nd ed. 20 vols. (Oxford: Oxford University Press, 1989).

families get enraged with me for "interfering with the medical process." I've told doctors I believe Jesus can heal their patients, only to have them lecture me about the "placebo effect."[203] I've risked relationship security by encouraging friends and family members to press in to Jesus for healing like never before. But do you know what? *It was all worth it.*

Paul stopped at nothing to preach the gospel, and it *cost him something.* And as you pursue Jesus like never before, it will cost you something too.

Put yourself out there. Pray with boldness and great faith! Cast your reservations to the side. The greatest gift you can ever give another person who is suffering with sickness and disease is to *refuse* to stop praying for God to bless them with a miracle.

Pray this over yourself. "God, I know You wrought unusual miracles by the hands of Paul. And now I am asking You to do the same thing through me! I know it will be costly, but I am ready, in Jesus' name."

---

[203] The placebo effect is a phenomenon in which a patient's belief that (s) he will improve can actually improve a patient's condition despite no medication having been applied.

CHAPTER FOURTEEN

WHY GOD HEALS

Why should we make such a big stink about physical healing? If our souls are saved and we're heaven-bound, isn't healing just icing on the cake? Should we really put our foot down and *insist* that churches contend for healing? Can't we all just worship Jesus regardless of our stance on miracles and get along?

For me, here is all that matters at the end of the day: If physical healing was important to Jesus, it should be important to us. It should be important to you! It is important to me.

Many modern churches don't even believe that healing is possible anymore.[204] But part of my mission in life is to change that. If some Christians are seeing healing happen, there is *absolutely no reason* you shouldn't see Jesus heal in your body too. He is the same "yesterday, today, and forever" (Heb. 13:8). So if He did it for someone else, He will do it for you!

Healing As A Testimony

There are people in your life who won't believe in Jesus until you *show them* He is real. Showing is different than telling. Don't settle for an intellectual argument in your attempts to lead people to Jesus. Even the

---

[204] This is known as cessationist theology. Cessationist theology "teaches that although Jesus healed people in biblical times, miracles had subsequently ceased and should not be expected today" [C. G. Brown, "Theologies of Medicine and Miracles," *Society* 2 (2019): 141. https://doi-org.ezproxy.nyack.edu/10.1007/s12115-019-00341-0]. Continuationists, on the other hand, contend that miracles are still for today!

215

apostle Paul, the greatest apologist since Jesus and the prolific writer of almost half of the books in the New Testament, did not trust himself to win people to Jesus with words alone:

> And my speech and my preaching were not with persuasive words
> of human wisdom, but in demonstration of the Spirit and of power,
> that your faith should not be in the wisdom of men but in the power
> of God.   —1 Corinthians 2:4-5

God wants to lead people to Jesus through you.[205] But it's not going to happen because you tell people something they're never *heard before*. It will happen when you show people something they've never *seen before*.

God trusts *you* to show other people that He is real by allowing His power to flow through you. So it's time to get over your doubts, insecurities, and fears, and go out and pray for someone!

For the Unbeliever

You know people in your life who aren't Christians (yet). God is willing to show those people a miracle so they can get over their insecurities and fears and finally believe that He is who He says He is.

Mark 2 tells the story of a man who was paralyzed. He heard that Jesus was preaching nearby, so his friends brought him to Jesus to be healed:

> And again He entered Capernaum after some days, and it was heard
> that He was in the house. Immediately many gathered together, so
> that there was no longer room to receive them, not even near the
> door. And He preached the word to them. Then they came to Him,

---

[205] "No one can come to Me unless the Father who sent Me draws him; and I will raise him up at the last day." —Jn. 6:44

bringing a paralytic who was carried by four men. And when they could not come near Him because of the crowd, they uncovered the roof where He was. So when they had broken through, they let down the bed on which the paralytic was lying.

When Jesus saw their faith, He said to the paralytic, "Son, your sins are forgiven you."   —Mark 2:1-5

Here we see the power of spiritual hunger. There wasn't any room in the house where Jesus was preaching, but that didn't discourage this man and his friends. They made a way. They ripped a hole in the roof and lowered the man down right on his bed.

We also see the power of godly friendship. This man's friends *insisted* on getting him to Jesus. They didn't walk away, and they didn't give up. They knew that only Jesus had the remedy to what ailed their friend, and they stopped at nothing to get him to Him. Are you contending for your friends who don't know Jesus with the same devotion and hunger?

This was an amazing miracle! But not everyone in the room was happy to see Jesus heal.

And some of the scribes were sitting there and reasoning in their hearts, "Why does this Man speak blasphemies like this? Who can forgive sins but God alone?"   —Mark 2:6-7

The religious leaders didn't understand the connection between healing and salvation. They thought that *maybe* Jesus was an anointed prophet who could heal. But who did this Man think He was *forgiving sins?*

But Jesus showed them that there is an inextricable link between healing and salvation that we have to understand:

But immediately, when Jesus perceived in His spirit that they reasoned thus within themselves, He said to them, "Why do you reason about these things in your hearts? Which is easier, to say to the paralytic, 'Your sins are forgiven you,' or to say, 'Arise, take up your bed and walk'? But that you may know that the Son of Man has power on earth to forgive sins" —He said to the paralytic, "I say to you, arise, take up your bed, and go to your house." Immediately he arose, took up the bed, and went out in the presence of them all, so that all were amazed and glorified God, saying, "We never saw anything like this!" —Mark 2:8-12

Jesus did the *seen* to prove He is capable of the *unseen*. He healed this paralyzed man's body to prove to everyone in the room that He had power to save his soul!

Healing and salvation happened on the same day. Provision for *both* the salvation of your soul *and* the healing of your body was made by the blood of Jesus on the cross. If salvation is still for today (it is!), then healing is still for today! We should not pick and choose which aspects of the atonement we want to receive, and which we want to discard.

Jesus does the *tangible* to prove that He is capable of the *intangible*. He heals *bodies* to show that He has the power to redeem *souls*. The religious leaders balked at the prospect of believing that Jesus was able to forgive sins (v 7)! But Jesus showed them that He had the *power* to forgive sins by showcasing His *power* to heal bodies.

You have people in your life who simply *will not* be open to a spiritual conversation until they see that God cares about their physical, tangible needs. Have you ever seen Maslow's hierarchy of needs?[206]

---

[206] Reprinted with permission from https://www.simplypsychology.org/maslow.html

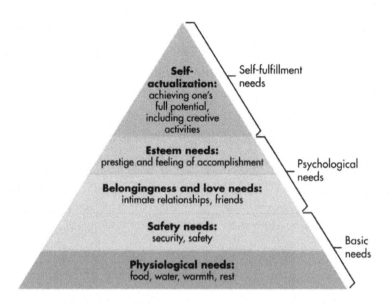

Psychologists understand that people aren't open to "self-actualization" (for our purposes, "salvation") until their physiological needs are met. So why is that so hard for Christians to understand? We structure our church homeless outreaches around praying for the homeless instead of giving them somewhere to sleep. We structure our missionary trips around preaching the gospel instead of giving people something to eat! But why should someone listen to your gospel presentation before you demonstrate a willingness to care about what's most important and pressing to *them*? When we meet an urgent physical need, people will be open to a spiritual conversation.

As Theodore Roosevelt famously said, people don't care how much you know until they know how much you care. It's not that we *shouldn't* preach the gospel and encourage people to receive Jesus. Of course that is the goal! But first we have to give people a good reason to listen to what we have to say. The way Jesus got their attention was by *healing the sick* and *casting out demons*. Why have we lost sight of those priorities in church?

Wanting to be healed is not selfish. Seeking God for what you need is not selfish! If Jesus didn't want you to seek Him for what you need, why would He have asked a blind man, "What do you want Me to do for you?"

> So Jesus answered and said to him, "What do you want Me to do for you?" The blind man said to Him, "Rabboni, that I may receive my sight." Then Jesus said to him, "Go your way; your faith has made you well." And immediately he received his sight and followed Jesus on the road. —Matthew 10:51-52

Jesus didn't make this man come to church. He didn't ask him to sit and listen to a sermon before he brought his request to God! Jesus *healed,* and this formerly blind man "followed Jesus" (v. 52).

Do you see how effective Jesus' ministry model is? We get it backwards. We insist people receive Jesus *before* they get healed. But Jesus used healing as *evidence* that people should believe that He is God. He healed first, and the result was that people "followed [Him] on the road" (v. 52)!

Which Is Easier?

Which is easier, to pray for salvation or to pray for healing? Of course praying for salvation is easier! If I pray for you to get saved and receive Jesus, I can tell you you're going to heaven until I'm blue in the face, but you are going to have *no clue* if my prayer actually worked until you die! And by then it will be too late for you to get back at me if I'm wrong.

Praying for healing, on the other hand, seems *hard.* Why? Because if I pray for you to get healed, *something has to happen.* This is why we pray for salvation so easily in church, but back away from healing prayer. But according to Jesus, we have it all wrong. Physical healing should be *easier*, not harder, than saving a soul! Fixing the flesh should be *easier* than fixing the spirit! Jesus is willing to do the former to *prove* that He is capable of doing the latter. The only problem is, we have to let Him.

It's time to stop being afraid of praying for healing. Healing is *not about you*. It's all about Him! You have *nothing* to be afraid of, because healing has *nothing* to do with you! All you have to do is show up and let Jesus do what He does best. When we step out on His Word, He will *never* leave us hanging.

Several months ago I preached at our Friday Night God Encounter service. As I got up to take the microphone, I was overwhelmed by a strong impression from the Lord that He wanted me to pray for healing. He specifically showed me[207] two women in the room who were suffering from barrenness. One of these women was a complete stranger. The other was a member at our Manhattan location. She was married, but I had no idea she and her husband were trying to have a baby.

In that moment, I was excited. It's so *thrilling* when God speaks! But I'm not going to lie to you, I was also afraid. What if I spoke out this word on barrenness and the women were mad that I had exposed what might have been a secret? What if I was *wrong* and I wasn't really hearing from God at all? What was my relationship with that woman and her husband going to be like if I completely missed the mark?

I made a conscious decision to push down my fear and step out in faith. I declared that God was going to heal barrenness tonight. I asked who needed prayer to have a child. The first woman raised her hand. I laid hands on her, and she started sobbing as a I began to pray.

---

[207] When I say God "showed me," I am referencing an open vision. As I turned around to face the crowd of people in the room, the Holy Spirit emphasized several people and spoke to me about their condition. They just seemed to stand out in the crowd, as if they were highlighted by God.

But the other woman said nothing. I preached my message, and then returned to my seat, slightly vexed. Why would God highlight her to me if she didn't need prayer? After the message, the worship team started to play another song. As they slipped from the first verse into the chorus, I felt a tap on my shoulder.

The Manhattan member, who hadn't raised her hand in prayer, sat down next to me with tears in her eyes. "My husband and I want to have a baby," she said. I smiled and nodded in agreement. We prayed, and believed a miracle had happened.

Several months later, I was in the shower when the Lord told me to text that woman's husband. *Are you pregnant yet or what?* I asked.

It looks like it may be twins, he replied.

Jesus promised His disciples that when we take a step out in faith, He will meet us with supernatural results:

> And they went out and preached everywhere, the Lord working with them and confirming the word through the accompanying signs. Amen.   *—Mark 16:20*

You are still His disciple! And He still has not changed.

The Importance of Scientific Proof

Healing is a testimony that Jesus is real. And that is why it is so important to get *medical evidence* that you are healed. When Jesus healed ten lepers, He told them to go and confirm their healing:

> Now it happened as He went to Jerusalem that He passed through the midst of Samaria and Galilee. Then as He entered a certain village, there met Him ten men who were lepers, who stood afar off. And they lifted up their voices and said, "Jesus, Master, have mercy on us!"

So when He saw them, He said to them, "Go, show yourselves to the priests." And so it was that as they went, they were cleansed.

—*Luke 17:11-14*

Back then, the priest was the trusted authority who could confirm that someone had been healed. The priest was the one would tell you when you were healthy enough to be in community. So when Jesus sent the lepers to the priest, part of what He was really telling them was, "Go and get confirmation that you are healed so that your testimony will be stronger than just giving your side of a story." The lepers had to trust that their healing would materialize as they went to get proof of verification!

If you say, "I got healed," but you can't prove it, the strength of your testimony is limited. Staunch atheists are not going to accept your subjective comment that you "feel better" as proof that Jesus is real. But when you have *medical evidence,* scientific proof, that Jesus has healed you, your testimony becomes unstoppable.

There is a growing movement of people in the church who seek to evaluate claims of Christian healing with the same standard of objective evidence required to publish medical data in a peer-reviewed scientific journal. The Global Medical Research Institute[208] is leading the charge.

What would the scientific community do if the church presented verifiable, testable evidence that Jesus heals? How many conversations would that open up about the reality of heaven and hell, even with people who don't *want* to believe that Jesus is real? What if we were able to *show the world* that Jesus really heals, instead of just trying to convince the world that He wants to?

---

[208] https://www.globalmri.org/. The Global Medical Research reviews evidenced-based testimonies from various ministries applying rigorous methods of research to show the effects of "proximal intercessory prayer" in the resolution of conditions that would otherwise typically have a poor prognosis.

If you need healing, go to the doctor *before* receiving prayer. Get medical documentation of your condition, along with what doctors say is required for healing to take place. Once you get healed, go to the doctor *after* receiving prayer too. Get medical documentation of your healing. You will have a record that God has just done what science says is impossible!

Do you remember Amanda's story from Chapter 4, "Do You Want to Be Healed?" Amanda received an amazing miracle. Her left leg grew out *six inches* in front of our eyes. So what did she do? She went to her doctor to *test the results.* She walked into the doctor's office and didn't tell her doctor a thing—she just asked him to measure her legs! They were *even,* and he was in shock because he had been treating her his whole life!

This is the equivalent of the Old Testament priest pronouncing someone clean. Now Amanda has a testimony that is *confirmed by medical evidence* so that no one can ever point a finger and say that it didn't happen!

GMRI recently published an article in a scientific journal that tells the story of a man healed from gastroparesis.[209] This man was hospitalized as an infant at two weeks of age. He had a feeding tube installed in his body and *could not eat solid food* for sixteen years. His family was Christian, but described themselves as cessationists (i.e., they did not believe that God still works miracles).

But one day, they attended a Pentecostal church. A healing evangelist was speaking, who told the story of his own miraculous healing after a massive truck fell on his abdomen and severed his intestines. While the preacher was telling his story, the man (then a teenager) "felt a pulsating sensation in his abdominal region." After the sermon, he and

[209] Gomez, C., Zaritsky, D. & Brown, J. "Case report of gastroparesis healing: 16 years of a chronic syndrome resolved after proximal intercessory prayer," *Complementary therapies in Medicine* 43, (2019): 289-294.

the evangelist spoke. They bonded instantly because of all the surgeries each of them had experienced. And when the evangelist laid hands on the boy, he felt "a shock starting from his right shoulder going down in a diagonal angle across his abdomen."[210] That night, he ate a meal for the first time in sixteen years without any complications. He continues to eat solid food to this day.

What makes this testimony so powerful is that there is *scientific proof* that healing took place. The patient went and saw his pediatric gastroenterologist, who had been seeing him for sixteen years and was intimately acquainted with his condition. The doctor *verified* that "symptoms had resolved," which is a very scientific way of saying that he was completely and totally healed! So now, whenever someone asks, this man has *proof* that God healed him! And whenever the scientific community doubts that Jesus is the Healer, this story stands in stark contrast to that claim.

So, have you been healed? Go and show yourself to the doctor. Do you know someone who has been healed? Encourage him or her to go get medical confirmation of their results! If we want the rest of the world to take our claim that Jesus heals seriously, we have to meet them where they are and prove it.

If You Believe

Jesus will show healing to unbelievers to prove He is real. But what if you already believe?

If you are already Christian, it's time to make a choice. Knowing what God's Word says about Jesus as the Healer, will you make a deliberate determination to believe what His Word says? The longer you've been a Christian, the stronger the tendency is to settle into *powerless Christianity*.

---

[210] Gomez, Zaritsky & Brown, "Case report of gastroparesis healing," 291.

We get comfortable coming to church and going home the same. We lose our hunger for miracles over time!

The people of Israel had the same problem. Do you remember when Moses sent spies into Canaan to survey the Promised Land? They came back with a *good report*. God "showed them the fruit of the land" (Deut. 13:26). They found a cluster of grapes that was so big that they needed to carry it between two of the men on a pole (Deut. 13:23). God was truly about to take His people into a land flowing with "milk and honey" (Deut. 13:27)!

But there was one problem. There were enemies in the Promised Land. The descendants of Anak were there (v 28). The Amalekites, Hittites, Jebusites, and Amorites (v 29) all stood in their way! And because the children of Israel faced some obstacles between them and their destiny, they *forgot about God's faithfulness*. They forgot about God's power! So instead of charging into the Promised Land based on the good report, they chickened out:

> *But the men who had gone up with him said, "We are not able to go up against the people, for they are stronger than we." And they gave the children of Israel a bad report of the land which they had spied out, saying, "The land through which we have gone as spies is a land that devours its inhabitants, and all the people whom we saw in it are men of great stature. There we saw the giants (the descendants of Anak came from the giants); and we were like grasshoppers in our own sight, and so we were in their sight."* —Numbers 13:31-33

I wonder how many times you and I have failed to take hold of the promises of God because we focus on the obstacles instead of the opportunity at hand. Jesus is the Healer, and He wants to show us healing! But we choose to believe *negative reports* over His Word.

I don't know about you, but God has done some amazing things in my life! But as many times as I have seen Him heal, I still have to deal with a nagging voice almost every time I go to pray for someone who needs a miracle. *What if God doesn't do it?*

But we should focus on the *opposite question*. *What if He does do it?* What if someone's life is dramatically changed because you had the courage to pray for them without thinking about what might happen if nothing happened! And what if that person gave his or her life to Jesus because it was the first time in their life that they saw the power of God?

God has moved in your life before. I know He has! But Scripture warns us in advance that when we face impossible odds, we tend to forget that we serve the God of the impossible.[211] We forget to remember what God has already done in our lives:

> *"So it shall be, when the Lord your God brings you into the land of which He swore to your fathers, to Abraham, Isaac, and Jacob, to give you large and beautiful cities which you did not build, houses full of all good things, which you did not fill, hewn-out wells which you did not dig, vineyards and olive trees which you did not plant—when you have eaten and are full—then beware, lest you forget the Lord who brought you out of the land of Egypt, from the house of bondage."* —Deuteronomy 6:10-12

God has done amazing things in your life. He has healed you! He has saved you! He has delivered you and made you free. But if you want to see Him do it again, you have to *remember and celebrate* everything He has already done.

It's time to ask God to help you remember all the amazing things He has done in your life. You don't need another miracle to know He is

---

[211] "For with God nothing will be impossible." —Lk. 1:37

God! You need to declare He is God to see another miracle. And as you celebrate all the many ways God has already moved, He will move again.

You Can Do It Too

I'm glad you're reading this book. But if you believe that Jesus heals, now you need an *outlet*. You need a forum to convert your faith into action.

Every time I conduct training for our Healing Rooms, I ask our new volunteers why they signed up for training. At our last training session, a woman named Martha told me she signed up because, "I believe Jesus is the Healer. He is the great physician!" I prodded a little: "But how do you know?" I wanted to see if her statement was based on hope or experience.

She told me that she had been suffering for over one year with muscle spasms before she came to our Healing Rooms for prayer. She was instantly healed as one of our volunteers laid hands on her. "That's how I know," she said. I nodded in agreement. As I took a survey of everyone else in the room, I found that nine out of ten people were there for training because Jesus had healed them. They had an *experience* where they encountered the Healer, and now they wanted the theology to back it up! They wanted an outlet to pray so Jesus could do for others what He had already done for them.

And Jesus will do the same with you. He heals to prove that He is real. And if you want to show the world that Jesus is real, I believe one of the *best ways* to do it is by showing the world that He heals.

CHAPTER FIFTEEN

WHOM DOES GOD HEAL?

I'm going to start this chapter with a bold statement.

I believe God's will is to heal *all* His children *all* the time.

Now here is why that statement is so bold. If you're like me, you have prayed for people who haven't been healed. You've seen people who have never recovered from an ailment. And our typical yet unfortunate response is to adjust our theology to match our life experience, instead of asking God to elevate our life experience to match His Word! When we go through something in life that doesn't line up with the Word of God, we assume that God's Word must not be true.

But what if God's Word is true, and your life experience is the lie?[212] What if you have an adversary, Satan, whose very job is to try to convince you not to believe in God's Word?

Wouldn't it make so much more sense to take God at His Word and ask Him to give you a life that matches what you see in His Word, instead of downgrading your theology to match the negative experiences you've gone through? Wouldn't it be so much better to learn from the life of Jesus, and ask God to give you a life that matches His?

Jesus Heals All

Here is what I see in the life of Jesus: Jesus healed *all* who 1) came to Him or 2) were brought to Him. But don't just take my word for it:

---

[212] "Indeed, let God be true but every man a liar." —Rom. 3:4

> *When evening had come, they brought to Him many who were*
> *demon-possessed. And He cast out the spirits with a word, and*
> *healed all who were sick, that it might be fulfilled which was spoken*
> *by Isaiah the prophet, saying: 'He Himself took our infirmities and*
> *bore our sicknesses.'"* —Matthew 8:16-17, emphasis added

Verse 16 says that Jesus healed "all" who were sick. Jesus healing "all" was the prophetic fulfillment of Isaiah's promise that we read about in Chapter One.[213]

All means *all*. If Jesus only healed *some*, Scripture would say so. But Scripture says that Jesus healed *all*. So you must make a very careful deliberation here. If you refuse to believe that Jesus healed *all*, you are refusing to take God at His Word. You can reject God's Word. He gives you that choice! But let's not agree to live a powerless life because we don't believe God's Word, but then pretend that we do.

Now, there are those who maintain that "all" doesn't really mean "all." The Greek word for "all" in the original text is *pas*. Strong's concordance lists the definition as "each, every, any, all, the whole, everyone, all things, [and] everything." [214] But even in the margins of Strong's concordance there is a caveat of doubt, taken from Charles Spurgeon's sermon called "Particular Redemption" in 1858:

> Does the whole world there mean everybody? The words
> "world" and "all" are used in some seven or eight senses in
> Scripture, and it is very rarely the "all" means all persons,
> taken individually. The words are generally used to signify

---

[213] "Surely He has borne our griefs and carried our sorrows; yet we esteemed Him stricken, smitten by God, and afflicted." —Isa. 53:4

[214] "G3956 - pas - Strong's Greek Lexicon (KJV)." Blue Letter Bible. Accessed 11 Aug, 2020. https://www.blueletterbible.org//lang/lexicon/lexicon.cfm?Strongs=G3956&t=KJV

that Christ has redeemed some of all sorts— some Jews, some Gentiles, some rich, some poor, and has not restricted His redemption to either Jew or Gentile ..." [215]

Even the writer of the concordance entry is hedging his bets! He does not bother to explain that, in proper context, Spurgeon is elaborating on Calvinism versus Arminianism and the subject of predestination, as opposed to physical healing. Spurgeon was saying that Jesus will not save "all" souls, because some souls will not want to be saved and will not receive Him. He is making no comment on Jesus' willingness or ability to heal, but rather our willingness to receive healing. So the reader is left confused. Did Jesus heal *all*, or did He not?

But we know better. The same Greek word *pas* is also used in Galatians 3:22 to define that *every human being* needs Jesus:

> But the Scripture has confined all under sin, that the promise by faith
> in Jesus Christ might be given to those who believe.
> —*Galatians 3:22, emphasis added*

And then the same word is used again to explain that *everyone* who calls on the name of Jesus is saved:

> "For you are all sons of God through faith in Christ Jesus."
> —*Galatians 3:26, emphasis added*

So why do we so quickly concede that "all" means "all" when it comes to salvation, but claim that "all" only means "some" when it comes to

---

[215] Eric W. Hayden, *Spurgeon on Revival: A Pattern for Evangelism Today* (City: Publisher, year), 110.

healing? Why do we refuse to believe that Jesus is good to all His people all the time?

Here we see the inextricable link between healing and salvation yet again. Healing and salvation happened on the same day![216] Jesus made provision for *both* when He died two thousand years ago on the cross. And if you receive one, yet fail to receive the other, you have not yet received everything that Jesus died for you to have.

Every Scripture verse that shows Jesus healing illustrates this same principle that "all" means "all" when it comes to Jesus' willingness and ability to heal:

> *When the sun was setting, all those who had any that were sick with various diseases brought them to Him; and He laid His hands on every one of them and healed them. And demons also came out of many, crying out and saying, "You are the Christ, the Son of God!" And He, rebuking them, did not allow them to speak, for they knew that He was the Christ.* —*Luke 4:40-41, emphasis added*

> *Then Jesus went about all the cities and villages, teaching in their synagogues, preaching the gospel of the kingdom, and healing every sickness and every disease among the people.* —*Matthew 9:35, emphasis added*

> *But when Jesus knew it, He withdrew from there. And great multitudes followed Him, and He healed them all.* —*Matthew 12:15, emphasis added*

---

[216] Please see Chapter One and the discussion on Isaiah 53 for a full analysis of this statement.

And the whole multitude sought to touch Him, for power went out
from Him and healed them all.   —*Luke 6:19, emphasis added*

[H]ow God anointed Jesus of Nazareth with the Holy Spirit and with
power, who went about doing good and healing all who were oppressed
by the devil, for God was with Him.   —*Acts 10:38, emphasis added*

Notice in these verses that Jesus not only healed "all" people, He also healed "every" type of disease (Matt. 9:35)! The manner of your affliction does not intimidate Jesus! He doesn't care if you have cancer or a common cold. He doesn't care if your doctor says your condition is terminal, or if the world says you have a fighting chance. His response to what ails you is always the same: He heals!

The Whole World

Now there is an important distinction to note as we discuss who received healing from Jesus. Jesus *did not* heal the whole world. He made *healing provision* for the whole world. But He healed "all" who *came to Him*.[217]

This is extremely important. Because the immediate argument to the statement "Jesus heals all," is, "Well then why are there people in the world who are still sick?" And the answer is, "Because many of them haven't come to Jesus for healing." Maybe they've given Him their heart, but they still haven't had the revelation that Jesus heals and given Him their body! There is more of His presence to enjoy. There is more of His healing to receive! There is always more intimacy with Jesus to be experienced.

In Matt. 12:15, Jesus healed those who "followed Him." In Luke 6:19, He healed those who "sought to touch Him." Those who were healed

---

[217] Or, in the case of Matt. 8:16, above, He healed those who were "brought to Him."

first had to *seek* Jesus. They had to know He was the Healer and follow Him!

And this is what makes your mission so absolutely critical. There are people all over the world—many of whom are already *in your church*—who aren't convinced Jesus is the Healer. *And you get to tell them.* In Matt 8:16 and Luke 4:40, Jesus healed those who were "brought to Him." From this moment forward, that is your role—to bring people who have not heard that Jesus heals directly to Him.

If Jesus healed "all" then, He heals all now. His will has not changed.[218] Our problem, then, is not that He no longer heals! It is that we have stopped *coming to Him* for healing. We have stopped *placing a demand* on His anointing to heal.

I have nothing against medicine, but we should never go to medicine for healing before we go to Jesus. I *love* doctors! But we should never go to a doctor for healing before we go to Jesus. I eat a healthy diet and exercise *all the time*. But none of that is a substitute for sitting at the feet of my Divine Physician every day.

When Jesus walked the earth, few medical options were available for healing. People sought Jesus because they had no other choice—they could either be healed by Him, or they could die! But now we live in a world *full of choices*. And unfortunately many of us have chosen to seek someone or something else for our healing.

Have you ever wondered why miracles are so hard to come by in the United States, yet they seem to pop like popcorn on the mission field? I witness this phenomenon whenever we take a team to Guatemala. Church members who have never laid hands on the sick all of a sudden start seeing miracles overnight!

One of the women on our most recent trip to Guatemala named Leslie had never seen anyone healed when she prayed. So she was

---

[218] "Jesus Christ is the same yesterday, today, and forever." —Heb. 13:8

understandably anxious when, on the first night of our week-long trip, the preacher opened up the altar for prayer, promised that Jesus was going to heal, and invited his "American friends" to come forward and pray for the sick.

Leslie took her position at the front of the sanctuary and turned to face the congregation. An older woman limped straight to Leslie, guided by several ushers from the church. She spoke no English and broken Spanish. She looked up at the ceiling and avoided eye contact as she asked Leslie to pray for her leg in Spanish, pointing to the leg that was causing her limp.

Leslie spoke Spanish, so she knew what was expected of her. And she was terrified! What if nothing happened when she prayed? But she didn't have time to think, so she started declaring God's Word over that woman. She thanked God out loud that His Holy Spirit was in her. She knew all she had to do to exercise the Creative Power Formula[219] was to release the Word of God over this woman and expect creation to take shape according to God's command.

As Leslie was praying, the old woman latched onto her arm. She started to shake her leg. A smile crept across her face. She put all her weight back on the leg that had been causing her limp. She was healed! The woman was in shock. The ushers were in shock! Leslie was in shock! So she grabbed that woman's hands and started jumping up and down at the altar, "[L]eaping and praising God" (Acts 3:8).

But God wasn't done. Now the old woman was filled with faith. She wanted more! She explained to Leslie that she had cataracts in her eyes that made her legally blind. Leslie realized that was why she hadn't made eye contact earlier. So, Leslie, filled with faith, started declaring the Word of God over her again. And that blind eye opened right up. The old woman saw! She looked Leslie right in the eyes and smiled. Then

---

[219] See Chapter 9.

she told the ushers what had happened. And then she and Leslie started jumping up and down all over again!

Do you see what can happen when you release the Word of God over bodies that need to be healed? Do you see what can transpire when you embrace this revelation that God wants to heal *all* of His children *all* the time? Leslie could have convinced herself that maybe God didn't want to heal this woman. Maybe today wasn't her day. Maybe Leslie wasn't anointed enough to heal. She could have been praying in doubt instead of by faith! But instead she took God at His Word and charged right into miracle territory, and that woman was miraculously healed in front of the whole church as a result.

Your level of experience doesn't matter. Your tenure in ministry is irrelevant! You are filled with the Spirit of the Living God and you are armed with His Word. And all you need to do is release His Word over broken bodies to see them completely healed.

So why is it that miracles seem to happen so quickly overseas? It's because we think we're so smart in the West! We think that having more treatment options makes us more likely to be healed. Did you know that the more education you have, the *less likely* you are to believe in miracles?[220] Having more information and options doesn't automatically make you any more likely to be healed! But *knowing Jesus more does.*

Jesus Is Willing

The level of healing you experience in your life and in your ministry will depend on what you decide to believe about divine healing. Will you spend your whole life wondering if God heals and waiting for Him to

---

[220] Barna Group. "Most Americans Believe in Supernatural Healing." (Sep. 29, 2016). https://www.barna.com/research/americans-believe-supernatural-healing/

prove it to you? Or will you first make a determination to believe that He is the Healer, and let the proof accumulate in the wake of that choice?

Matthew describes a leper coming to Jesus. He is plagued not only by disease, but also by the same question that may be plaguing you as you read this book: Does Jesus really heal?

> *When He had come down from the mountain, great multitudes followed Him. And behold, a leper came and worshiped Him, saying, "Lord, if You are willing, You can make me clean."*
>
> —*Matthew 8:1-2*

Lord, *if* You are willing. Was Jesus willing to heal? Would He be able to heal? But look at Jesus' swift and decisive response:

> *Then Jesus put out His hand and touched him, saying, "I am willing; be cleansed." Immediately his leprosy was cleansed.* —*Matthew 8:3*

Jesus didn't leave the leper hanging. He didn't leave him in doubt! He didn't send him home and tell him to come back another day. He met this man where he was with the healing he needed. "I am willing," He said. "Be cleansed." And "immediately" the man was healed.

This leper had every right to ask Jesus if He was willing to heal. Why? Because there was no written record of Jesus' healing ministry at that time. But you and I have *lost the right* to wonder if Jesus heals. Why? Because Jesus already answered the leper's question—not only with words, but with *action*.

If you want to be healed, you have to understand that Jesus is *willing*. That is a critical first step in your healing process, but it is an unavoidable foundation upon which you must build. For if you know Jesus wants to heal you more than you want to be healed, what else can stand in your way?

Do I Deserve Sickness?

Sometimes when we see sick people, we think they *deserve* what they are going through. Have you ever heard about someone passing away and immediately wondered what they were up to? *Was he drinking too much? Smoking too much? Cheating on his wife? What was he doing to make God strike him down like that in his prime?*

This is known as the "punishment concept" of disease. Janell Carroll defines this as "the idea that people who [have] become infected with certain diseases . . . did something wrong and are being punished."[221] Carroll notes that, especially for those who have contracted AIDS or another sexually transmitted infection (i.e., illnesses associated with shame), other people tend to judge them and assume they "got what they deserved." Loretta Kopelman suggests that this is a defense mechanism we employ to justify ourselves. [222] If we believe someone is sick because they deserve it as a consequence of their behavior, we tell ourselves that we are safe as long as we don't engage in whatever they were doing!

But this attitude is simply not biblical. Your healing has nothing to do with your behavior. It has everything to do with your faith![223] Do you remember when Job's friends assumed he was going through

---

[221] Janell L. Carroll, *Sexuality Now: Embracing Diversity* (New York, NY: Cengage Learning) Kindle Edition, 392.

[222] L. Kopelman, "The punishment concept of disease." *AIDS, ethics, and public policy.* C. Pierce & D. Vandeveer (Eds.), (Belmont, CA: Wadsworth, 1988).

[223] "But let him ask in faith, with no doubting, for he who doubts is like a wave of the sea driven and tossed by the wind." —Jas. 1:6

tragedy because he deserved it?[224] And do you remember God's response?

> *And so it was, after the Lord had spoken these words to Job, that the Lord said to Eliphaz the Temanite, "My wrath is aroused against you and your two friends, for you have not spoken of Me what is right, as My servant Job has."*　　　　　　　　　　　　—Job 42:7

In the theological construct, this type of thinking is known as "retribution theology."[225] If we get sick, we assume that God is punishing us for something we have done. But Jesus spoke against this:

> *Or those eighteen on whom the tower in Siloam fell and killed them, do you think that they were worse sinners than all other men who dwelt in Jerusalem? I tell you, no; but unless you repent you will all likewise perish."*　　　　　　　　　　　　—Luke 13:4-5

You didn't get sick because you were a "worse sinner!" Sickness exists because we are *all sinners.* And the remedy to sickness is not good behavior. It is not pointing a finger at someone who is sick, assuming they deserve it, and trying to avoid what they do! The *only answer* is to come to Jesus and ask Him to do what only He can do—*heal.*

Do I Deserve Healing?

Bartimaeus was a man who didn't "deserve" healing:

---

[224] See Job chapters 4-23
[225] See pages 28 and 34.

Now they came to Jericho. As He went out of Jericho with His disciples and a great multitude, blind Bartimaeus, the son of Timaeus, sat by the road begging. And when he heard that it was Jesus of Nazareth, he began to cry out and say, "Jesus, Son of David, have mercy on me!"

Then many warned him to be quiet . . .   —*Mark 10:46-48a*

As far as everyone around him was concerned, blind Bartimaeus had no right to call out to Jesus. They told him to be quiet! They hushed him. Who did this lowly beggar think he was, calling out to Jesus without an invitation?!

But Bartimaeus didn't care what other people thought:

...but he cried out all the more, "Son of David, have mercy on me!"
     —*Mark 10:48b*

And you shouldn't care what other people think either! Because when you "cry out all the more," Jesus responds to your passionate faith:

So Jesus stood still and commanded him to be called.

Then they called the blind man, saying to him, "Be of good cheer. Rise, He is calling you."

And throwing aside his garment, he rose and came to Jesus.

So Jesus answered and said to him, "What do you want Me to do for you?"

The blind man said to Him, "Rabboni, that I may receive my sight."

Then Jesus said to him, "Go your way; your faith has made you well." And immediately he received his sight and followed Jesus on the road. —Mark 10:49-52

Do not let other people quiet you in your quest for healing, because even as other people try to shush you, Jesus will reward you for crying out. He will reward you for *persistent faith*, whether other people say you "deserve" healing or not.

Do you remember the Gentile woman from Canaan who pursued Jesus for healing? At first, Jesus paid her no mind:

Then Jesus went out from there and departed to the region of Tyre and Sidon. And behold, a woman of Canaan came from that region and cried out to Him, saying, "Have mercy on me, O Lord, Son of David! My daughter is severely demon-possessed."

But He answered her not a word.

And His disciples came and urged Him, saying, "Send her away, for she cries out after us." —Matthew 15:21-23

This woman didn't *deserve* healing! She was a Gentile, and Jesus was only sent to the Jews. She wasn't one of God's people, so Jesus framed His response to her accordingly:

But He answered and said, "I was not sent except to the lost sheep of the house of Israel." —Matthew 15:24

241

But look at this woman's persistent response:

> *Then she came and worshiped Him, saying, "Lord, help me!"*
>
> *But He answered and said, "It is not good to take the children's bread and throw it to the little dogs."*
>
> *And she said, "Yes, Lord, yet even the little dogs eat the crumbs which fall from their masters' table."* —Matthew 15:25-27

She knew other people would say she didn't "deserve" healing because of her background! Even Jesus reminded her that she was not one of God's chosen people. But *she didn't care.* She continued to pursue Jesus with passionate faith; and before she went home, she got what she came for that day:

> *Then Jesus answered and said to her, "O woman, great is your faith! Let it be to you as you desire." And her daughter was healed from that very hour.* —Matthew 15:28

How many of us give up right away when Jesus "answers us not a word" (v. 23)? But this woman learned a powerful lesson. When it seems like healing isn't happening and God is not hearing your cries, that is *not* the time to withdraw and walk away! That is the time to press in and pursue God for your healing more than ever before.

You Don't Deserve It

Here is the truth of the matter: *No one* deserves healing. I don't! And neither do you. We are all sinful *messes* when left to our own devices:

[F]or all have sinned and fall short of the glory of God.

—Romans 3:23

Yet Jesus *gave it to us* all the same. Of course you're not worthy of healing! But this is the gospel.

You don't deserve to be healed, just as you don't deserve to be saved! But Jesus died on the cross—He took what you "deserve" —so that you can receive the reward that only He deserves:

> *[W]ho Himself bore our sins in His own body on the tree, that we, having died to sins, might live for righteousness—by whose stripes you were healed.*   *—1 Peter 2:24*

Healing is for you, just as much as salvation is for you. Healing is for today, just as much as salvation is for today! So why not you? And why not now?

Whom Does God Use to Heal?

Maybe you've already accepted that God is the Healer. Maybe you're convinced that He heals, but you haven't seen Him heal through you. Now I want to encourage you to take a bold step of faith. If you already believe God heals, now it's time to accept the truth that God will *use you* to *heal others*.

I love reading about Jesus' disciples. I think we are supposed to read their stories in Scripture and think, "God could do the same thing with me!" We should read about the disciples and be overwhelmed with excitement because the same Holy Spirit who lived in them lives in us!

It's notable to me that Jesus' disciples were a rag-tag band of men who had *zero* formal theological education. They hadn't been to Bible school! I promise you they didn't have PhDs in New Testament theology because the New Testament hadn't been written yet. But despite their lack of formal training, God used them *powerfully*. They had the "one thing"[226] that matters most: the presence of Jesus!

The Holy Spirit used Philip powerfully:

> *Therefore those who were scattered went everywhere preaching the word. Then Philip went down to the city of Samaria and preached Christ to them. And the multitudes with one accord heeded the things spoken by Philip, hearing and seeing the miracles which he did. For unclean spirits, crying with a loud voice, came out of many who were possessed; and many who were paralyzed and lame were healed. And there was great joy in that city.* — Acts 8:4-8

He used Peter powerfully:

> *And believers were increasingly added to the Lord, multitudes of both men and women, so that they brought the sick out into the streets and laid them on beds and couches, that at least the shadow of Peter passing by might fall on some of them.* —Acts 5:14-15

The *only special thing* about these men was that they had been with Jesus[227] and they had His Holy Spirit. And if you call yourself a Christian, you meet those same qualifications. You have access to His presence in prayer! And you are filled with His Holy Spirit.

Scripture says that healing will follow "those who believe:"

---

[226] "But one thing is needed, and Mary has chosen that good part, which will not be taken away from her." —Lk. 10:42

[227] "Now when they saw the boldness of Peter and John, and perceived that they were uneducated and untrained men, they marveled. And they realized that they had been with Jesus." —Acts 4:13

"And these signs will follow those who believe: In My name they will cast out demons; they will speak with new tongues; they will take up serpents; and if they drink anything deadly, it will by no means hurt them; they will lay hands on the sick, and they will recover."

—Mark 16:17-18

Anyone who believes can lay hands on the sick and they will recover. The disciples proved it so that you could follow in their footsteps. And centuries later, you are the answer to the disciples' prayer:

Then He said to His disciples, "The harvest truly is plentiful, but the laborers are few. Therefore pray the Lord of the harvest to send out laborers into His harvest."   *—Matthew 9:37-38*

You are the laborer Jesus prayed would go out into His harvest! *You* are God's chosen vessel to bring salvation to the lost, and healing to the sick! *You*—yes, little old you!—are the best weapon God has in His sovereign plan to bring His presence to the world.

By now you know that God heals. And now you know that you are the one He has been looking for to heal His people. So what's stopping you from praying in faith that everyone around you will be healed? The question is no longer, "Why would God use me?" It is instead, "Why *wouldn't* He use me?" And I, for one, don't have a good answer to that question. He will use you because you were born for such a time as this.[228]

Do you remember when Jesus could do "no mighty work" in Nazareth?[229] Your Nazareth is *in your own mind.* You talk yourself out

---

[228] "For if you remain completely silent at this time, relief and deliverance will arise for the Jews from another place, but you and your father's house will perish. Yet who knows whether you have come to the kingdom for such a time as this?" —Est. 4:14

[229] "Now He could do no mighty work there, except that He laid His hands

of a miracle before God can do anything! You know where you've been! You know what you've done, and you are your biggest critic. Jesus didn't have to deal with a guilty conscience! And neither should you. If you want to see healing happen everywhere you go, you are going to have to accept the reality that your résumé—whether it's *great* or whether it's *terrible* —does not matter when it comes to being used by God.

When you believe that God can use you, He will. God uses those who are available, regardless of their qualifications. And it's time for you to step up and accept His calling for your life.

---

on a few sick people and healed them." —Mk. 6:5

CHAPTER SIXTEEN

WHATEVER IT TAKES

The most miraculous healings I've ever witnessed have happened when I'm the most desperate I've ever been. Almost exactly five years ago, we had a young couple stop by our church with their newborn baby. She wasn't more than three weeks old. They came up after Sunday service holding their baby, and told me what was going on.

Their daughter Sarah had been diagnosed with biliary atresia several weeks after birth. Biliary atresia is a rare disease of the liver that blocks bile flow from the liver to the gallbladder. If the disease is not addressed immediately, the end result will be severe liver damage and eventually liver failure. Doctors had told them their daughter would likely need a liver transplant to overcome this rare disease. Even if a transplant happened, the doctors promised the parents that she would have a drastically shortened lifespan.

As the parents told me about their precious daughter's medical condition, we all wept. But I also made a silent determination in my heart: *Lord, I am willing to do whatever it takes to see a miracle here.* Before we prayed, I looked Sarah's parents in the eyes, and said, "Whatever happens when we pray, know this: We are by your side, whatever it takes for a miracle to happen."

I prayed my best prayer in that moment, but nothing happened. I was discouraged, and so were Sarah's parents, but I reiterated my promise to them that we would keep praying and doing whatever the Holy Spirit asked us to do until a miracle happened.

The next week, they came back. We prayed after service, just as we had the week before. *Nothing happened.* I had seen plenty of miracles happen as we prayed at the altar! But in this case, it seemed like we were coming up emptyhanded, again and again.

In the coming weeks, I prayed for Sarah every chance I could get. I kept asking the Lord, "What am I missing here?" You see, sometimes we can actually be the roadblock to healing because we think God is going to heal the same way we've seen Him heal before. But what He asks from us most of all is an open, receptive heart that is ready to hear what the Holy Spirit is whispering, and a determined will that is ready to follow His instructions.

About six weeks later, Sarah's parents got good news. They had found a liver for a transplant. But something still wasn't settled in my heart. The parents scheduled the surgery, but I met with them and asked for their permission to continue to pray and believe that a surgery wasn't going to be required. I believed that Sarah was going to be supernaturally healed.

In the next week, I tried everything I could think of in prayer. I recited every healing prayer model I had ever heard. I stayed up and prayed for Sarah late at night, and woke up and prayed for her early in the morning. I asked her parents to bring Sarah to the church during the week and we all prayed and took Communion. I had our entire Healing Rooms staff praying for her! I didn't know exactly how her healing was going to happen, but I knew I was willing to do whatever it took to see it come to pass.

The surgery was scheduled for a Tuesday. On the Sunday before the surgery, Sarah still hadn't been healed. With her parents' permission, I informed our church congregation what was going on. Everyone in attendance at service stretched out their hands towards Sarah and we prayed in faith that God would move in the eleventh hour. I asked the parents to keep me updated if anything changed before the surgery. I wanted to have faith for Sarah to be healed, but I didn't want to derail their hope for a successful surgery.

On Monday morning, I got a call from Sarah's dad. "You're not going to believe this," he said. I dropped to my knees in anticipation. I didn't know what I was about to hear, but I knew it was going to be good news!

Sarah and her parents had gone to the hospital to prep for surgery the next day. Doctors had told them they would run some last-minute tests. And do you know what the doctors found? *Nothing.* Nothing! All of Sarah's bile ducts were perfect in every scan. The doctors were in shock. They told the parents they had *never* seen anything like it before.

The surgery was *completely canceled* one day before it was scheduled to happen. I've never been so happy in my life.

So what happened here? Did Sarah get prayer from someone so undeniably anointed that a miracle just had to happen? Hardly. Did God give me or her parents specific instructions as to what to do so she would be healed? I can't say that He did. The difference maker was that we decided to do *whatever it takes* to see Sarah healed. We *never gave up.* When God asked us to move, whether it was an inch-long adjustment or a mile-long leap of faith, we moved. And as a result, Sarah was healed.

Part of our calling as Christians is to stand side by side with people as they pursue their healing. We are to walk with people through pain and suffering with a steadfast commitment to do whatever God asks until healing happens. You are surrounded by people in your church and in your city who are *desperate* for healing. Will you make a commitment to walk with them and stay with them until healing happens, *whatever it takes?*

Press On

The apostle Paul made a decision. He was not Jesus. He was far from perfect! God still had work to do in him. So he made the choice to "press on":

*Not that I have already attained, or am already perfected; but I press
on, that I may lay hold of that for which Christ Jesus has also laid
hold of me.*   —*Philippians 3:12*

He knew that God had more for him to experience. And by this point in
our healing journey together, I'm hoping you've come to the same place.

Here is God's promise for you in Scripture when it comes to healing:

"[T]hey will lay hands on the sick, and they will recover."
                                                        —*Mark 16:18b*

Has every single person you've ever prayed for been healed? My guess
is, probably not. But that doesn't mean that God is no longer the Healer!
It means that you and I have *work to do*.[230] And I don't know about you,
but I have made up my mind that I am willing to do *whatever it takes* to
see people healed when I pray for them.

Whatever It Takes

For many years, the Old Testament prophet Elisha was "just" a servant.
Scripture says that Elisha "poured water on the hands of Elijah" (2 Kings
3:11). Whatever Elijah needed, Elisha took care of it.

But when Elijah passed away, Elisha inherited a "double portion"
of the anointing Elijah carried (2 Kings 2:9). Elijah had seen incredible
miracles! But God's promise to Elisha was that because of his persistent
service, he would see *double*.

We know Elisha for healing Naaman (2 Kings 5). We know him for
opening the eyes of his servant (2 Kings 6:17). But before Elisha moved

---

[230] Of course, by "work" here I mean yielding to the Holy Spirit more and
more every day, as opposed to putting forth effort in and of ourselves.

powerfully in the Lord, he had to demonstrate to God that he was willing to do *whatever it took* to see the miraculous unfold.

In 2 Kings 4, Elisha befriended a Shunammite woman. They developed such a friendship that "as often as he passed by, he would turn in there to eat some food" (2 Kings 4:8). This woman was so good to Elisha that he wanted to bless her back. He asked his servant Gehazi what he could do for her "and Gehazi answered, 'Actually, she has no son, and her husband is old'" (2 Kings 4:14). Elisha told the Shunammite woman she would have a son, and even though she couldn't even believe it, she conceived and gave birth.

But one day, out of nowhere, her son got very sick and died. So the Shunammite woman went straight to Elisha:

And so she departed, and went to the man of God at Mount Carmel.

So it was, when the man of God saw her afar off, that he said to his servant Gehazi, "Look, the Shunammite woman! Please run now to meet her, and say to her, 'Is it well with you? Is it well with your husband? Is it well with the child?' "

And she answered, "It is well." Now when she came to the man of God at the hill, she caught him by the feet, but Gehazi came near to push her away. But the man of God said, "Let her alone; for her soul is in deep distress, and the Lord has hidden it from me, and has not told me." —2 *Kings 4:25-27*

What I want you to see here is that God did not warn Elisha that something had happened to this woman's son. Elisha was just as surprised when the Shunammite woman came to him as you or I would have been. But he made an immediate, irreversible decision when he heard the news.

He decided to do *whatever it took* to make sure healing happened. He dropped what he was doing and pursued the will of God on behalf of the Shunammite woman and her family:

> *Then he said to Gehazi, "Get yourself ready, and take my staff in your hand, and be on your way. If you meet anyone, do not greet him; and if anyone greets you, do not answer him; but lay my staff on the face of the child."*

> *And the mother of the child said, "As the Lord lives, and as your soul lives, I will not leave you." So he arose and followed her. Now Gehazi went on ahead of them, and laid the staff on the face of the child; but there was neither voice nor hearing. Therefore he went back to meet him, and told him, saying, "The child has not awakened."*
> —*2 Kings 4:29-31*

First, Elisha sent Gehazi off ahead of him. He gave Gehazi his staff, hoping that if Gehazi laid the staff "on the face of the child " (v 29), he would be healed. But when Gehazi did as Elisha instructed, *nothing happened.*

What would you do in that situation? Would you turn around and go home? Would you give the Shunammite woman some well-thought-out theological argument that everyone has a time to die, and maybe it was just her son's time to go home? Well, that wasn't what Elisha did! Watch this:

> *When Elisha came into the house, there was the child, lying dead on his bed. He went in therefore, shut the door behind the two of them, and prayed to the Lord.*　　　　　—*2 Kings 4:32-33*

I believe Elisha's prayer went something like this: "Lord, what am I missing?" He had already tried the staff trick,[231] and it hadn't worked! So his next step was to check in with God and reiterate his holy determination to be used by God *however God required* to see healing happen. So God gave him instructions:

> *And he went up and lay on the child, and put his mouth on his mouth,*
> *his eyes on his eyes, and his hands on his hands; and he stretched*
> *himself out on the child, and the flesh of the child became warm.*
> —2 Kings 4:34

Finally Elisha saw some light at the end of the tunnel. The boy wasn't healed! But his flesh "became warm." So Elisha became more determined than ever:

> *He returned and walked back and forth in the house, and again went*
> *up and stretched himself out on him; then the child sneezed seven*
> *times, and the child opened his eyes.* —2 Kings 4:35

God rewarded Elisha's persistence! He rewarded his determination to seek God and do whatever He said, no matter how absolutely ridiculous it might seem. Imagine the uproar Elisha would have created if he had done what he did to that boy in this day and age? People would have ridiculed him and possibly even prosecuted him for putting his mouth on the mouth of the child and laying down on top of him! But what God said, Elisha did.

---

[231] "And you shall take this rod in your hand, with which you shall do the signs." —Ex. 4:17. Moses was Elisha's biblical precedent of someone who powerfully yielded a staff with miraculous results.

And he called Gehazi and said, "Call this Shunammite woman." So he called her. And when she came in to him, he said, "Pick up your son." So she went in, fell at his feet, and bowed to the ground; then she picked up her son and went out. —2 Kings 4:36-37

That boy was healed because Elisha made a deliberate decision as soon as he heard the news to do whatever it took to see him healed. He had no advance warning. God didn't give him a plan! But he ran *towards* the sickness instead of away from it. And when he arrived on the scene where healing was required, God told Elisha exactly what was required for healing to happen.

Now, if even a great Old Testament prophet like Elisha had to experiment and try some different things out for healing to happen, how much more will you? Every healing will look different. God is not a God of formula! You can't just lay your staff on everyone and have them healed. But when you make up your mind to stick around as long as it takes for healing to take place, God will use you.

If healing doesn't happen the first time you pray for someone, *don't back down!* Sometimes people are healed instantly! Sometimes healing takes some time.[232] But what's most important is that whenever you encounter resistance to healing, you decide to press in all the more.

Radical Desperation

Everyone who was healed in Scripture demonstrated a radical desperation to be healed.

When Jairus came to Jesus and asked Him to heal his daughter, he had exhausted all his options. As a "ruler" and a Jewish religious leader,

---

[232] Scripture delineates between "gifts of healings" (1 Cor. 12:9) and "the working of miracles" (1 Cor. 12:10). The implication is that while miracles are instantaneous, healing often takes time.

he was supposed to have all the answers![233] But when sickness hit under his own roof, he had no idea what to do. So he sacrificed his pride and came to Jesus:

> *While He spoke these things to them, behold, a ruler came and worshiped Him, saying, "My daughter has just died, but come and lay Your hand on her and she will live." So Jesus arose and followed him, and so did His disciples.* —Matthew 9:18-19

When the woman with the issue of blood stopped Jesus on His way to Jairus' house, she risked her very life. Had she been caught as an "unclean" person in public, she would have been killed! But she was desperate to come into contact with the Healer:

> *And suddenly, a woman who had a flow of blood for twelve years came from behind and touched the hem of His garment. For she said to herself, "If only I may touch His garment, I shall be made well." But Jesus turned around, and when He saw her He said, "Be of good cheer, daughter; your faith has made you well." And the woman was made well from that hour.* —Matthew 9:20-22

When a blind man named Bartimaeus heard Jesus passing by, he cried out:

> *Now they came to Jericho. As He went out of Jericho with His disciples and a great multitude, blind Bartimaeus, the son of Timaeus, sat by the road begging. And when he heard that it was Jesus of Nazareth,*

---

[233] "And behold, one of the rulers of the synagogue came, Jairus by name." —Mk. 5:22

he began to cry out and say, "Jesus, Son of David, have mercy on me!"

Then many warned him to be quiet; but he cried out all the more, "Son of David, have mercy on me!" — Mk. 10:46-48

People told him to keep it appropriate. To be quiet! Why should he expect the Prophet to stop for him? But he cried out all the more. And God rewarded his insistence on getting his healing, *no matter the cost:*

So Jesus answered and said to him, "What do you want Me to do for you?"

The blind man said to Him, "Rabboni, that I may receive my sight."

Then Jesus said to him, "Go your way; your faith has made you well." And immediately he received his sight and followed Jesus on the road. —Mark 10:51-52

The "garment" Bartimaeus threw aside to get to Jesus (v 50) was his begging garment. Without it, he could not legally beg! Bartimaeus was making the desperate declaration that, because he had Jesus, he wouldn't need to beg anymore.

Healing Will Cost You Something

If you want to see healing in your ministry like never before, it is going to cost you something. It might cost you your pride like Jairus. It might cost you your safety and security like the woman with the issue of blood.

It might require you to toss aside an economic safety net like Bartimaeus! But I'm here to tell you that whatever it costs, *it is worth it.*

Healing is not free. It always *costs* something. It's true that, for us, the price for healing has been paid by the blood of Jesus:

> *[K]nowing that you were not redeemed with corruptible things, like silver or gold, from your aimless conduct received by tradition from your fathers, but with the precious blood of Christ, as of a lamb without blemish and without spot.* —1 Peter 1:18-19

Jesus didn't pay for your healing with something temporal like silver or gold. He purchased your healing with something infinitely more costly: His precious blood.

Jesus already paid the price! But you have to count the cost.[234] You have to position yourself for God's healing anointing to flow through you by living a life that prizes the sacrifice Jesus made for you on the cross. It's not that you're paying the price yourself, it's that you are *recognizing the value* of the price that has been paid and responding to His purchase.

What can you give God that you have never given Him before? Can you offer Him hours of your time like never before, sitting at His feet in the "secret place"?[235] Can you offer Him a reckless devotion to praying for the sick, no matter the resistance you face? Can you give Him a commitment to walk side by side with someone who desperately needs to be healed, but just doesn't have the faith to believe it will happen for

---

[234] "For which of you, intending to build a tower, does not sit down first and count the cost, whether he has enough to finish it . . . " —Lk. 14:28

[235] "But you, when you pray, go into your room, and when you have shut your door, pray to your Father who is in the secret place; and your Father who sees in secret will reward you openly." —Matt. 6:6

him or herself? Can you trust Him that His word is true, no matter how hard it is for you to believe? [236]

As you pursue healing at any cost, God will respond to your sacrifice.

God Responds to Sacrifice

All throughout Scripture, we see the pattern that God responds to sacrifice. When a plague was ripping through Israel, King David responded by making an offering to God:

> And Gad came that day to David and said to him, "Go up, erect an altar to the Lord on the threshing floor of Araunah the Jebusite." So David, according to the word of Gad, went up as the Lord commanded.   —2 Samuel 24:18-19

When Araunah saw David coming, he was willing to give David whatever he needed:

> Now Araunah said to David, "Let my lord the king take and offer up whatever seems good to him. Look, here are oxen for burnt sacrifice, and threshing implements and the yokes of the oxen for wood. All these, O king, Araunah has given to the king." And Araunah said to the king, "May the Lord your God accept you."
>   —2 Samuel 24:22-23

But David understood a principle that you and I should take to heart. If it's not *costly*, it's not a sacrifice.

---

[236] "Indeed, let God be true but every man a liar." —Rom. 3:4

Then the king said to Araunah, "No, but I will surely buy it from you for a price; nor will I offer burnt offerings to the Lord my God with that which costs me nothing." So David bought the threshing floor and the oxen for fifty shekels of silver. And David built there an altar to the Lord, and offered burnt offerings and peace offerings. So the Lord heeded the prayers for the land, and the plague was withdrawn from Israel. —2 Samuel 24:24-25

David gave a costly offering, and God responded by removing the disease that was ravaging the land. When it comes to healing, the sacrifice God expects you and me to offer Him is a life that is fully yielded to Jesus Christ.

Healing is not *easy* and it is not *convenient.* Jesus is looking for a body of believers who are willing to do *whatever it takes* for His will to come to pass on this earth.

CHAPTER SEVENTEEN

SPIRITUAL WEAPONS

D o you remember the story of the RMS *Titanic*? Construction of *Titanic* started in March, 1909 at the Harland and Wolff shipyard in Belfast, Ireland. Over two years later, on March 31, 1911, *Titanic* was complete. More than 100,000 people came to see the ship launched into the water. It was a magnificent sight, and *Titanic* was certainly the most elegant passenger ship the world had ever seen.

On April 10th, 1912, *Titanic* departed Southampton, England on its maiden voyage to New York City, carrying 2,240 passengers and crew. Many of those on board were "high-ranking officials, wealthy industrialists, dignitaries and celebrities."[237] Also on board was Thomas Andrews, the ship's builder and master architect.

Four uneventful days into what should have been a seven-day voyage, *Titanic*'s crew received sporadic reports of ice in the water from other ships nearby. The captain and crew saw nothing but calm, clear water, but at 11:30 p.m. a lookout spotted an iceberg straight ahead forming out of the haze above the water. The engines were reversed and the ship turned to avoid direct impact. The ship seemed to turn in time, barely grazing the side of the iceberg instead of hitting it straight on.

The captain and crew assumed they had avoided disaster. They celebrated what seemed to be a near miss on this great vessel that had

---

[237] "Titanic." *The History Channel* March 10, 2020. Retrieved from https://www.history.com/topics/early-20th-century-us/titanic

been dubbed "practically unsinkable" by *Shipbuilder* magazine.[238] They had no idea that the iceberg had a jagged and giant underwater spur, which unapologetically tore a 300-foot gash in the ship's hull.

The rest of the story is absolute tragedy. Once the gash was discovered and he assessed the damage, Thomas Andrews announced the ship would only remain afloat for several hours, to the shock and horror of everyone on board. Life boats were jettisoned from the ship less than half-full, leaving many women and children on board. Passengers who had safely escaped begged the captains of their lifeboats to turn back, but the captains refused out of fear they would be swamped by desperate passengers trapped in the icy waters.

Titanic plunged beneath the ocean's surface at 2:20 a.m. on April 15th, 1912. 1,517 of the ship's passengers and crew members lost their lives.

There were many reasons *Titanic* sank. But the most notable reason is the captain and crew had no way of telling what was *beneath the surface*. They were making decisions based on the information that was *visible*, because they had no way of telling what was going on underwater.[239] That is a huge problem because most of an iceberg's mass is located *below* the surface—approximately 90% according to the US Geological Survey.[240] If *Titanic*'s crew had had access to technology that would have allowed them to see what was happening underwater, the catastrophic loss of life would have been completely avoided.

Joseph Vadus was the leader of the team that discovered *Titanic*'s wreck in 1985. According to Vadus, "Using only lookouts, there wasn't enough time to veer the ship away from the iceberg. [But today], they

---

[238] "Titanic's Lost Sister." *PBS*. Originally aired January 28, 1997.

[239] Radar would not be invented until 1935, more than twenty years later.

[240] United States Geological Survey. (n.d.). "Ninety percent of an iceberg is below the waterline." Retrieved from https://www.usgs.gov/media/images/ninety-percent-iceberg-below-waterline

have sonar that could detect an iceberg under water . . . and radar could have detected it more than 100 miles away."[241]

What's Happening Underwater

The sickness or disease you are facing is just like that iceberg that *Titanic* plowed into. You can get a doctor's report that will tell you what is happening above the waterline (physically). But if you want to know what's lurking underwater, you need a spiritual inventory. You need to check in and ask God what is going on that needs to be dealt with beneath the surface!

In Matthew 17, a desperate father asked Jesus to heal his son.

> *"Lord, have mercy on my son, for he is an epileptic and suffers severely; for he often falls into the fire and often into the water. So I brought him to Your disciples, but they could not cure him."*
>
> —*Matthew 17:15-16*

Above the water, this boy was suffering from epileptic seizures. So the disciples treated what they could see. But it *wasn't enough*. They couldn't cure him with their limited vision! But Jesus saw *beneath the surface:*

> *Then Jesus answered and said, "O faithless and perverse generation, how long shall I be with you? How long shall I bear with you? Bring him here to Me." And Jesus rebuked the demon, and it came out of him; and the child was cured from that very hour.*
>
> —*Matthew 17:17-18*

---

[241] Gaudin, Sharon, "Titanic was high-tech marvel of its time." *CIO Magazine*, April 13, 2012. Retrieved from https://www.cio.com/article/2397238/titanic-was-high-tech-marvel-of-its-time.html

The disciples prayed for epilepsy to be cured, but Jesus "rebuked the demon . . . and the child was cured" (v 18). Do you see the difference? The disciples treated the symptom, but Jesus pulled up the root. And *that is the level of vision* we need in the church today.[242]

When you are struggling with sickness, ask Jesus, "Lord, what do I need to see that's happening beneath the surface?" Maybe you're the victim of demonic oppression. Maybe there is anger, bitterness, and unforgiveness that need to be dealt with beneath the surface of your heart. You *must* deal with whatever is beneath the surface, or else your hope of healing will sink!

And whenever you pray for other people, ask the Holy Spirit, "Lord, what do I need to see that's happening in this person's life?" Part of your mission is to command their body to be healed, but another essential part of your task is to minister to their spirit so that whatever is allowing sickness and disease to take hold can be cast out in Jesus' name.

Spiritual Sonar

God has given you vision to see beneath the surface. Amos 3:7 says, "Surely the Lord God does nothing, unless He reveals His secret to His servants the prophets." God wants to speak to you! He wants to show you what He is about to do so you can pray accordingly! He wants you to know what is lurking in the depths of hearts so you can adjust course.

You might say, "Well I'm not a prophet, so why would God speak to me?" But Luke 7:28 says that "he who is least in the kingdom of God" is a greater prophet than even John the Baptist. 2 Kings 6 shows us that

---

[242] The most phenomenal resource of which I am aware that will help you in this department is the book *How to Minister to Specific Diseases* by the International Association of Healing Rooms: https://healingrooms.com/cart/how-to-minister-to-specific-diseases-electronic-version-.html

God opens the eyes of His servants![243] So as you maintain a relationship with the Holy Spirit and rely on Him to tell you what is really going on, He will show you everything you need to know.

Even Jesus said He could do "nothing" except what "He sees the Father do; for whatever He does, the Son also does in like manner" (Jn. 5:19). Our mission is not to *know* how to heal, but to rely on the Holy Spirit to *show us* what needs to be healed so we can access it in prayer!

Spiritual Weapons

Healing is rarely a completely physical battle. Accordingly, God has given you the *weapons* you need to fight back against the work of the enemy. Don't spend your life praying physical prayers based on what you see with your eyes and wondering why they don't work. Instead, initiate a life of partnership with God's Holy Spirit so He can show you what to pray out of your *spirit!*[244]

> *For though we walk in the flesh, we do not war according to the flesh. For the weapons of our warfare are not carnal but mighty in God for pulling down strongholds . . .*   —2 Corinthians 10:3-4

If you're going to win the spiritual battle that is happening underneath the surface of your sickness, you're going to have to be properly armed. You're not just doing battle "according to the flesh" (v 3). You are not

---

[243] "And Elisha prayed, and said, 'Lord, I pray, open his eyes that he may see.' Then the Lord opened the eyes of the young man, and he saw. And behold, the mountain was full of horses and chariots of fire all around Elisha." —2 Kings 6:17

[244] "God is Spirit, and those who worship Him must worship in spirit and truth." —Jn. 4:24

restricted to the tools of science and medicine![245] So, are you properly armed?

> *Put on the whole armor of God, that you may be able to stand against the wiles of the devil. For we do not wrestle against flesh and blood, but against principalities, against powers, against the rulers of the darkness of this age, against spiritual hosts of wickedness in the heavenly places. Therefore take up the whole armor of God, that you may be able to withstand in the evil day, and having done all, to stand.*
> —*Ephesians 6:11-13*

There are entire books written about Ephesians 6 and what it means to be equipped with the "whole armor of God" (v. 11). This is not one of those resources. However, our discussion of healing would be incomplete if I didn't arm you with the two most practical and powerful tools you have readily available in your healing arsenal as a follower of Jesus Christ.

The Name of Jesus

First, you have the name of Jesus. Take a moment to pause in your reading. Just say His name. Say "Jesus" out loud. Notice how laughter fills your heart. Notice how confidence wells up inside of you. Observe the manner in which your physical body feels strengthened and made whole, without you even technically praying a prayer!

Why does that happen? Because there is *power* in the name of Jesus:

---

[245] Please note, however, that science and medicine are extremely powerful tools that can work in tandem with, and not at odds with, spiritual prayer. What a shame it would be to shun the advice of your physician if God is planning to work through your physician to heal you!

And being found in appearance as a man, He humbled Himself and became obedient to the point of death, even the death of the cross. Therefore God also has highly exalted Him and given Him the name which is above every name, that at the name of Jesus every knee should bow, of those in heaven, and of those on earth, and of those under the earth, and that every tongue should confess that Jesus Christ is Lord, to the glory of God the Father. — *Philippians 2:8-11*

You carry the very name and nature of the Son of God! And because you have a relationship with Jesus, you are able to wield His name with authority and power. Not everyone can use the name of Jesus, because not everyone has a relationship with Him![246] But you are a child of God who *knows* Jesus because you've had an *experience* with Him.

As you call out the name Jesus over your body, you will be healed. And as you proclaim the name Jesus over the body of any person for whom you pray, he or she will be healed in His name!

In Acts 3, Peter and John went to the temple to pray. They found a man who had been laid at the gate of the temple to beg for change. The man saw them and asked them for money. But Peter and John gave him a *completely different* kind of change:

And fixing his eyes on him, with John, Peter said, "Look at us." So he gave them his attention, expecting to receive something from them. Then Peter said, "Silver and gold I do not have, but what I do have I give you: In the name of Jesus Christ of Nazareth, rise up and walk." And he took him by the right hand and lifted him up, and immediately his feet and ankle bones received strength. — *Acts 3:4-7*

---

[246] See Acts 19:11-20. The sons of Sceva and a group of itinerant Jewish exorcists tried to cast out demons in the name of Jesus, but because they didn't have a relationship with Him, their attempts backfired!

Peter and John didn't recite a scripted prayer. They *proclaimed the name of Jesus.* They weren't doctors! But they were armed and equipped with a much greater gift. And because they used the name of Jesus out of the power they had through *relationship* with Him, this man who had been paralyzed was instantly healed!

> *So he, leaping up, stood and walked and entered the temple with them—walking, leaping, and praising God. And all the people saw him walking and praising God. Then they knew that it was he who sat begging alms at the Beautiful Gate of the temple; and they were filled with wonder and amazement at what had happened to him.*
>
> *—Acts 3:8-10*

Not only was this man *healed* and transformed in his body—he was also healed and transformed in his heart. Because of the strength and power in the name of Jesus, this child of God was transformed from a destitute beggar into a charismatic evangelist.

Everyone who saw this man who had been paralyzed made perfectly whole was astonished. So Peter explained to them exactly how his healing had happened:

> *And His name, through faith in His name, has made this man strong, whom you see and know. Yes, the faith which comes through Him has given him this perfect soundness in the presence of you all.*
>
> *—Acts 3:16*

I have no problem with prayer models. But I do get the overwhelming sense that we have made healing too complicated in the church. When you release the name of Jesus over bodies that need to be healed, they will come back to life!

"Most assuredly, I say to you, he who believes in Me, the works that I do he will do also; and greater works than these he will do, because I go to My Father. And whatever you ask in My name, that I will do, that the Father may be glorified in the Son. If you ask anything in My name, I will do it." —John 14:12-14

The Blood of Jesus

The second powerful weapon you have in your arsenal is the blood of Jesus. There is no substance in the universe more powerful than His blood! Have you appropriated the blood of Jesus over your body? Do you plead the blood of Jesus over the bodies of men and women for whom you pray?

If you're new to Christianity, that might sound a little creepy. What does it mean to apply the blood of Jesus to my body and my life? All it means is saying this in prayer, "Lord, I plead the blood of Jesus over my body right now!" And as you do, His blood that makes men and women whole will wash you perfectly clean, and make you perfectly holy.

Blood was important under Levitical law. God set up a whole sacrificial system for His people under which they had to be cleansed by sacrificial blood. If any man or woman sinned unintentionally, [247] the required remedy was blood:

Then likewise he sprinkled with blood both the tabernacle and all the vessels of the ministry. And according to the law almost all things

---

[247] There was no remediation for anyone who sinned intentionally. Numbers 15:30-31 says, "But the person who does anything presumptuously, whether he is native-born or a stranger, that one brings reproach on the Lord, and he shall be cut off from among his people. Because he has despised the word of the Lord, and has broken His commandment, that person shall be completely cut off; his guilt shall be upon him." Aren't you glad you live on this side of the cross?

are purified with blood, and without shedding of blood there is no
remission.   *—Hebrews 9:21-22*

Without blood, there can be no remission of sin! There can be no healing of the body. But under the old covenant, the blood of animals could never fully "take away sins":

> *For it is not possible that the blood of bulls and goats could take away*
> *sins.*   *—Hebrews 10:4*

Old covenant blood could only wash you clean for a time, not forever! But under our new covenant with God through Jesus Christ, we have been set free by *better blood*. We have been set free, once for all, by the blood of Jesus!

> *By that will we have been sanctified through the offering of the body*
> *of Jesus Christ once for all.*   *—Hebrews 10:10*

You have been set free *forever* by the "precious blood" of Jesus Christ Himself:

> *And if you call on the Father, who without partiality judges*
> *according to each one's work, conduct yourselves throughout the*
> *time of your stay here in fear; knowing that you were not redeemed*
> *with corruptible things, like silver or gold, from your aimless conduct*
> *received by tradition from your fathers, but with the precious blood of*
> *Christ, as of a lamb without blemish and without spot.*
>   *—1 Peter 1:17-19*

Jesus is sinless and spotless. He lived a life completely free of sickness and disease! Do you ever see Jesus going to the doctor in the Gospels? Do you ever hear Him so much as complaining about a headache? *I don't think so.* Why? Because He has perfect blood running through His veins. And when you believe in Him, *so do you.*

His Blood Makes Us Free

Almost a decade ago, we had a woman in our church named Kaitlin who was diagnosed with terminal cancer. Kaitlin's exact diagnosis was stage IV colon cancer. The American Cancer Society notes that colorectal cancer is the "second most common cause of cancer death" in the United States.[248] The prognosis for colon cancer is particularly grim. In Kaitlin's case, doctors told her that, in an absolute best-case scenario, she had several months to live.

Kaitlin had always lived a healthy life. She was in good shape. She ate well! She often ran marathons and competed in road bike races. So imagine her surprise when a doctor told her he thought she was going to die. But Kaitlin wasn't going down without a fight.

The doctor recommended radiation treatment. Kaitlin felt absolute peace from the Lord to undergo medical treatment, but she knew that wouldn't be enough. This is wisdom: Do what the doctor is telling you to do to combat the tip of the iceberg (physical symptoms), but rely on the Holy Spirit to tell you what to do to take care of what's beneath the surface.

So, she started taking Communion every day.[249] Why? Because as you take Communion, you are pleading the blood of Jesus over your

---

[248] American Cancer Society (2020). Key Statistics for Colorectal Cancer. Retrieved from https://www.cancer.org/cancer/colon-rectal-cancer/about/key-statistics.html Para. 3

[249] For more on the pivotal role Communion plays in healing, see Chapter 20.

body. You are declaring that His blood makes *every part of you*—body, soul, and spirit—perfectly well and whole.

This is how the apostle Paul taught Communion to the early church:

> *For I received from the Lord that which I also delivered to you: that the Lord Jesus on the same night in which He was betrayed took bread; and when He had given thanks, He broke it and said, "Take, eat; this is My body which is broken for you; do this in remembrance of Me." In the same manner He also took the cup after supper, saying, "This cup is the new covenant in My blood. This do, as often as you drink it, in remembrance of Me."*

> *For as often as you eat this bread and drink this cup, you proclaim the Lord's death till He comes.*   —1 Corinthians 11:23-26

When Jesus died on the cross in your place, His body was broken so that yours doesn't have to be. The cross was an especially cruel and torturous form of the death penalty—it's where we get the word "excruciating"! He did that on purpose, so that you and I would never have to suffer unnecessary symptoms of sickness and disease. He poured out His blood so that we would have His blood available to plead and declare over our own bodies. And as often as we do it, we "proclaim [His] death til he comes" (v. 26).

Communion is so much more than a ritual. It is a prophetic act. It is a declaration that Jesus' blood covers your sickness. That His death *as your sickness and pain*[250] forever removed your burden to bear something that God's Word says no longer belongs to you!

Kaitlin took Communion every day. And after five months, she was completely healed. It's been over ten years since she was given a

---

[250] See our discussion of Isaiah 53:4-6 in Chapter One.

death sentence by doctors. She has competed in road races, bike races, swimming races, and triathlons all over the country since then. Ten years later, there is still *no trace* of cancer in her body. Because when the blood of Jesus is running through your veins, you don't have to fear disease and death.

CHAPTER EIGHTEEN

HEALING AND PROPHECY

There is no voice more powerful than God's. David tells us in Psalm 29 just how powerful His voice is:

The voice of the Lord is over the waters;
The God of glory thunders;
The Lord is over many waters.
The voice of the Lord is powerful;
The voice of the Lord is full of majesty.

The voice of the Lord breaks the cedars,
Yes, the Lord splinters the cedars of Lebanon.
He makes them also skip like a calf,
Lebanon and Sirion like a young wild ox.
The voice of the Lord divides the flames of fire.

The voice of the Lord shakes the wilderness;
The Lord shakes the Wilderness of Kadesh.
The voice of the Lord makes the deer give birth,
And strips the forests bare;
And in His temple everyone says, "Glory!"

—Psalm 29:3-9

God's voice is powerful. His voice is full of majesty! His voice is strong enough to break down any stronghold (v. 5). His voice will make your enemies "skip like a calf" (v. 6). It is His voice that "divides the flames of fire" (v. 7).[251] His voice shakes the wilderness and gets you out of any rut that you feel is keeping you from your Promised Land! The voice of the Lord gives birth to new life (v. 9), and causes everyone who hears Him to erupt in glorious praise.

Why is that important? Because *you* have the ability to release God's voice.[252] You have the ability to release God's Word over the bodies of people who desperately need healing. He has given His voice to you, and it is time for you to rise up and use it! [253]

Did you know that Jesus has the ability to cancel storms with His voice?

On the same day, when evening had come, He said to them, "Let us cross over to the other side." Now when they had left the multitude, they took Him along in the boat as He was. And other little boats were also with Him. And a great windstorm arose, and the waves beat into the boat, so that it was already filling. But He was in the stern, asleep on a pillow. And they awoke Him and said to Him, "Teacher, do You not care that we are perishing?"

Then He arose and rebuked the wind, and said to the sea, "Peace, be still!" And the wind ceased and there was a great calm. But He said to them, "Why are you so fearful? How is it that you have no faith?"

---

[251] And it was His voice that caused "divided tongues, as of fire, to rest upon each" of the disciples in the Upper Room (Acts 2:3).

[252] "Voice" is the Hebrew *qowl*,which can be translated "proclamation of God." "H6963 - qowl - Strong's Hebrew Lexicon (KJV)." Blue Letter Bible. Accessed 11 Aug, 2020. https://www.blueletterbible.org//lang/lexicon/lexicon.cfm?Strongs=H6963&t=KJV

[253] "So shall My word be that goes forth from My mouth; it shall not return to Me void, but it shall accomplish what I please, and it shall prosper in the thing for which I sent it." —Is. 55:11

And they feared exceedingly, and said to one another, "Who can this be, that even the wind and the sea obey Him!" —Mark 4:35-41

The wind and the sea listened to Jesus! Why? Because they knew the sound of His voice. He was there when they were created:

In the beginning God created the heavens and the earth. The earth was without form, and void; and darkness was on the face of the deep. And the Spirit of God was hovering over the face of the waters. Then God said, "Let there be light"; and there was light. —Genesis 1:1-3

Jesus is God. When creation happened, He was there:

In the beginning was the Word, and the Word was with God, and the Word was God. He was in the beginning with God. All things were made through Him, and without Him nothing was made that was made. —John 1:1-3

So when the wind and the wave hear the voice of Jesus, the same God who spoke them into existence, they obey! And in the same way, when broken bodies hear the voice of Jesus, the same God who formed them in their mothers' womb, [254] they will obey.

So how do we make sure broken bodies hear the voice of Jesus?

Healing and Prophecy

There is an important link between healing and prophecy. If you're praying for people and they're not getting healed, you may be missing this link!

---

[254] "Before I formed you in the womb I knew you; before you were born I sanctified you; I ordained you a prophet to the nations." —Jer. 1:5

"Gifts of healings" is a spiritual gift:

[F]or to one is given the word of wisdom through the Spirit, to another the word of knowledge through the same Spirit, to another faith by the same Spirit, to another gifts of healings by the same Spirit, to another the working of miracles, to another prophecy, to another discerning of spirits, to another different kinds of tongues, to another the interpretation of tongues. But one and the same Spirit works all these things, distributing to each one individually as He wills.
—1 Corinthians 12:8-11

A gift is not a wage. It is important that we never think we can *earn* a gift. We must simply receive it. And if we are not *experiencing* the fruit of a gift in our daily lives, it is our responsibility to go and ask the Giver for the gift that we are missing.

But did you know that not all spiritual gifts are created equal?

Pursue love, and desire spiritual gifts, but especially that you may prophesy.
—1 Corinthians 14:1

The apostle Paul is trying to save us some time here. We should pursue love! And one of the most effective ways we can love the people around us is to show them the power of God by exercising spiritual gifts! But Paul tells us to keep one spiritual gift in particular on our radar—prophecy. We should "desire" them all! But receiving one special gift will enhance the others.

Prophecy is simply allowing Jesus to speak through you. Prophecy is the bridge between the natural and the supernatural. Prophecy happens when God speaks to you, so you can tell someone else what He says! And the best way to love someone is to tell them what God is saying about them.

Naaman the Syrian

Do you remember Naaman the Syrian from Chapter 3?

> *Now Naaman, commander of the army of the king of Syria, was a great and honorable man in the eyes of his master, because by him the Lord had given victory to Syria. He was also a mighty man of valor, but a leper. And the Syrians had gone out on raids, and had brought back captive a young girl from the land of Israel. She waited on Naaman's wife.* —2 Kings 5:1-2

God had His eye on Naaman. Naaman had everything! Except for that *one thing.* He had victory, honor, and prestige! But he didn't have his health. But lucky for Naaman, he had a young Hebrew girl living in his house who, even though she had been enslaved, still wanted to make sure Naaman saw the power of God:

> *Then she said to her mistress, "If only my master were with the prophet who is in Samaria! For he would heal him of his leprosy." And Naaman went in and told his master, saying, "Thus and thus said the girl who is from the land of Israel."* —2 Kings 5:3-4

Notice that Naaman didn't need a healing evangelist! He needed a "prophet" (v. 3). Why? Because there is a *link* between healing and prophecy!

> *Then the king of Syria said, "Go now, and I will send a letter to the king of Israel." So he departed and took with him ten talents of silver,*

six thousand shekels of gold, and ten changes of clothing. Then he brought the letter to the king of Israel, which said, "Now be advised, when this letter comes to you, that I have sent Naaman my servant to you, that you may heal him of his leprosy."

And it happened, when the king of Israel read the letter, that he tore his clothes and said, "Am I God, to kill and make alive, that this man sends a man to me to heal him of his leprosy? Therefore please consider, and see how he seeks a quarrel with me." —2 Kings 5:5-7

Just because you have a title in your church doesn't mean you can heal. How embarrassing! Even the King of Israel didn't have the faith to heal Naaman! But there was someone else who did:

So it was, when Elisha the man of God heard that the king of Israel had torn his clothes, that he sent to the king, saying, "Why have you torn your clothes? Please let him come to me, and he shall know that there is a prophet in Israel." —2 Kings 5:8, emphasis added

Elisha had the *one thing* that is required for healing to take place: He had the word of the Lord.

When God sends someone to you who needs healing, how do you respond? Do you respond like the King of Israel? "Lord, I can't heal him! Only You can do that!" Or do you respond like Elisha? "Lord, send him to me! And he will know that God still heals."

I pray that *every single believer* would respond like Elisha. I pray that we would stop running away from opportunities to heal people, and instead run *towards them!*

Look at what the prophet did when Naaman arrived:

Then Naaman went with his horses and chariot, and he stood at the door of Elisha's house. And Elisha sent a messenger to him, saying, "Go and wash in the Jordan seven times, and your flesh shall be restored to you, and you shall be clean." —2 *Kings 5:9-10*

God is not a God of formula. Elisha didn't come outside and pray for Naaman with a scripted prayer that he found in a healing manual somewhere. He didn't anoint Naaman with oil, or even lay his hands on Naaman's skin! Elisha did something far more powerful: He *sought the Lord* for a fresh, spoken word[255] from heaven that would be just what Naaman needed to hear. Elisha knew exactly how Naaman's healing was going to happen, because God had *showed him in advance.*[256]

You know the rest of the story. Naaman was furious at first, but eventually did what Elisha asked him to do. And the result was nothing short of supernatural:

So he went down and dipped seven times in the Jordan, according to the saying of the man of God; and his flesh was restored like the flesh of a little child, and he was clean. —2 *Kings 5:14*

What a miraculous healing! And it all started because Elisha got a fresh word from heaven and released it over Naaman. It all started because a *prophet* believed that he could *heal.*

---

[255] This is the *rhema* (i.e. spoken or uttered) word of God (Romans 10:17), as opposed to the *logos* (i.e. written) word of God (John 1:1).
[256] See Chapter 3, "Your Healing Is Unique," for a more in-depth analysis of Naaman's healing.

Jesus Wants to Speak Through You

Again, you might say, "Well that's great for Elisha. But I'm not a prophet." But Jesus Himself calls you a "greater prophet"[257] than John the Baptist. John the Baptist was the greatest Old Testament prophet, but you are "greater" because you are filled with the Holy Spirit![258]

You are going to see Jesus heal like never before when you stop trying to *figure out how God heals,* and just start asking Him what He wants you to do in that moment. Your healing ministry is not a test! It is a *gift.* And God will show you how He wants to heal the people around you, so that you can show them what intimacy with God looks like firsthand.

What Should I Say?

Jesus reminded His disciples just how powerful their voices are:

> *"For assuredly, I say to you, whoever says to this mountain, 'Be removed and be cast into the sea,' and does not doubt in his heart, but believes that those things he says will be done, he will have whatever he says."* —*Mark 11:23*

When you speak, mountains move! But you can't just tell the mountain whatever you want to say. Jesus didn't just tell His disciples to speak to the mountain—He also told them exactly what to say. They couldn't just say, "Mountain, move!" They were instructed to say, "Be removed and be cast into the sea."

---

[257] "For I say to you, among those born of women there is not a greater prophet than John the Baptist; but he who is least in the kingdom of God is greater than he." —Lk. 7:28

[258] "But if the Spirit of Him who raised Jesus from the dead dwells in you, He who raised Christ from the dead will also give life to your mortal bodies through His Spirit who dwells in you." —Rom. 8:11

This isn't a prescription for ritual, memorized prayer. It is a reminder to always ask Jesus what He wants you to say over a person when you pray. You have to say what He gives you to say! That is the definition of prophecy.

Did you know that God is willing to turn every conversation into a prayer session? Nehemiah was "cupbearer to the king" (Neh. 1:11) of Persia. One day while Nehemiah was serving the king, Artaxerxes asked him why he looked "sad in his presence" (Neh. 2:1). So Nehemiah told him:

> *And the king said to me, "Why is your face sad, seeing you are not sick? This is nothing but sadness of the heart." Then I was very much afraid. I said to the king, "Let the king live forever! Why should not my face be sad, when the city, the place of my fathers' graves, lies in ruins, and its gates have been destroyed by fire?" Then the king said to me, "What are you requesting?" So I prayed to the God of heaven.*
> *—Nehemiah 2:2-4*

Nehemiah needed to know what to say! So he "prayed to the God of heaven" *in the middle of his conversation with the king.* He knew better than to answer from his flesh! But he didn't have to stop and physically remove himself from the room to accurately hear what God was saying in that moment. He checked in with the Lord and then immediately delivered his response:

> *And I said to the king, "If it pleases the king, and if your servant has found favor in your sight, that you send me to Judah, to the city of my fathers' graves, that I may rebuild it." And the king said to me (the queen sitting beside him), "How long will you be gone, and*

when will you return?" So it pleased the king to send me when I had
given him a time.   *—Nehemiah 2:5-6*

When someone tells you they're sick, hold back your reply for a moment. Check in with the God of heaven. What does the Holy Spirit want you to say? What is God showing you about that person that will help direct your prayers? And what is stopping you from allowing the Lord to turn that conversation into a prayer session so that God can put His power on display, right then and there?

Let me give you an example of how this all plays out in real time. The first time our Healing Rooms were ever open, we had a woman come in for prayer who was visiting from Africa. Her daughter was a medical school student in New York City and a member of our church. The mother was only here for one week, but she had heard about the Healing Rooms and came in for prayer.

She presented for prayer with visible bone spurs. I was leading a team of three people assigned to pray for her. She was in agonizing pain, wincing with every step as she walked into the room. We asked her to sit down, and one of our volunteers held her feet in his hands. We commanded the bone spurs to retract into her feet with full faith that, as we spoke, her feet would respond. But nothing happened.

I took a moment to pause and check in with the Lord. All of a sudden, I saw a picture[259] of two long snakes, almost like eels, wrapped around her feet. The Lord reminded me of this Scripture:

How then shall they call on Him in whom they have not believed?
And how shall they believe in Him of whom they have not heard?

---

[259] When I saw "I saw a picture," I mean the Lord gave me an open vision. What I "saw" in the spirit realm was superimposed over what I saw with my natural eyes. I was still there in the moment, but God was showing me a spiritual reality that took precedence over the natural reality.

And how shall they hear without a preacher? And how shall they preach unless they are sent? As it is written:

"How beautiful are the feet of those who preach the gospel of peace, who bring glad tidings of good things!"   —Romans 10:14-15

I asked the woman if she had people in her family who had yet to receive Jesus. She did. I asked her if she had been trying to share the gospel with them. She had. But the members of her extended family who needed to receive Jesus didn't live close to her. She needed to travel to spend time with them, and the bone spurs were making that increasingly difficult.

Do you see what was happening here? God had given her a mandate to share the gospel, but the enemy was getting in the way! He was attacking her destiny by hitting her feet, the one area of her body she needed most to travel and minister to other people. God showed me what was happening in the spirit so I could pray accordingly.[260]

Our prayer immediately changed based on what I had seen. Instead of commanding the bone spurs to move and invoking Mark 11:23,[261] we released her feet from the bondage Satan was trying to force her to live under in Jesus' name. We cast those slimy serpents off her body and out of her life in Jesus' name! And as we did, we *watched in awe* as those bone spurs retracted into her body *right in front of our very eyes*. We celebrated the healing that had taken place! And then we encouraged her in her mission to share the gospel, and promised her that Satan no longer had any authority to interfere with that objective.[262]

---

[260] Remember to "look beneath the surface" from Chapter 17!

[261] "For assuredly, I say to you, whoever says to this mountain, 'Be removed and be cast into the sea,' and does not doubt in his heart, but believes that those things he says will be done, he will have whatever he says." —Mk. 11:23

[262] "Behold, I give you the authority to trample on serpents and scorpions,

Do you see why it's so critical to *hear from God* as you pray for other people? If we hadn't stopped to check in with Jesus mid-prayer, we might have completely missed what God was doing! If we had kept commanding physical restoration without first providing spiritual deliverance, the opportunity for healing could have passed. We would have left discouraged that nothing had taken place. But when you ask God what He is doing, — even in the middle of a sentence — He will tell you!

Increasing in the Prophetic

So if prophecy and healing are linked, what are some practical steps you can take to increase in the prophetic?

1) Spend time with Jesus.

If you want to hear what Jesus is saying, you need to get close to Him. There is no shortcut for intimacy with Jesus. Do you remember Mary and Martha? Martha was running around serving Jesus! But Jesus reminded her that there is only "one thing" that really matters:

> *"But one thing is needed, and Mary has chosen that good part, which will not be taken away from her."* —*Luke 10:42*

Mary "sat at Jesus' feet and heard His word" (v. 39). If you want to hear His Word, you have to sit at His feet! You can go to all the training courses you want, and collect all the healing certifications you can find! But the "one thing" you need most to hear God's voice and heal the sick is time spent at the feet of Jesus.

---

and over all the power of the enemy, and nothing shall by any means hurt you." —Lk. 10:19

2) Ask Him for increase.

Jesus responds to requests:

> *"So I say to you, ask, and it will be given to you; seek, and you will find; knock, and it will be opened to you. For everyone who asks receives, and he who seeks finds, and to him who knocks it will be opened."* —Luke 11:9-10

And when you ask to *increase* in the anointing, God will never let you down:

> *"If you then, being evil, know how to give good gifts to your children, how much more will your heavenly Father give the Holy Spirit to those who ask Him!"* —Luke 11:13

It is *good* and *holy* for you to seek God for what you need to heal His people! You are not seeking to increase your ministry—you are seeking to show a generation of people who don't know Jesus His glory. Someone has to heal the sick in Jesus' name! If you don't do it, who will?

3) Practice.

I live in New York City. There is *no better place* to practice the gifts of prophecy and healing. Every time I walk by someone on the street, I ask God to show me something about them. Sometimes I share it, and sometimes I don't. Whatever the Holy Spirit says, I do. Whether I share the word or not, the exercise keeps me *reliant on God* to hear what He is saying about someone, instead of assuming I already know what they need.

The best way to increase in the prophetic is to start prophesying. And know that as you step out and do what God has called you to do, He will never let you down.

> *The things which you learned and received and heard and saw in me,*
> *these do, and the God of peace will be with you.* —Philippians 4:9

CHAPTER NINETEEN

POWER OF COMMUNION

I have saved perhaps the simplest material for last because it is so effective, yet so often overlooked. There is *power* in Communion.

Several years ago, one of our church members approached me excitedly after service one Sunday and said, "I have a testimony!"

"Tell me!" I cajoled.

"Did you know the stuff you guys [our preaching team] preach actually works?"

I bit my tongue. "Oh yeah?"

We had just finished a preaching series on the power of Communion. One of the topics we focused on in the series was that whenever you are sick, one of the *best and most effective ways* you can pursue healing is to take Communion as often as possible.

"My mom was in the hospital last week," she said. "She's had a blood disease for some time, and her immune system is really weak, so she gets a lot of infections. When she got checked into the hospital I went to see her. She looked terrible. She had lesions all over her face. You could *see* the infection all over her."

I tried my best to be comforting and consoling. "Oh my Lord . . ."

But before I could launch into counseling mode, she continued. "But after I went to see her, I listened to one of the messages on Communion. I heard you guys says that God can heal you as you take Communion. So I went to the bodega[263] and bought some matzo and grape juice. I took it to the hospital. I told my mom about the message and we listened to

---

[263] A local corner deli or grocery store in New York City.

it together. She didn't know what to think of it at first. I don't think she really believed it! Then we took Communion. And *nothing happened.*"

I looked at her, eager for her to resolve the tension. "Wait . . . nothing happened?" I asked, confused.

"Nothing happened!" she announced again, beaming.

"I don't understand," I admitted.

"So the next day I went to the hospital to visit my mom again. I remembered [the preaching team] saying you should take Communion as often as you want, so I brought back the matzo and grape juice and went to take communion with my mom again.

"But when I got there, she was *gone.*"

"Gone?" I asked.

"Gone!" she said. "She was *gone* because they *discharged her* the morning after we took Communion, because later that night, after I left, the entire infection had disappeared!"

Now I understood! Isn't God amazing? This young woman took hold of a scriptural truth, by faith, and she made a decision: *I'm going to bless my family with this.* She *refused* to let the enemy keep her mom sick. She went into battle with one of the most powerful spiritual weapons we have at our disposal. She took the body and the blood of Jesus Christ and proclaimed His death, burial, and resurrection over her mother's body. And because she did it by faith, her mother was miraculously healed.

The Power of Communion

Communion is not a lifeless ritual. It is not just a formal procedure that the church carries out once per month to entice everyone to show up for service. Communion is the *lifeblood* of your relationship with Jesus:

> For I received from the Lord that which I also delivered to you: that the Lord Jesus on the same night in which He was betrayed took

bread; and when He had given thanks, He broke it and said, "Take, eat; this is My body which is broken for you; do this in remembrance of Me." In the same manner He also took the cup after supper, saying, "This cup is the new covenant in My blood. This do, as often as you drink it, in remembrance of Me." For as often as you eat this bread and drink this cup, you proclaim the Lord's death till He comes.

—1 Corinthians 11:23-26

In the passage above, the apostle Paul is speaking to the early church at a time when they had *forgotten* the importance of Communion. And Paul was reminding them *why* the church practiced Communion in the first place.

Why Take Communion?

1) Jesus took Communion.

First, we take Communion because Jesus took Communion. In Matthew 26, Jesus gathered His disciples for the Passover meal in an upper room at Jerusalem. The disciples were about to betray Jesus. He was trusting them with His life! And none of them would prove worthy of that trust. So before the disciples entered what would be the most stressful and trying period of their lives, Jesus wanted to make sure they did one thing—take Communion:

And as they were eating, Jesus took bread, blessed and broke it, and gave it to the disciples and said, "Take, eat; this is My body."

Then He took the cup, and gave thanks, and gave it to them, saying, "Drink from it, all of you. For this is My blood of the new covenant, which is shed for many for the remission of sins. But I say to you,

I will not drink of this fruit of the vine from now on until that day when I drink it new with you in My Father's kingdom."

And when they had sung a hymn, they went out to the Mount of Olives. —*Matthew 26:26-30*

The disciples would forget what it was like to have Jesus with them as they waited for Him to be raised from the dead. And Communion would be their reminder.

2) We need the reminder.

Second, we take Communion because we need the reminder. Communion is a physical act that reminds us of a spiritual truth. Jesus gave His body on the cross as a substitute for us. He gave His body to sickness and disease so that we don't have to allow ours to be consumed. He allowed His body to be overcome so that we could be healed and made whole.

And in the same manner, He poured out His blood to establish a "new covenant" (v 28). The writer of Hebrews calls our new covenant with God through the blood of Jesus Christ a "better covenant, which was established on better promises" (Heb. 8:6). That means God will not punish His people with sickness and disease anymore![264] What's more, when the enemy comes with a counterfeit and tries to convince God's people that their pain and suffering is from Him, God will *remove* that which is not His.

When we take Communion, we are reminded of just how much God loves us. We are reminded that *our body* is one of the vessels that was designed to receive God's infinite love in the form of healing. There is something special about physical reminders of love.

---

[264] "I will put none of the diseases on you which I have brought on the Egyptians. For I am the Lord who heals you." —Ex. 15:26

When my wife and I got married, I had her initials and birthdate engraved onto the inside of my wedding ring. She did the same for me. We didn't do it because it's cute—we did it so we would have a tangible reminder that God created us for each other. He designed us as counterparts who are "suitable and complementary" for each other (Gen. 2:18 AMP).

When life gets busy and our kids drive us up the wall (Sorry, kiddos—we love you!), we leave love notes for each other. Why? Because they are *tangible reminders* of the love that we have for each other. On days when things aren't going as well as they could be, all I have to do is look down and be reminded that my wife loves me. And when I remember that there is someone who loves me, supports me, and is rooting for me, I have exactly what I need to charge ahead.

Communion is God's love note to you. As you take it, be reminded that you don't have to sacrifice your body to appease the wrath of God any more.[265] Be reminded that Jesus poured out His blood so that you could receive the benefits of salvation:

> *Bless the Lord, O my soul;*
> *And all that is within me, bless His holy name!*
> *Bless the Lord, O my soul,*
> *And forget not all His benefits:*
> *Who forgives all your iniquities,*
> *Who heals all your diseases,*
> *Who redeems your life from destruction,*
> *Who crowns you with lovingkindness and tender mercies,*
> *Who satisfies your mouth with good things,*
> *So that your youth is renewed like the eagle's.*
>
> —*Psalm 103:1-5*

---

[265] You are still called to give your body as a "living sacrifice" (Rom. 12:1), but to God, not to sickness.

3) Communion is prophetic.

Communion is a prophetic act! Look again at the apostle Paul's encouragement to the church at Corinth:

> *For as often as you eat this bread and drink this cup, you proclaim the Lord's death till He comes.* —*1 Corinthians 11:26*

Proclamation is prophecy. When you take Communion, you are proclaiming the Lord's death until He arrives. You are binding sickness when you eat of the body and declare, "Jesus already died for this!" And you are releasing healing when you drink of the blood and proclaim, "Jesus already rose for this!"

What areas of your life need the blood of Jesus? What segments of your life need to be baptized in resurrection power? The way you prophesy to those areas and invite the resurrection life of Jesus is to "eat this bread and drink this cup" (v. 26). As you take Communion, you are proclaiming the death of Jesus over every area of your life where the influence of heaven has yet to come!

So are you sick? Take Communion and declare that Jesus died to heal you. Are you poor? Take Communion and declare that, "The blessing of the Lord makes one rich, and He adds no sorrow to it" (Prov. 10:22). Do you want your family members saved? Take Communion and believe that it is the "goodness of God" manifested in the death of His only Son on the cross that will lead your family members to repentance (Rom. 2:4)!

The Best Medicine

Whatever ails you, Communion is just what the Doctor ordered. It is your medicine! When you experience sickness in your body, Communion is the first meal you should take in.

But you don't have to wait until you're *sick* to take Communion. Take it when you're healthy! And the same meal that heals your disease will make you impervious to disease in the first place.

The apostle Paul cautioned the church not to take Communion "in an unworthy manner":

> *"Therefore whoever eats this bread or drinks this cup of the Lord in an unworthy manner will be guilty of the body and blood of the Lord. But let a man examine himself, and so let him eat of the bread and drink of the cup. For he who eats and drinks in an unworthy manner eats and drinks judgment to himself, not discerning the Lord's body. For this reason many are weak and sick among you, and many sleep."*
> —1 *Corinthians 11:27-30*

Some denominations of the church have misinterpreted the phrase "unworthy manner." Some churches have restricted Communion to those who are free from sin, living holy and blameless lives. But if we had to wait until we were perfect to take Communion, we would all be waiting until we got to heaven!

Do you wait until you're healed to go to the hospital? Of course not! You go to the hospital to get better. In the same way, whenever you're struggling with anything less than perfection—perfect health, perfect holy living, or even a perfect thought life—you go to the Communion table to dine with God to get better!

Taking Communion in a "worthy manner" does not mean waiting to take it until you are completely healthy and free from sin. It means *fully appreciating* the power of what you are doing. When Paul told the church they were taking Communion in an "unworthy manner," he simply meant that they were not *properly valuing* the meal.

They were eating divided, instead of united:

For there must also be factions among you, that those who are
approved may be recognized among you. —*1 Corinthians 11:19*

They were eating in a rush, instead of savoring the meal:

For in eating, each one takes his own supper ahead of others; and one
is hungry and another is drunk. —*1 Corinthians 11:21*

They were keeping Communion for themselves, instead of sharing its power with the world:

What! Do you not have houses to eat and drink in? Or do you despise
the church of God and shame those who have nothing?
—*1 Corinthians 11:22*

This is why, according to Paul, people were dying in the church:

For this reason many are weak and sick among you, and many sleep.
—*1 Corinthians 11:30*

But what is the opposite of death? Life! So if taking Communion *improperly* (not fully valuing its significance) leads to death, than taking it *properly* (understanding the weight and significance of the action as you take it) leads to life!

You *need* Communion. Communion heals your body and cleanses your soul! And the best part is, Communion is not just a healing response—it is also a preventative measure. It is what keeps you healthy when the rest of the world is getting sick. It is what keeps you sane when the rest of the world is going crazy! It is what keeps you grounded when the rest of the world is losing hope.

Take Communion Every Day

As I'm writing this chapter, the novel coronavirus[266] is devastating the globe. For about ten days, our kids have been out of school and I have been working from home. People are getting sick around us left and right! And do you know what we are resolving to do each and every single day as a family?

You guessed it. We are going to take Communion. We are going to *prophesy* healing and protection over our bodies as we feast on the body and blood of Jesus Christ. Why? Because Jesus told us to:

> *Then Jesus said to them, "Most assuredly, I say to you, unless you eat the flesh of the Son of Man and drink His blood, you have no life in you. Whoever eats My flesh and drinks My blood has eternal life, and I will raise him up at the last day. For My flesh is food indeed, and My blood is drink indeed. He who eats My flesh and drinks My blood abides in Me, and I in him. As the living Father sent Me, and I live because of the Father, so he who feeds on Me will live because of Me. This is the bread which came down from heaven — not as your fathers ate the manna, and are dead. He who eats this bread will live forever."* — John 6:53-58

We are going to declare that Jesus already died on the Cross as COVID-19, and that means there is no virus left for us. And as we do, we know that the *goodness* and the *protection* of God will be activated over our lives:

> *A thousand may fall at your side,*
> *And ten thousand at your right hand;*
> *But it shall not come near you.* — Psalm 91:7-11

---

[266] SARS-CoV-2 and the resulting respiratory disease, COVID-19.

Take Communion as often as you can. Take it every day if you have time! Let the promises of God for resurrection and abundant life wash over you. Believe that sickness and disease died when the body of Jesus was broken! Believe that healing was released for all God's people when His blood was poured out. And as you do, the work of the enemy will no longer have any power over you, in Jesus' name.

CHAPTER TWENTY

DEALING WITH DOUBT

A s we near the end of our healing journey together, my guess is you have a lingering question in your mind:

Why do some people get healed, but others don't?

First, I want to encourage you to embrace that question. Don't run from it.

Second, I am *not* going to try and give you an easy answer. You should grapple with that question for the rest of your human life. It should generate *tension*, a seeming contradiction between your faith and your experience. We like to run from tension, but the truth is, we need tension to grow.

Julius Wolff was a German anatomist and surgeon whose professional career spanned the second half of the 19th century. He is most famous for Wolff's law, which stipulates that bones in a healthy person will adapt to the load under which they are placed.[267] From a natural perspective, if you never lift anything healthy, your bones won't grow in density! They won't adapt to carry more weight. And if you never subject your body to any heavy lifting at all, your bones will atrophy— they will actually grow weaker and *less dense* over time.

Think about how that principle applies to your journey into healing with Jesus. If you never expose yourself to people who need healing, your

---

[267] Anahad O'Connor, "The Claim: After Being Broken, Bones Can Become Even Stronger." New York Times, October 18, 2010. Retrieved 2010-10-19.

anointing to heal is not going to grow. If you want to stay so safe that you never take a risk in praying for someone with an incurable condition, you're never going to see a miracle! It is only by exposing yourself to a load that feels greater than your capacity to carry that you invite the Holy Spirit to help you bear the weight.[268]

Some people ask why some people get healed while others don't, and because they can't find an easy answer to that question, they run from it. They *stop asking*. And over time, they atrophy. Before they know it, their faith to see miracles dries up and is gone. They adopt a theology that assumes that Jesus just doesn't heal any more. The age of signs and miracles must have ended when the last apostle who saw Jesus with his own eyes died.

But that's not a healthy response! If healing was important to Jesus, the Head, healing should be important to the church—His body! And the only way we are going to *grow* into our destiny is to confront the difficult questions, like the one posed above, head on. If we want to grow in our gifting and our anointing, we have to grapple with the weight of the reality that prayers aren't always answered in the way we hope they will be.

Maybe you're still struggling with sickness in your own body. You think the fact that you have a cane, walk with a limp, or sometimes experience debilitating pain prevents you from being a witness to Jesus' healing power. But don't let the enemy talk you out of your destiny!

Do you remember Abraham and Abimelech? God promised Abraham and Sarah a child,[269] but after *decades*, the baby still hadn't arrived. So

---

[268] "And He said to me, 'My grace is sufficient for you, for My strength is made perfect in weakness.' Therefore most gladly I will rather boast in my infirmities, that the power of Christ may rest upon me." —2 Cor. 12:9

[269] "And behold, the word of the Lord came to him, saying, 'This one shall not be your heir, but one who will come from your own body shall be your heir.' Then He brought him outside and said, 'Look now toward heaven, and

God sent Abraham into a foreign nation where a man named Abimelech was king and all the women were barren, and asked Abraham to pray that the wombs of Abimelech's people would be opened:

> *So Abraham prayed to God; and God healed Abimelech, his wife, and his female servants. Then they bore children; for the Lord had closed up all the wombs of the house of Abimelech because of Sarah, Abraham's wife.* —Genesis 20:17-18

God was testing Abraham's faith. Would Abraham trust God enough to go and pray something over someone else that he hadn't yet received for himself? Or would he run away from the challenge because he struggled to believe God still healed?

We are in the same boat as Abraham. So you've never seen someone healed?! Will you have the faith to step out and pray that someone else will see what you have yet to see yourself? Today is the perfect day to ask God for a miracle. Our mandate is to "lay hands on the sick, and they will recover" (Mk. 16:18b). Does the reality that some people may not recover mean that our mandate has been canceled? I don't think so. Does the fact that it may seem like we're losing a battle mean we should hang up our weapons and retreat from the war? Absolutely not!

What Happens When Healing Doesn't Happen

The coronavirus pandemic broke out in New York City in a big way starting in March, 2020. Our church made a declaration over our members and our families: "Not a single one of us will die from this disease." We made that declaration by faith, because we believe that "death and life is in the power of the tongue" (Prov. 18:21).

---

count the stars if you are able to number them.' And He said to him, 'So shall your descendants be.'" —Gen. 15:4-5

Several weeks into the pandemic, I got a text message from one of our members. Her mom, Carol, had been showing symptoms of respiratory distress for several days, so she was on her way to the emergency room. We made a decision to pray and agree that no matter the diagnosis, Carol would be completely healed.

When Carol arrived at the hospital, she was immediately hooked up to every machine imaginable so doctors could monitor her condition. She was elderly, so the prognosis wasn't good. Over the next several days, her condition worsened. She was put on a ventilator for breathing assistance, which meant her chance of survival was only about twelve percent.[270]

But we kept praying. We kept declaring the word we believed Jesus had given us for our church. And about two weeks later, we got the good news we had been praying for. Carol was headed home. She had beaten the odds! Yes, she received medical care, but I believe the most powerful contributor to her recovery was dedicated prayer.

At the same time we were celebrating Carol's healing, I received dire news from another one of our members named Larry that his wife, Cindy, had again been diagnosed with terminal cancer. Since her initial diagnosis, we had prayed that Cindy would be completely healed, and after several months of prayer, we received news that Cindy's cancer was gone! But now, several months later, Cindy had gotten a report that the cancer was back and more aggressive than ever. It had spread from her lungs to her brain and liver, and was quickly taking over the rest of her body.

Larry and Cindy invited me over to their apartment to pray. Because we were in the midst of the coronavirus outbreak in New York City, I

---

[270] For the period from March 1, 2020, through April 4, 2020, the overall death rate for COVID-19 patients was 21%, but for patients requiring mechanical ventilation, the death rate rose to 88%. Source: https://www.usnews.com/news/health-news/articles/2020-04-22/most-covid-19-patients-placed-on-ventilators-died-new-york-study-shows

stood inside the doorway with a medical-grade N95 mask on. I wore gloves as I stretched out my hand towards Cindy and prayed from across their living room. Understandably, Larry and Cindy requested that I didn't come any closer since Cindy was in the "high-risk" category and needed to be sheltered from any possible coronavirus contamination.

I prayed my best prayer. We all felt the presence of God. We made a decision to decree and declare that Cindy would be completely healed. But about two weeks later, I got a call from Larry. Cindy had gone home to be with Jesus. She had slipped into life after death peacefully as she rested one night, her body succumbing to cancer.

I had a difficult choice to face at that moment. I had just seen Carol healed! But I had just seen Cindy pass away. Did the fact that Carol was healed but Cindy wasn't mean that God didn't want Cindy healed? Did it mean that God had changed His mind about healing in the span of one week? Did He stop after Carol? Should I adjust my theology and my prayer life to accommodate the reality that Cindy didn't get the result we were praying for? Or could it possibly mean that there are some things 1) beyond my control and 2) outside of my understanding?

Faith means persevering *in spite of* not always seeing what you're hoping for.

> *Now faith is the substance of things hoped for, the evidence of things not seen.* —Hebrews 11:1

Faith is what happens when you make a decision to believe for things that have been promised, even if you don't immediately get what you expect. So I made a decision to press in for healing, more than ever before. And immediately my faith was tested yet again.

Several days after Cindy passed away, I got a message from one of our members. Her brother-in-law, Marcos, was in the hospital with COVID-19. Here is the text message she sent me:

> Please keep Marcos in prayer. [My husband Charlie] just got news that his brother Marcos is dying. The doctors are taking the ventilator out today; it has been two weeks since he has been on a ventilator. He now has an infection and his kidneys are shutting down and his white cells count is high. The doctor gave him a blood transfusion but it did not work. Now the doctors are making him comfortable until he dies. Thank you for your prayers.

I immediately called Charlie, who is one of our volunteers at the Healing Rooms. I've seen Charlie pray some bold prayers! I've seen legs grow out as Charlie prayed. I've seen bone spurs shrink as Charlie held broken feet in his hand! Charlie is one of the most anointed men of God I know.

But Charlie was understandably upset. When sickness hits your own household, a new level of faith is required. So we had a decision to make. Would we swallow the doctor's report and accept some vaguely comforting thing that people usually say at times like these like, "Well, maybe it's just his time?" Or would we believe in the Word of God and contend for the healing Jesus promised?

We declared that Marcos would completely recover. We prayed that Marcos would not only be healed, but that he would leave the hospital and live for Jesus like never before! We asked that Marcos' healing would be a testimony of God's goodness to the rest of Charlie's extended family, and that everyone who didn't know Jesus would be drawn to Him.[271]

And then we waited. I continued to pray for Marcos for ten days, but I heard nothing. Finally, we got the answer we had been praying for. I received the following text from Charlie's wife:

> To everyone who prayed and is still praying for Charlie's brother Marcos thank you. Praise report, Charlie's brother was moved on Friday from the hospital to a facility in the Bronx called Bronx Rehabilitation Center & Nursing Facility. He is very much awake and the respirator was removed. The doctor did a tracheotomy on his throat instead and put a feeding tube in his stomach. I am not sure if the tubes were removed before he was moved. He is awake and the nurses and doctors all clapped and cheered as he left. Now he needs speech therapy and muscle therapy for his legs. Thank You (smiley face emoji)

We laughed. We cried. We celebrated! God had done it again. And then several days after that, we got even more good news. The breathing and feeding tubes had been removed, and Marcos was on his way to full recovery.

Imagine the disservice it would have been to Marcos and his family if we had refused to believe God wanted to heal Marcos because of what happened with Cindy. Isn't it so silly and misguided to change our theology just because of one bad experience? *But this is what we do.* We "try healing" as if it's some type of exotic food at a buffet, and if it doesn't work, we decide it just must not be "for us" and never try it again!

---

[271] "No one can come to Me unless the Father who sent Me draws him; and I will raise him up at the last day." —Jn. 6:44

But healing comes to those who *persevere.* Healing comes to those who *keep knocking:*

> *"So I say to you, ask, and it will be given to you; seek, and you will find; knock, and it will be opened to you. For everyone who asks receives, and he who seeks finds, and to him who knocks it will be opened."* —Luke 11:9-10

No matter your personal history in the healing department, *trust God.* There are a litany of reasons someone you knew may not have gotten healed. That is a whole separate book I may write one day. But the reasons some people *don't* get healed are far less relevant than the overwhelming reason some people *do:* Jesus is the Healer.

Adjusting Your Theology

When healing doesn't happen, please do not adjust your theology to match your life experience. Scripture says that God holds His Word above His name:

> *I will worship toward Your holy temple,*
> *And praise Your name*
> *For Your lovingkindness and Your truth;*
> *For You have magnified Your word above all Your name.*
> —Psalm 138:2

And so should we. There is nothing God exalts more highly than His Word! So shouldn't we value and treasure His Word with exactly the same level of reverence and awe?

Instead of bringing your interpretation of Scripture *lower* to match your life experience, ask God to bring your life experience *higher* to match

His Word. Ask Him to put a greater level of expectation for miraculous healing on you than you've ever had before! Your healing muscles will get stronger and start to grow. You'll move from healed headaches and cured fevers to lame bodies walking and mental illness eradicated!

God is faithful. He will do everything He promised to do. All He asks of us is that we take Him at His Word.

ALL THE WORLD

C hurch, you are now armed with something incredibly power-ful. You have knowledge that almost *all* of the world—and even much of the church! —still does not possess. You know that God heals. So, knowing what you know, what are you going to do with that information?

We know the enemy is prowling around the earth, looking for people he can attack with sickness and disease:

> *Be sober, be vigilant; because your adversary the devil walks about like a roaring lion, seeking whom he may devour. Resist him, steadfast in the faith, knowing that the same sufferings are experienced by your brotherhood in the world.* —*1 Peter 5:8-9*

I've always heard the verse above used as a caution to stay on guard. We must guard ourselves against the enemy! Stay awake! Stay ready for his attack! But did you know the verse above isn't just *for you?* It's for the people who don't know God is the Healer yet. The mandate is for *you* to go out and protect *others.*

The enemy is on the attack. He attacks with sickness and disease. He attacks with deception, trying to convince God's people that healing is not really for us! And *you* are now the one whom God has armed with the knowledge and power that God is the Healer, so that you can go out and bless the world!

Have you ever watched a lion hunt? Many lions make their home in the Okavango Delta in Botswana, Africa. For most of the year, the

Okavango is dusty and dry. It's located in the middle of the Kalahari desert, which is one of the largest subtropical deserts in the world.

But every year, the Okavango River overflows with rainwater. Refreshing floodwaters spill into the Okavango Delta, turning what was once a dry and thirsty land into one of the most diverse habitats on earth. Tens of thousands of animals flock to the Delta to enjoy the luscious fruits that spring up when the deluge of rainwater arrives.

But lions are waiting when the herds arrive. The lions wait in the tall grass for herds of water buffalo to rush towards the water. And just when the buffalo are most optimistic and finally have the water in their sights, the lions pounce.

The lions don't attack the *strongest* in the herd. They don't go after the adults with the highest chance of survival. They go after the *young.* They prey on the *weak.* And here's the unfortunate truth: When the lions pounce out of the grass, the other members of the herd scatter. They don't stop to help when one of their young or weak get snatched by a lion. They run and hide, distancing themselves from the attack as much as possible, so they don't get attacked too.

But we are made in the image of God. We are not like animals! And it is now *your responsibility* to make sure that when the enemy lunges at someone with sickness or disease, you don't run away—you *charge back.*

1 Peter 5 (above) is not just a passage on personal spiritual warfare! Its primary purpose is to provide a lesson on *leadership:*

> *The elders who are among you I exhort, I who am a fellow elder and a witness of the sufferings of Christ, and also a partaker of the glory that will be revealed: Shepherd the flock of God which is among you, serving as overseers, not by compulsion but willingly, not for dishonest gain but eagerly . . .* —1 Peter 5:1-2

Scripture is reminding us to shepherd well. To protect the sheep! When a lion attacks, it is now *your responsibility* to make sure he doesn't get what he came for. When sickness and disease lash out and rear their ugly heads, *you* are now the one who gets to come in and "lay hands on the sick, and they will recover" (Mk. 16:18).

It will not always be easy. Running into the hospital—*towards the battle*—as the rest of the world runs away will not always be fun. But others will join you to lighten the load:

> *[N]or as being lords over those entrusted to you, but being examples to the flock . . .*   —*1 Peter 5:3*

And when all is said and done, you will receive a reward.

> *[A]nd when the Chief Shepherd appears, you will receive the crown of glory that does not fade away.*   —*1 Peter 5:4*

God is the Healer. And as He is, so are you in this world.[272] Now go out and lay hands on everything that moves, in Jesus' name.

---

[272] "[B]ecause as He is, so are we in this world." —1 Jn. 4:17

APPENDIX

100 HEALING VERSES

You have now reached what I believe is the most valuable portion of this book. Below are one hundred Scriptures that speak directly to physical healing. They are organized by book of the Bible as they appear in Scripture.

Your task now is to *internalize* these verses – to receive them by believing they are for you, and to memorize them so they flow out of you whenever you open your mouth to pray. I cannot over-emphasize the importance of this process. Make these verses part of you. Do whatever it takes to get this done and spend time every day declaring these verses over your body along with the many more promises for healing God has written in His Word.

Each Scripture contains a 2-4 sentence description describing its importance to the healing process. This will help to give you a proper context for the verse and guide you in praying it over your life.

Please note that this is not an exhaustive list. I have employed hundreds of verses in the writing of this manuscript. It would do you well to internalize not only the list below, but also the rest of the healing verses found in this text. In fact, each of our life's goal should be to internalize all 31,102 verses of the 66 books found in the Bible.

When I first started learning about God's will to heal, I took every healing Scripture I could find and wrote them out on 3x5 index cards. I declared them out loud over myself until I had them memorized and could recite them at will. I highly encourage you to do the same. You will be full of life in your own body, and full of anointing to minister to every person you come across.

1) Genesis 18:14

> *14 "Is anything too hard for the Lord? At the appointed time I will return to you, according to the time of life, and Sarah shall have a son."*

Why It's Important: Do you have a *big* prayer request? *Nothing* is too hard for God! He will do what He has promised to do "according to the time of life." He might not work according to your schedule! But He always works according to His Word.

2) Exodus 15:26

> *26 ...and [God] said, "If you diligently heed the voice of the Lord your God and do what is right in His sight, give ear to His commandments and keep all His statutes, I will put none of the diseases on you which I have brought on the Egyptians. For I am the Lord who heals you."*

Why It's Important: Healing is not just what God does. It is who He is! Healing is an inseparable part of God's character and His nature. If He did it in Scripture, He will do it in your life. You are a living epistle (2 Cor. 3:2)! And God is writing a healing story through you. God's people acquired sickness by living outside of His covenant. The way that we acquire health is by choosing to live inside of His covenant by faith in Jesus Christ.

3) Exodus 23:25-26

> *25 "Worship the Lord your God, and his blessing will be on your food and water. I will take away sickness from among you, 26 and none will miscarry or be barren in your land. I will give you a full life span."*

Why It's Important: When you worship God, He will take away sickness and disease from you. He will take away barrenness and miscarriage! He will give you long life, because it aligns with His will.

4) Numbers 23:19

> 19 *"God is not a man, that He should lie, nor a son of man, that He should repent. Has He said, and will He not do? Or has He spoken, and will He not make it good?"*

Why It's Important: God does not lie. He "cannot" lie (Titus 1:2)! Everything He has spoken will come to pass, and all that He has promised will be fulfilled.

5) 2 Kings 4:14-17

> 14 *So he said, "What then is to be done for her?" And Gehazi answered, "Actually, she has no son, and her husband is old." 15 So he said, "Call her." When he had called her, she stood in the doorway. 16 Then he said, "About this time next year you shall embrace a son." And she said, "No, my lord. Man of God, do not lie to your maidservant!" 17 But the woman conceived, and bore a son when the appointed time had come, of which Elisha had told her.*

Why It's Important: God will promise you things that sound too good to be true! But God is not mocked (Gal. 6:7). He is not a man that He should lie (Num. 23:19)! You will conceive and give birth to everything He tells you is yours. Barrenness – whether spiritual or physical – cannot persist in God's presence.

315

6) 2 Kings 5:8

8 So it was, when Elisha the man of God heard that the king of Israel had torn his clothes, that he sent to the king, saying, "Why have you torn your clothes? Please let him come to me, and he shall know that there is a prophet in Israel."

Why it's Important: Where the Word is, healing follows. The king of Israel was afraid to heal the sick because he did not have God's Word! But Elisha was unafraid because the Word was with him and in him. You have the Word! Go heal the sick. Invite people to come to you for healing with the same boldness as Elisha.

7) 2 Kings 5:14

14 So he went down and dipped seven times in the Jordan, according to the saying of the man of God; and his flesh was restored like the flesh of a little child, and he was clean.

Why it's Important: Your healing will be unique! Naaman didn't get the dramatic healing he was looking for. He simply had to do what God said, and he was healed. Your healing might be simple! Or it might be complicated. But it will *always and only* happen according to the word and will of God.

8) 2 Kings 20:7

7 Then Isaiah said, "Take a lump of figs." So they took and laid it on the boil, and he recovered.

Why It's Important: This is one example of God healing in Scripture with medication. God can heal you any way He chooses: with or without the help of a physician, and with or without medication. The most important key to your healing process is this: listen to God, and do what He says.

9) Job 1:1

1 There was a man in the land of Uz, whose name was Job; and that man was blameless and upright, and one who feared God and shunned evil.

Why it's Important: If you remember one thing about Job, remember this! His sickness was not a result of bad behavior. He was blameless and upright, and God loved him! His sickness was the result of an attack from Satan. And God took his sickness away. Satan – not God – is the author of sickness and disease. Don't accept what Satan wants you to have if Jesus already died for you to be free!

10) Psalm 6:2

2 Have mercy on me, O Lord, for I am weak; O Lord, heal me, for my bones are troubled.

Why It's Important: We are weak; but God is strong! We deserve death for our sin; but His mercy brings healing and strength when we need Him most.

11) Psalm 91:5-6

5 You shall not be afraid of the terror by night, nor of the arrow that flies by day, 6 nor of the pestilence that walks in darkness, nor of the destruction that lays waste at noonday.

Why It's Important: Whether night or day, light or darkness: you do not have to be afraid because God is with you! Pestilence (v 6) is no threat to you because Jesus already died as your disease.

12) Psalm 91:10-11

10 No evil shall befall you, nor shall any plague come near your dwelling; 11 For He shall give His angels charge over you, to keep you in all your ways.

Why It's Important: Scripture says that angels are "ministering spirits sent forth to minister for those who will inherit salvation" (Heb. 1:14). That means *you* when you receive Jesus as your personal Lord and Savior. God will dispatch His angels to protect you no matter what comes your way!

13) Psalm 91:16

16 "With long life I will satisfy him, and show him My salvation."

Why It's Important: Is God's will still to show you His salvation? It sure is. Then His will is still to satisfy you with long life! We cannot accept the spiritual component of His promise for salvation while ignoring the physical component of health and wellness. God wants you to have a long, fruitful life free of sickness and disease.

14) Psalm 103:1-3

1 Bless the Lord, O my soul; and all that is within me, bless His holy name! 2 Bless the Lord, O my soul, and forget not all His benefits: 3 Who forgives all your iniquities, who heals all your diseases...

Why It's Important: God heals "all your diseases." Healing is one of the benefits of salvation! We should never forget it. The same God who forgives our sins, heals our diseases! Healing and salvation happened on the same day.

15) Psalm 105:37

37 He also brought them out with silver and gold, and there was none feeble among His tribes.

Why It's Important: God brought Israel out of Egypt with 1) great wealth and 2) perfect health. There was "none" feeble among them. Not one sick. Not one too weak to continue the journey! All of His people were well.

16) Psalm 107:20

20 He sent His word and healed them, and delivered them from their destructions.

Why It's Important: God's medicine is His Word. The remedy to sickness and disease is the Word of God! Study His word (2 Tim. 2:15). Read it over your body. Let it heal you from your disease and deliver you from your destruction. Every disease – whether physical or mental – must bow to the name of Jesus (Phil. 2:9-11)!

17) Proverbs 17:22

22 A merry heart does good, like medicine, but a broken spirit dries the bones.

Why It's Important: Your attitude has an impact on your healing. Is your heart merry because you believe you will be healed? Is your spirit whole because you trust in the Lord your God?

18) Proverbs 18:21

21 Death and life are in the power of the tongue, and those who love it will eat its fruit.

Why It's Important: The words you speak over your body *matter*. Are you speaking death, or are you speaking life? Are you inviting sickness, or are you declaring healing? Whatever you speak, you will eat the fruit thereof.

19) Isaiah 53:4-6

4 Surely He has borne our griefs and carried our sorrows; yet we esteemed Him stricken, smitten by God, and afflicted. 5 But He was wounded for our transgressions, He was bruised for our iniquities; the chastisement for our peace was upon Him, and by His stripes we are healed. 6 All we like sheep have gone astray; we have turned, every one, to his own way; and the Lord has laid on Him the iniquity of us all.

Why It's Important: "Griefs" and "sorrows" refer specifically physical sickness and pain in the original Hebrew language.[273] When Jesus died on the cross, He died *as* your sickness and *as* your pain! God laid every sickness that would ever be known to man on the person of Jesus Christ. And if Jesus already took the burden, that means there is none left for you! He died so that you could be made well in His name. By His stripes you are healed!

20) Isaiah 55:11

11 So shall My word be that goes forth from My mouth; it shall not return to Me void, but it shall accomplish what I please, and it shall prosper in the thing for which I sent it.

---

[273] "Griefs" is the Hebrew *choliy* (Strong's H2483) which literally translates to sickness; "Sorrows" is the Hebrew *makob* (Strong's H4341) which literally translates to physical pain. See Chapter 1, "God Wants to Heal You."

Why It's Important: The best way you can pray for healing – or for *anything* for that matter – is by bringing God's Word back to Him. God gave You His Word for a reason! He wants you to bring it back to Him in prayer. And as you do, it will accomplish the purpose for which God intended it. His Word will bring healing, and it will bring life!

21) Isaiah 57:18-19

> *18 I have seen his ways, and will heal him; I will also lead him, and restore comforts to him and to his mourners. 19 "I create the fruit of the lips: Peace, peace to him who is far off and to him who is near," says the Lord, "And I will heal him."*

Why It's Important: God has seen your ways! He knows just how imperfect you are. *But He will still heal you.* Your healing does not depend on your righteousness. It depends on the righteousness of Christ! Whether you feel close to Jesus or far away, He will heal you.

22) Isaiah 58:6-8

> *6 "Is this not the fast that I have chosen: to loose the bonds of wickedness, to undo the heavy burdens, to let the oppressed go free, and that you break every yoke? 7 Is it not to share your bread with the hungry, and that you bring to your house the poor who are cast out; when you see the naked, that you cover him, and not hide yourself from your own flesh? 8 Then your light shall break forth like the morning, your healing shall spring forth speedily, and your righteousness shall go before you; the glory of the Lord shall be your rear guard.*

Why It's Important: Healing happens when you fast! Healing happens when you share your resources with people who have none. When you make the

Gospel come alive with your action, healing will follow. When you fast for the right reason – to be closer to Jesus and not to be noticed by man – your healing will come in a hurry. God will heal you, and He will protect you!

23) Isaiah 61:1-3

1 "The Spirit of the Lord God is upon Me, because the Lord has anointed Me to preach good tidings to the poor; He has sent Me to heal the brokenhearted, to proclaim liberty to the captives, and the opening of the prison to those who are bound; 2 To proclaim the acceptable year of the Lord, and the day of vengeance of our God; to comfort all who mourn, 3 to console those who mourn in Zion, to give them beauty for ashes, the oil of joy for mourning, the garment of praise for the spirit of heaviness; that they may be called trees of righteousness, the planting of the Lord, that He may be glorified."

Why It's Important: God anointed Jesus with the Holy Spirit to heal. You are anointed with the same Holy Spirit as Jesus (Romans 8:11)! Just as He was anointed to heal, so are you in Him.

24) Habakkuk 3:5

5 Before Him went pestilence, and fever followed at His feet.

Why It's Important: The Old Testament prophet Habakkuk tells us exactly what happens to sickness around Jesus in this Messianic prophecy. Sickness flees before Jesus, and never returns! Sickness and disease cannot stay where Jesus has been.

25) Zechariah 4:6

6 So he answered and said to me: "This is the word of the Lord to Zerubbabel: 'Not by might nor by power, but by My Spirit,' says the Lord of hosts."

Why It's Important: Your healing is not going to happen by the strength of man. It's not going to happen as a result of your own self-effort! It is going to happen by the Holy Spirit. God can do in a moment what you could never accomplish in years!

26) Malachi 4:2

2 But to you who fear My name the Sun of Righteousness shall arise with healing in His wings; and you shall go out and grow fat like stall-fed calves.

Why It's Important: Jesus has healing in His wings! When we approach God with a reverential fear – an awesome sense of wonder at His miracle-working power – we activate the healing that is included in our relationship with Him!

27) Matthew 4:23

23 And Jesus went about all Galilee, teaching in their synagogues, preaching the gospel of the kingdom, and healing all kinds of sickness and all kinds of disease among the people.

Why It's Important: Teaching, preaching and healing go hand in hand. When you preach the Gospel, people should be healed! Jesus was not restricted or intimidated by any kind of sickness or disease. He healed "all kinds" of sickness and "all kinds" of disease everywhere the Word was released.

28) Matthew 6:33

33 But seek first the kingdom of God and His righteousness, and all these things shall be added to you.

Why It's Important: Seek God first! The goal is *not* to be healed; it is to *meet* the God who heals. As you seek Him first, every other material *need* (as differentiated from a *want)* will be added to you.

29) Matthew 8:2-3

2 And behold, a leper came and worshiped Him, saying, "Lord, if You are willing, You can make me clean." 3 Then Jesus put out His hand and touched him, saying, "I am willing; be cleansed." Immediately his leprosy was cleansed.

Why It's Important: This leper had every right to ask Jesus His will when it came to healing, because it had never been written and recorded! But you and I have lost that right. We know God's will because we have His word! As soon as we come and worship, Jesus is *always* willing to heal.

30) Matthew 8:8

8 The centurion answered and said, "Lord, I am not worthy that You should come under my roof. But only speak a word, and my servant will be healed."

Why It's Important: One word from Jesus is all you need to be healed! Jesus has all authority (Matt. 28:18). When He speaks, your body will listen. Your flesh will come back to health and sickness will flee at the power of His word!

31) Matthew 8:13

13 Then Jesus said to the centurion, "Go your way; and as you have believed, so let it be done for you." And his servant was healed that same hour.

Why It's Important: What happens in your life depends on your faith. The centurion made a decision to believe – he had faith! – and it was done "that same hour." The moment you truly believe, your healing is secure.

32) Matthew 8:16-17

> *16 When evening had come, they brought to Him many who were demon-possessed. And He cast out the spirits with a word, and healed all who were sick, 17 that it might be fulfilled which was spoken by Isaiah the prophet, saying: "He Himself took our infirmities and bore our sicknesses."*

Why It's Important: Jesus' healing ministry was the fulfillment of Old Testament prophecy. Jesus is the fulfillment of God's Word! Everything God has ever promised His people, from deliverance to healing, is found in the Person and presence of Jesus.

33) Matthew 9:28-29

> *28 And when He had come into the house, the blind men came to Him. And Jesus said to them, "Do you believe that I am able to do this?" They said to Him, "Yes, Lord." 29 Then He touched their eyes, saying, "According to your faith let it be to you."*

Why It's Important: Do you believe Jesus is able to heal you? That determination is the beginning of your healing process.

34) Matthew 10:1

> *1 And when He had called His twelve disciples to Him, He gave them power over unclean spirits, to cast them out, and to heal all kinds of sickness and all kinds of disease.*

Why It's Important: Are you a disciple? Then Jesus has given you "power over unclean spirits...and to heal all kinds of sickness and all kinds of disease." Recall Matthew 4:23, where Jesus healed "all kinds of sickness and all kinds of disease." He has given the same power to you when you are in close proximity to Him.

35) Matthew 10:8

> *8 "Heal the sick, cleanse the lepers, raise the dead, cast out demons. Freely you have received, freely give."*

Why It's Important: Jesus doesn't just tell us to *pray for* the sick. He tells us to *heal* the sick! Our mission is not just to preach the Gospel. It is, in addition, to heal, cleanse, raise, and cast out. Jesus would not have told us to do it unless He had already given us everything we would need to get it done!

36) Matthew 11:4-5

> *4 Jesus answered and said to them, "Go and tell John the things which you hear and see: 5 The blind see and the lame walk; the lepers are cleansed and the deaf hear; the dead are raised up and the poor have the gospel preached to them."*

Why It's Important: John the Baptist wanted to know if Jesus was really God. So Jesus replied: "Go and tell John the things which you hear and see!" God proves He is real by demonstrating the miraculous. He proves He is the Healer by healing! He will show you, along with everyone around you, that He is real by *what He does.*

37) Matthew 15:28

28 Then Jesus answered and said to her, "O woman, great is your faith! Let it be to you as you desire." And her daughter was healed from that very hour.

Why It's Important: This woman approached Jesus for healing. He turned her away because she was a Gentile: she was not one of God's people! But she was persistent; and her persistence was rewarded. Persistence is evidence of great faith! Never give up. Continue to approach God for healing, and He will answer your cry.

38) Matthew 28:18-20

18 And Jesus came and spoke to them, saying, "All authority has been given to Me in heaven and on earth. 19 Go therefore and make disciples of all the nations, baptizing them in the name of the Father and of the Son and of the Holy Spirit, 20 teaching them to observe all things that I have commanded you; and lo, I am with you always, even to the end of the age." Amen.

Why it's Important: Jesus has all authority "in heaven and on earth." And what did He do with His all-encompassing authority? *He gave it to you* (Lk. 9:1-3, Lk. 10:1-9). Go, therefore! Wherever you release the Word of God, He will be with you to confirm His word.

39) Mark 2:5

5 When Jesus saw their faith, He said to the paralytic, "Son, your sins are forgiven you."

Why It's Important: This paralyzed man was incapable of *acting on* his faith. He was paralyzed! So his friends showed their faith in his healing. And *it was enough*. When Jesus saw the faith of this man's friends, the man was healed and his sins were forgiven!

40) Mark 5:25-30

> *25 Now a certain woman had a flow of blood for twelve years, 26 and had suffered many things from many physicians. She had spent all that she had and was no better, but rather grew worse. 27 When she heard about Jesus, she came behind Him in the crowd and touched His garment. 28 For she said, "If only I may touch His clothes, I shall be made well." 29 Immediately the fountain of her blood was dried up, and she felt in her body that she was healed of the affliction. 30 And Jesus, immediately knowing in Himself that power had gone out of Him, turned around in the crowd and said, "Who touched My clothes?"*

Why It's Important: Doctors could not cure her! But Jesus did. This woman illegally pressed through a crowd to get to Jesus; and He rewarded her faithful boldness with a face-to-face encounter with the King of Glory. You are one touch away from your healing!

41) Mark 5:41-42

> *41 Then He took the child by the hand, and said to her, "Talitha, cumi," which is translated, "Little girl, I say to you, arise." 42 Immediately the girl arose and walked, for she was twelve years of age. And they were overcome with great amazement.*

Why It's Important: Jairus' daughter was dead. But according to Jesus, "The child [was] not dead, but sleeping" (Mk. 5:39). Heaven's perspective is different! When you adopt Heaven's perspective in place of your own, you will see incredible miracles in your life. Jesus had only to command this girl to arise, and she was raised up completely whole.

42) Mark 8:22-25

22 Then He came to Bethsaida; and they brought a blind man to Him, and begged Him to touch him. 23 So He took the blind man by the hand and led him out of the town. And when He had spit on his eyes and put His hands on him, He asked him if he saw anything. 24 And he looked up and said, "I see men like trees, walking." 25 Then He put His hands on his eyes again and made him look up. And he was restored and saw everyone clearly.

Why It's Important: Jesus didn't heal this man in front of a crowd of people. He didn't heal this man conventionally! He didn't heal this man on the first prayer. Jesus had to honor God's plan to see healing happen, and so too do we.

43) Mark 9:23-24

23 Jesus said to him, "If you can believe, all things are possible to him who believes." 24 Immediately the father of the child cried out and said with tears, "Lord, I believe; help my unbelief!"

Why It's Important: Healing requires faith! But it doesn't require perfect faith. This father's son was healed: not because he had perfect faith, but because he asked Jesus to help his unbelief. God will meet you where you are with "healing in His wings" (Mal. 4:2).

44) Mark 9:28-29

28 And when He had come into the house, His disciples asked Him privately, "Why could we not cast it out?" 29 So He said to them, "This kind can come out by nothing but prayer and fasting."

Why It's Important: If we want to move like Jesus moved, we have to cultivate a *lifestyle* of prayer and fasting! The disciples lacked power in their prayers because they did not pair their prayers with fasting. When you mix these powerful ingredients together, miracles will follow!

45) Mark 10:52

52 Then Jesus said to him, "Go your way; your faith has made you well." And immediately he received his sight and followed Jesus on the road.

Why It's Important: In Mark 10, a blind man named Bartimaeus came to Jesus to receive his sight. Jesus said to him, "Your faith has made you well!" What healed this man: the presence of Jesus, or this man's faith? YES! Your faith, paired with the presence of Jesus, creates a supernatural reaction whereby you receive the healing for which you have been praying.

46) Mark 11:23-24

23 "For assuredly, I say to you, whoever says to this mountain, 'Be removed and be cast into the sea,' and does not doubt in his heart, but believes that those things he says will be done, he will have whatever he says. 24 Therefore I say to you, whatever things you ask when you pray, believe that you receive them, and you will have them."

330

Why It's Important: Jesus didn't instruct His disciples to *think* to the mountain; He told them to *speak* to the mountain! Open your mouth and pray what God told you to pray. If you believe that your healing is "done," you will have whatever you say!

47) Mark 16:17-18

> 17 *"And these signs will follow those who believe: In My name they will cast out demons; they will speak with new tongues; 18 they will take up serpents; and if they drink anything deadly, it will by no means hurt them; they will lay hands on the sick, and they will recover."*

Why It's Important: It is the mandate of *every believer* ("those who believe") to heal the sick. Healing is not just a reward for those who are exceptionally dedicated to Jesus; it is the portion for everyone who calls on His name. Declare this over yourself: I will lay hands on the sick, and they will recover!

48) Luke 4:38-39

> 38 *Now He arose from the synagogue and entered Simon's house. But Simon's wife's mother was sick with a high fever, and they made request of Him concerning her. 39 So He stood over her and rebuked the fever, and it left her. And immediately she arose and served them.*

Why It's Important: Church service was done. But Jesus was not done healing! He brought healing right into Simon Peter's home after service, and He will bring healing right into yours. Jesus was not gentle with the fever. He rebuked it, and it left! And in response, Simon Peter's mother in law consecrated herself for a life of service.

49) Luke 4:40-41

40 When the sun was setting, all those who had any that were sick with various diseases brought them to Him; and He laid His hands on every one of them and healed them. 41 And demons also came out of many, crying out and saying, "You are the Christ, the Son of God!" And He, rebuking them, did not allow them to speak, for they knew that He was the Christ.

Why It's Important: Jesus healed *all*. Everyone He prayed for! The nature and type of the disease were irrelevant. He laid His hands on "every one" of them and healed them. Demonic oppression immediately ceased. And He will do the *same thing* in your life!

50) Luke 6:17-19

17 And He came down with them and stood on a level place with a crowd of His disciples and a great multitude of people from all Judea and Jerusalem, and from the seacoast of Tyre and Sidon, who came to hear Him and be healed of their diseases, 18 as well as those who were tormented with unclean spirits. And they were healed. 19 And the whole multitude sought to touch Him, for power went out from Him and healed them all.

Why It's Important: When people got close to Jesus, power went out from Him and healed them all! The exercise for us, then, is not to beg for healing; it is simply to get close to Jesus and receive what He already wants us to have.

51) Luke 9:1-2, 6

1 Then He called His twelve disciples together and gave them power and authority over all demons, and to cure diseases. 2 He sent them to preach the kingdom of God and to heal the sick . . . 6 So they departed and went through the towns, preaching the gospel and healing everywhere.

Why It's Important: Jesus gave His disciples His 1) power and 2) authority. Then, He sent them out to do what He did: to preach the gospel and to heal the sick! Jesus has called you to heal the sick, and He has given you everything you need to get it done.

52) Luke 9:11

11 But when the multitudes knew it, they followed Him; and He received them and spoke to them about the kingdom of God, and healed those who had need of healing.

Why It's Important: People came to Jesus to hear the Gospel, and they left healed. When someone comes to you to hear about Jesus, don't let them leave without their healing!

53) Luke 10:8-9

8 Whatever city you enter, and they receive you, eat such things as are set before you. 9 And heal the sick there, and say to them, 'The kingdom of God has come near to you.'

Why It's Important: Healing the sick was an essential component of Jesus' ministry, and He made it a critical component of the disciples' mission! Notice Jesus tells us to "heal" the sick, and not just pray for them. Also note that Jesus would not ask us to heal unless He planned to give us the resources to do it.

54) Luke 13:10-13

10 Now He was teaching in one of the synagogues on the Sabbath. 11 And behold, there was a woman who had a spirit of infirmity eighteen years, and was bent over and could in no way raise herself up. 12 But when Jesus saw her, He called her to Him and said to her, "Woman, you are loosed from your infirmity." 13 And He laid His hands on her, and immediately she was made straight, and glorified God.

Why It's Important: This woman could not raise herself up! But Jesus could raise her up. He makes everything crooked straight. Jesus didn't pity this woman. He didn't ignore her and pretend she was okay! He healed her, right then and there, so that God would be glorified.

55) Luke 11:9-10

9 "So I say to you, ask, and it will be given to you; seek, and you will find; knock, and it will be opened to you. 10 For everyone who asks receives, and he who seeks finds, and to him who knocks it will be opened."

Why It's Important: It is true that God, "…knows the things you have need of before you ask Him" (Matt. 6:8)! But that doesn't mean you don't have to ask. God gives to those who *ask,* not those who need! He reveals healing to those who seek. He opens to those who knock! "You do not have because you do not ask" (Jas. 4:2).

56) Luke 17:5-6

5 And the apostles said to the Lord, "Increase our faith." 6 So the Lord said, "If you have faith as a mustard seed, you can say to this mulberry tree, 'Be pulled up by the roots and be planted in the sea,' and it would obey you."

Why it's Important: Faith begets more faith. If you want great faith, come to God with whatever measure of faith you have! Whatever you bring Him, He will multiply and grow. Even faith that is far from perfect can uproot trees.

57) Luke 17:11-14

11 Now it happened as He went to Jerusalem that He passed through the midst of Samaria and Galilee. 12 Then as He entered a certain village, there met Him ten men who were lepers, who stood afar off. 13 And they lifted up their voices and said, "Jesus, Master, have mercy on us!" 14 So when He saw them, He said to them, "Go, show yourselves to the priests." And so it was that as they went, they were cleansed.

Why It's Important: The lepers were cleansed "as they went." They were cleansed as they stepped out and did what God told them to do! That is why *talking to Jesus* is so important! If you want to be healed, you have to go out and do what He tells you to do.

58) Luke 17:17-19

17 So Jesus answered and said, "Were there not ten cleansed? But where are the nine? 18 Were there not any found who returned to give glory to God except this foreigner?" 19 And He said to him, "Arise, go your way. Your faith has made you well."

Why It's Important: Ten lepers were healed! But only one "returned to give glory to God." Faith gets you healed! And faith keeps you healed.

59) John 6:2

2 Then a great multitude followed Him, because they saw His signs which He performed on those who were diseased.

Why It's Important: People followed Jesus because they saw what He did to sickness. Healing is a critical component of our witness! When people see that Jesus heals, they will stop at nothing to *know Him.*

60) John 9:1-3

1 Now as Jesus passed by, He saw a man who was blind from birth. 2 And His disciples asked Him, saying, "Rabbi, who sinned, this man or his parents, that he was born blind?" 3 Jesus answered, "Neither this man nor his parents sinned, but that the works of God should be revealed in him.

Why It's Important: Your sickness is nothing more than an opportunity for God to reveal His glory in you! Don't take it as a setback; attack it as a challenge.

61) John 9:6-7

6 When He had said these things, He spat on the ground and made clay with the saliva; and He anointed the eyes of the blind man with

the clay. 7 And He said to him, "Go, wash in the pool of Siloam"
(which is translated, Sent). So he went and washed, and came back
seeing.

Why It's Important: When this man was sent, he went! And he came back seeing. There is power in being sent by God to fulfill His Word! Whatever God says, do. You will be healed as you go.

62) John 10:10

10 The thief does not come except to steal, and to kill, and to destroy.
I have come that they may have life, and that they may have it more
abundantly.

Why It's Important: The enemy – not God – is the author of sickness and disease. Satan's goal in your life is simple and definitive. He wants to steal your salvation and your healing. He wants to kill you and destroy you! But Jesus came to cancel the work of the enemy and to give you abundant life! So please do not accept what Satan wants you to have as though it is a gift from God.

63) John 11:4

4 When Jesus heard that, He said, "This sickness is not unto death, but
for the glory of God, that the Son of God may be glorified through it."

Why It's Important: This is God's declaration over your life! Whatever you are struggling with is not going to kill you. It will be a launching pad for the glory of God to be put on full display in your life! Sickness is not an opportunity for doubt and death; it is an opportunity for God's glory and life!

64) John 11:41-42

41 Then they took away the stone from the place where the dead man was lying. And Jesus lifted up His eyes and said, "Father, I thank You that You have heard Me. 42 And I know that You always hear Me, but because of the people who are standing by I said this, that they may believe that You sent Me."

Why It's Important: Right before Jesus raised Lazarus from the dead, He gave us a lesson on prayer! Whenever you pray. God *always* hears. Pray your prayers with boldness and confidence, knowing that God hears you when you pray.

65) John 14:12-14

12 "Most assuredly, I say to you, he who believes in Me, the works that I do he will do also; and greater works than these he will do, because I go to My Father. 13 And whatever you ask in My name, that I will do, that the Father may be glorified in the Son. 14 If you ask anything in My name, I will do it."

Why It's Important: Jesus did some great works! But you will do *greater*. God will work miracles through you that are greater than you could ever imagine. But first you have to ask in the name of Jesus. You have not because you ask not!

66) Acts 3:6

6 Then Peter said, "Silver and gold I do not have, but what I do have I give you: In the name of Jesus Christ of Nazareth, rise up and walk."

Why It's Important: You don't have to be rich in resources to see healing happen. When you pray for other people, give what you have. Declare healing over them in the mighty name of Jesus!

67) Acts 3:16

> *16 And His name, through faith in His name, has made this man strong, whom you see and know. Yes, the faith which comes through Him has given him this perfect soundness in the presence of you all.*

Why It's Important: Faith in His name heals bodies. Faith in His name saves souls!

68) Acts 4:29-31

> *29 "Now, Lord, look on their threats, and grant to Your servants that with all boldness they may speak Your word, 30 by stretching out Your hand to heal, and that signs and wonders may be done through the name of Your holy Servant Jesus." 31 And when they had prayed, the place where they were assembled together was shaken; and they were all filled with the Holy Spirit, and they spoke the word of God with boldness.*

Why It's Important: When you pray for anointing to heal, the holy Spirit will show up! Signs and wonders will be done through the name of Jesus, and the city where you minister will shake with the power of God.

69) Acts 5:15

> *15 ...so that they brought the sick out into the streets and laid them on beds and couches, that at least the shadow of Peter passing by might fall on some of them.*

Why It's Important: Paul healed with his hankie (Acts 19:12). Peter healed with his shadow! God will use *all of you* to heal if you let Him.

70) Acts 6:8

8 And Stephen, full of faith and power, did great wonders and signs among the people.

Why It's Important: Once Stephen was full of faith, he was full of miracle-working power! Your job is to get full of faith by ingesting the Word of God. As you do, God will fill you with power for signs and wonders everywhere you go!

71) Acts 8:7-8

7 For unclean spirits, crying with a loud voice, came out of many who were possessed; and many who were paralyzed and lame were healed. 8 And there was great joy in that city.

Why It's Important: Do you want to see "great joy" in your city? Heal the sick. Deliver the possessed and the oppressed! Healing and deliverance are part of our mandate as disciples of Jesus.

72) Acts 10:38

38 ...how God anointed Jesus of Nazareth with the Holy Spirit and with power, who went about doing good and healing all who were oppressed by the devil, for God was with Him.

Why It's Important: It was the anointing – the manifest presence of God's Holy Spirit – that empowered Jesus to heal "all who were oppressed by the devil." The anointing removes oppression and eliminates possession. God is with you the same way He was with Jesus on this earth, because the same Spirit who raised Jesus from the grave lives in you (Rom. 8:11)!

73) Acts 14:8-10

8 And in Lystra a certain man without strength in his feet was sitting, a cripple from his mother's womb, who had never walked. 9 This man heard Paul speaking. Paul, observing him intently and seeing that he had faith to be healed, 10 said with a loud voice, "Stand up straight on your feet!" And he leaped and walked.

Why It's Important: When faith collides with the Word of God, healing happens. This man had never walked before! But God will facilitate the impossible in your life when you give Him the chance. Paul commanded, and this man's ankles responded.

74) Acts 19:11-12

11 Now God worked unusual miracles by the hands of Paul, 12 so that even handkerchiefs or aprons were brought from his body to the sick, and the diseases left them and the evil spirits went out of them.

Why It's Important: Paul had an encounter with Jesus (see Acts 9). The result of this interaction followed by radical devotion to Jesus was an anointing so strong that even handkerchief and aprons brought from Paul's body to the sick would heal and deliver. Why on earth can't God use you the same way?

75) Acts 22:12-13

12 "Then a certain Ananias, a devout man according to the law, having a good testimony with all the Jews who dwelt there, 13 came

to me; and he stood and said to me, 'Brother Saul, receive your sight.'
And at that same hour I looked up at him.

Why It's Important: Healing doesn't happen in a vacuum. God will send other people who will play a part – whether small or large – in your healing journey. Don't shut them out. Welcome them!

76) Romans 4:17-18

17 ...(as it is written, "I have made you a father of many nations")
in the presence of Him whom he believed—God, who gives life to the
dead and calls those things which do not exist as though they did;
18 who, contrary to hope, in hope believed, so that he became the
father of many nations, according to what was spoken, "So shall your
descendants be."

Why It's Important: God gives life to the dead. He calls those things which do not exist (yet) as though they did. When you speak perfect health and healing over your life, by faith, you are calling your recovery into existence!

77) Romans 6:12-14

12 Therefore do not let sin reign in your mortal body, that you
should obey it in its lusts. 13 And do not present your members as
instruments of unrighteousness to sin, but present yourselves to God
as being alive from the dead, and your members as instruments of
righteousness to God. 14 For sin shall not have dominion over you,
for you are not under law but under grace.

Why It's Important: You are the one who gets to decide if sin reigns in your life. You are the one who gets to decide if sickness reigns in your body! Say no to sickness and sin; and say yes to healing and resurrection life! You are no longer under the law but under grace!

78) Romans 8:2

> *2 For the law of the Spirit of life in Christ Jesus has made me free from the law of sin and death.*

Why It's Important: You are no longer irrevocably bound by sickness and disease. You are no longer bound by the law of sin and death! You are free; and your portion is now resurrection life.

79) Romans 8:32

> *32 He who did not spare His own Son, but delivered Him up for us all, how shall He not with Him also freely give us all things?*

Why It's Important: Jesus died for your healing! So why would God withhold what He has already given through the cross of Jesus Christ? Your healing happened two thousand years ago on the cross! All that's left is for you to receive it.

80) Romans 10:17

> *17 So then faith comes by hearing, and hearing by the word of God.*

Why It's Important: The "word" of God here is the Greek *rhema* (Strong's G4487), which means the spoken word of God. Do you want to build your faith? Listen to what God is saying to you in prayer! Allow Him to speak to you about your healing, and direct your prayers accordingly. Speaking in prayer must be preceded by listening in prayer.

81) Romans 16:20

20 And the God of peace will crush Satan under your feet shortly.

Why It's Important: "Shortly" means "with quickness or speed" (Strong's G5034; Greek *tachos*). Your healing is not hard! It's all about positioning. When you realize you are seated in Christ in heavenly places (Eph. 2:6) and Satan is under your feet, your healing will happen with quickness and speed!

82) 1 Corinthians 3:16-17

16 Do you not know that you are the temple of God and that the Spirit of God dwells in you? 17 If anyone defiles the temple of God, God will destroy him. For the temple of God is holy, which temple you are.

Why It's Important: Your body is not yours! You belong to God. You are the temple of His Holy Spirit. And anyone who tries to defile you – whether with sin or with sickness – will be destroyed! God will eradicate every sickness and disease that tries to attack His temple.

83) 1 Corinthians 6:18-20

18 Flee sexual immorality. Every sin that a man does is outside the body, but he who commits sexual immorality sins against his own body. 19 Or do you not know that your body is the temple of the Holy Spirit who is in you, whom you have from God, and you are not your own? 20 For you were bought at a price; therefore glorify God in your body and in your spirit, which are God's.

Why It's Important: Your body is the Lord's temple. You are not your own! You are *His.* He redeemed you. You were purchased by the blood of Jesus! And God will clean and heal that which belongs to Him.

84) 1 Corinthians 9:27

27 But I discipline my body and bring it into subjection, lest, when I have preached to others, I myself should become disqualified.

Why It's Important: Your body is not in charge. Your faith – not your form – decides whether you will be healed or sick! Don't let your body tell you whether or not healing is possible. Discipline your body! Bring it into subjection. Declare healing and wholeness, and you will be made well.

85) 1 Corinthians 12:7-11

7 But the manifestation of the Spirit is given to each one for the profit of all: 8 for to one is given the word of wisdom through the Spirit, to another the word of knowledge through the same Spirit, 9 to another faith by the same Spirit, to another gifts of healings by the same Spirit, 10 to another the working of miracles, to another prophecy, to another discerning of spirits, to another different kinds of tongues, to another the interpretation of tongues. 11 But one and the same Spirit works all these things, distributing to each one individually as He wills.

Why It's Important: Healing is a *spiritual gift.* You do not have to earn it, and you cannot buy it! You must simply receive it. Notice the distinction between "gifts of healings" (v 9) and the "working of miracles" (v 10). Healing can be gradual, and miracles are sudden! I pray God gives you faith for both.

86) Galatians 3:13-14

13 Christ has redeemed us from the curse of the law, having become a curse for us (for it is written, "Cursed is everyone who hangs on a tree"), 14 that the blessing of Abraham might come upon the Gentiles in Christ Jesus, that we might receive the promise of the Spirit through faith.

Why It's Important: Sickness is part of the curse. You were born into the curse of this fallen world as a son of Adam. But you have been redeemed from the curse as a son of God through Jesus Christ! Jesus became the curse – He became sickness! – on the cross so that you would receive divine health and abundant life.

87) Ephesians 2:8-9

8 For by grace you have been saved through faith, and that not of yourselves; it is the gift of God, 9 not of works, lest anyone should boast.

Why It's Important: Salvation comes by grace through faith. You didn't earn it! It was a gift. And the same goes for your healing. You cannot earn what God has already freely given. Instead, you must simply receive.

88) Philippians 4:8

8 Finally, brethren, whatever things are true, whatever things are noble, whatever things are just, whatever things are pure, whatever things are lovely, whatever things are of good report, if there is any virtue and if there is anything praiseworthy—meditate on these things.

Why It's Important: When you receive a bad report from the doctor, will you meditate on it? Or will you meditate on God's Word? Will you meditate on a piece of paper that says you are sick? Or will you meditate on the unchanging Word of God that says you are healthy and whole? Equally important as choosing to meditate on the right things, is choosing *not to meditate* on the wrong things. If it's not from God, it's not worthy of your focus!

89) 1 Thessalonians 5:23

> *23 Now may the God of peace Himself sanctify you completely; and may your whole spirit, soul, and body be preserved blameless at the coming of our Lord Jesus Christ.*

Why It's Important: God is holistic! He doesn't just want to heal your soul. He wants to heal your whole spirit, soul, and body. Why would you stop short of receiving everything Jesus died for you to have?

90) 2 Timothy 2:13

> *13 If we are faithless, He remains faithful; He cannot deny Himself.*

Why It's important: We should be full of faith for healing! But even when we're faithless, God is still faithful. He is Jehovah Rapha, the Healer! And He cannot deny who He is.

91) Hebrews 2:14-16

> *14 Inasmuch then as the children have partaken of flesh and blood, He Himself likewise shared in the same, that through death He might destroy him who had the power of death, that is, the devil, 15 and release those who through fear of death were all their lifetime subject to bondage. 16 For indeed He does not give aid to angels, but He does give aid to the seed of Abraham.*

Why It's Important: When Jesus died on the Cross, He *destroyed* the devil. He released you from the fear of death and bondage to disease! By faith in Him, we receive everything He died for us to have.

92) Hebrews 11:1-3

1 Now faith is the substance of things hoped for, the evidence of things not seen. 2 For by it the elders obtained a good testimony. 3 By faith we understand that the worlds were framed by the word of God, so that the things which are seen were not made of things which are visible.

Why It's Important: Your faith that you are healed is the evidence that your healing is already here! God created the world with His words. He will create your healing through your words! Speak healing out over your body by faith and your invisible words will turn into visible recovery.

93) Hebrews 11:6

6 But without faith it is impossible to please Him, for he who comes to God must believe that He is, and that He is a rewarder of those who diligently seek Him.

Why It's Important: God rewards faith. When you come to Him believing that He is the Healer, He will reward you with healing!

94) Hebrews 13:8

8 Jesus Christ is the same yesterday, today, and forever.

Why It's Important: God's will has not changed! If Jesus did it when He walked the earth, He will do it as you approach Him in faith. He is the same God Who Heals, and He always will be.

95) James 2:15-17

15 If a brother or sister is naked and destitute of daily food, 16 and one of you says to them, "Depart in peace, be warmed and filled," but you do not give them the things which are needed for the body, what does it profit? 17 Thus also faith by itself, if it does not have works, is dead.

Why It's Important: Some people will not be open to a spiritual conversation until they are physically healed. It is our role to give our "brother or sister…the things which are needed for the body." When someone needs healing, heal them in the name of Jesus! Your faith should produce healing everywhere you go.

96) James 4:7-8

7 Therefore submit to God. Resist the devil and he will flee from you. 8 Draw near to God and He will draw near to you.

Why It's Important: God's agenda is healing. We submit to His will by resisting the devil and his work, namely sickness. As we resist (i.e. refuse to accept sickness as "from God"), the devil will flee! As we draw near to the Healer, He will draw near to us.

97) James 5:13-15

13 Is anyone among you suffering? Let him pray. Is anyone cheerful? Let him sing psalms. 14 Is anyone among you sick? Let him call for the elders of the church, and let them pray over him, anointing him with oil in the name of the Lord. 15 And the prayer of faith will save the sick, and the Lord will raise him up. And if he has committed sins, he will be forgiven.

Why It's Important: The prescription for sickness is prayer! Call for the elders of the church and let them pray over you. Let them anoint you with oil in Jesus' name. Their faithful prayer will not only heal your body, it will redeem your soul! Here we also see the link between salvation and healing. Jesus made provision for both on the Cross!

98) 1 Peter 5:8-9

8 Be sober, be vigilant; because your adversary the devil walks about like a roaring lion, seeking whom he may devour. 9 Resist him, steadfast in the faith, knowing that the same sufferings are experienced by your brotherhood in the world.

Why It's Important: The enemy – the author of sickness and disease – walks about *like* a roaring lion. He is looking for people who will permit sickness and disease to exist in their life! But Jesus *is* a roaring lion. When you resist sickness, it will flee (James 4:7). Don't accept what God doesn't want you to have!

99) 3 John 1:2

2 Beloved, I pray that you may prosper in all things and be in health, just as your soul prospers.

Why It's Important: God's prosperous plan for your life involves good health! He not only wants to heal your soul; He also wants to heal your body. Healing and salvation happened on the same day, two thousand years ago on the cross!

100) Revelation 12:10-11

10 Then I heard a loud voice saying in heaven, "Now salvation, and strength, and the kingdom of our God, and the power of His Christ have come, for the accuser of our brethren, who accused them before our God day and night, has been cast down. 11 And they overcame him by the blood of the Lamb and by the word of their testimony, and they did not love their lives to the death."

Why It's Important: Satan is the author of sickness and disease. But He has been "cast down!" Satan no longer has power over your life because you are "hidden with Christ in God" (Col. 3:3). He no longer has authority to afflict you with sickness and disease. He has been cast down, and you have overcome by the blood of Jesus!

INTELLIGENT
CHARISMATIC ®

Changing the way you think about your faith.

For more resources, please visit pastormike.nyc.

Made in USA - Kendallville, IN
1212647_9780578793665
12.11.2020 2132